THE MARKETING GITA

Ancient Wisdom for Modern Business Success

DR. PRATEEK MAHESHWARI
SAGAR VENKATESHWAR

An imprint of
Srishti Publishers & Distributors

Srishti Publishers & Distributors
A unit of AJR Publishing LLP
212A, Peacock Lane
Shahpur Jat, New Delhi – 110 049

editorial@srishtipublishers.com

First Published by Bold,
an imprint of Srishti Publishers & Distributors in 2023

10 9 8 7 6 5 4 3

This is a work of non-fiction, based on the authors' experiences and life-learnings. It provides insights into marketing aspects taking help from Hindu mythology, but the recommendations given herein are in no way intended to be a substitute for professional advice and help. The mythological aspects are for reference purposes only and are not intended to hurt anyone's beliefs.

Printed and bound in India

Advance Praise

Our Vedas and Puranas have always been known as the comprehensive doctrine that have been the guiding post to lead our lives since time immemorial. The fact that it indoctrinates our path to lead day-to-day lives in a manner which is relevant now more than ever – especially in Kalyuga where there are so many distractions – is known to all. The Marketing Gita approaches marketing theory from a very innovative and imaginative spiritual twist. I would recommend you read it at least once.

Mohit Malhotra, CEO
Dabur India Limited

The world appears to suffer with an excess of intelligence and shortage of wisdom, more so in the world of business management. Marketing at the centre of it all, poses a still greater challenge of it being rather nebulous and not a definitive science…

Prateek and Sagar, have interestingly distilled the wisdom from the mythical stories of Vishnu's Dashavatar, and applied them to the pragmatic business world with all its marketing dilemmas, that managers often find themselves caught up in. The rich fables and stories are captivatingly told, and this book will surely impact the marketing minds particularly in India!!!

KV Rao, Resident Director ASEAN,
TATA Sons Pvt. Ltd., Singapore

As an industry leader, I found The Marketing Gita to be a refreshing and insightful departure from the usual marketing textbooks. The authors have successfully blended ancient wisdom with modern marketing practices, making it a valuable resource for marketers at any level. The book's examples and Indian case studies are relatable and relevant, providing practical insights into the challenges faced by marketing professionals and entrepreneurs alike.

Sundeep Singh
Managing Director, Accenture Consulting

I grew up listening and reading to the stories of Vishnu's Dashavataar, but it never occurred to me that how closely these stories are linked to modern-day business strategies. This book [The Marketing Gita] approaches business & marketing theory with several elements of surprises. It will make you to fall in love with marketing, for sure…

Keshav Maheshwari, MD
(ALLEN Overseas, Dubai UAE), a TEDx Speaker

The Marketing Gita *is a captivating read that offers valuable lessons for marketing professionals. The book's storytelling style is engaging and accessible. Sagar and Prateek have successfully integrated the mythical stories of Vishnu with practical marketing strategies, offering a fresh perspective on business management.*

Nishant Shekhar,
Managing Director and Partner
in a Global Management Consulting Company

Marketing is like storytelling, which comes from the imagination or features of a product or service. Drawing its principles and strategies from the Indian mythology is a unique art. We know Vedas are a source of knowledge about God and Universe as a whole. Authors have aptly drawn evolution from Lord Vishnu's various incarnations, Dashavatars. Purposeful appearances have been related with products and services with synthesis of ongoing marketing principles and practices. All details enlighten the subject – amply, interestingly.

Sunil Mantri
CEO, WH Smith India

Can't be a better and more engaging way to learn marketing and business concepts than that of reading The Marketing Gita. *The authors have taken the business learning to the next level. Must be in every marketing and business professional's reading list…*

Siraj Azmat Chaudhry
Country Chairman SATS India Pvt. Ltd, Independent Director on Boards, Ex- Chairman, Cargill India Pvt Ltd.

Simple, lucid, engaging, and intuitive… The excellent narration and flow make you read The Marketing Gita *in one sitting. It will be difficult for anyone to put down the book till one reaches the last page!!!*

I like how mythological stories can be used in the reality of business and classrooms for effective teaching. Must read!

Varsha Jain, AGK Chair Professor of Marketing,
MICA (Ahmedabad, India)

The Marketing Gita *is a must read for every marketing and sales professional. It is a brilliant reference for management students, entrepreneurs and business executives.*

Sridhar Srinivasan
President and CEO, Web Packaging Solutions (USA)

Provides pragmatic and unique insights into business and marketing practices using Vishnu's Dashavataar *as a base. It serves as a bridge between ancient mythology and the contemporary business world. Drawing upon timeless stories and applying them to real-world scenarios, this book offers a fresh perspective, unlocking the hidden power of mythological facts and their potential in shaping successful businesses today. Much appreciated work! It is a must-read for B-school students, marketing and sales professionals, entrepreneurs, business leaders, and anyone seeking fresh perspectives in the world of business…*

Rahul Jairath, National Sales Head,
Café Coffee Day Retail Chain

A simple and fascinating read. Great marketing insights and learning for every management & business student, professional, marketing practitioner entrepreneur, and anyone who enjoys reading.

Kalpak Chhajed, Co-founder
Shop101 and Dash101

Being passionate about myths and history, I came across the final draft of The Marketing Gita *and, went through the same with utmost curiosity to know how myths and marketing principles can be interrelated. The book does full justice to that. Kudos to the authors and best wishes for the success of their interesting, unconventional endeavour…*

Nirmal Kumar Maheshwari
Former Joint President (Projects),
Thai Acrylic Fibre (Aditya Birla Group), Thailand

To my beloved grandfather,
Late Shri S.N. Maheshwari.

To all the immortal storytellers
who inspire all the story lovers...

– Dr Prateek Maheshwari

To my grandfather, Subba Rao Nemani,
who made me the man I am today.

– Sagar Venkateshwar

Contents

Mathsya Koormo Varahashcha
Narasimhashcha Vaamana
Raamo Raamashcha Raamashcha
Krishna-Kalki-Janardhana:

Foreword

Sanatana Dharma, as the world's oldest religion Hinduism is called, has survived millennia with minor turbulences in its exalted history. Vedas, the holy texts of the religion, have been passed down generations orally. Not having engaged in outreach and missionary activities, Hinduism has flourished due to its inclusivity and timeless wisdom that has been passed on in the form of stories through generations.

Several literary texts are relevant in today's era and have managed to survive the battle against time due to their relatability to each generation's problems. Despite all the technological advancements, human nature is still similar in many ways, and history happens to be cyclical. Likewise, mythological stories carry relevance across time, and sometimes even across spaces. The situations may change, the variables may not be the same, the parameters may differ, yet the core underlying principle of the stories remains the same.

When it comes to a business, the theory still holds true. With numerous businesses that have had their day in the sun since the dawn of industrialization, the lessons are many to draw upon. However, it is close to impossible to keep a track of all the strategies and moves that one (an individual or a business) can apply to meet their objectives. Not to mention, it wouldn't be appropriate to replicate somebody's strategy without taking into cognizance one's own capability and context.

This is where mythological stories come into the forefront to provide a perspective. Even though most of the stories deal with the triumph of good over evil, the nature of the problem and the solution provided could be quite different. What matters is the ability to recognize the prevailing scenario, build a perspective and make moves accordingly. Sagar and Prateek have managed to beautifully weave together the discrete worlds of marketing and mythology to get a hang of the brand in its journey from inception to extinction. Using the stories of *Vishnu's* Dashavatar, they have managed to illuminate the process of building a brand and its associated challenges.

This book is a delightful read for anyone who is curious about what goes behind the glamour of marketing, or is interested in finding out how a business thrives from scratch, or is intrigued by the possibilities from mythology.

In the end, I have only one question for all of you - "Are you interested in traveling to Vaikuntha in a saga of brand and strategy?" If so, your quest can begin with *The Marketing Gita!*

Prof. Himanshu Rai
Director, IIM Indore

Why you should read this book

We have been admirers of the science of marketing from B-School and beyond. What we see in advertisements and campaigns for various brands barely scratches the surface. And one cannot deny that they are the most visible parts of marketing. People assume that it must be glamorous to be working for the marketing team of any brand as it involves interactions with celebrities and a lot of travel that unleashes one's inner wanderlust. At times, most of us also get carried away with such builds. However, the reality is far from such notions. Probably marketing and in extension marketers are the most misunderstood concept in the business and academic circles alike.

Various academicians have attempted to define marketing in their own ways and succeeded to a greater extent. However, the razor-thin differences between the classroom theories and the real world only grow with time when one leaves the comfort of university boundaries. Not to mention the rapid changes that are being witnessed across technology to consumer behavior. When one enters the corporate world, they can find a section of folks rooted firmly in the belief that marketing is an integral core function, while another section accepts that it is a glorious team that is impeccable to provide finishing touches to enable sales. Sudhir Sitapati, CEO of Godrej Consumer Products and HUL executive alumni, once claimed that HUL is a marketing company at its core and all other functions merely aid in ensuring that the product appropriately reaches the customer's doorstep. Few people move ahead with the understanding that marketing is nothing but a hogwash job and others assume that it is a quick fix that solves all the problems in a snap. There is also a minority who tends to believe that simply throwing away money blindly into advertising is enough to bring in sales. Imagine a candy shop owner who doesn't believe that chocolates taste yum and therefore, should be taken off the shelves, when the demand is rapidly building for chocolates. Or that candy shop owner doesn't have the right product and assumes that advertising aggressively would bring in the much-needed sales. These biases over marketing are rooted in their experiences and in turn affect the direction in which a business moves ahead. These could also be a consequence of not realizing the actual role marketing plays in setting up a business from the shadows. Hence it is imperative that business leaders and entrepreneurs recognize the importance of marketing.

Amidst all this, the fundamental question still remains – What is marketing?

Marketing at its very core is storytelling, but with a larger perspective, a wider canvas and a razor-sharp focus. It tells the story of a company that tries to generate value for its shareholders and investors. It scripts the screenplay of a product or a service that attempts to solve a consumer's problem from the start. It fills in the plot of numerous stakeholders along the value chain who ensure that the product is ready to face the market. Even if one stakeholder folds, the whole venture collapses like a bunch of dominos.

Marketing is not merely restricted to brand management or advertising or the development of communication materials or throwing out punch lines at the customers. It is much more than that. A brand happens to be a consequence of marketing actions, but marketing takes the pole position as it is responsible for a business from its very inception to its death. Starting from picking the right consumer insights to developing a successful prototype and testing it out to ensuring that a smooth pathway is laid out for the product to reach the consumer, marketing is involved in each step, directly or indirectly. Only when the foundation laid by marketing is firm that the other functions (sales, operations, finance, legal, etc.) can continue to build upon that in the value chain.

Marketing is the invisible hand that holds the narrative of a business from its formation to its ultimate demise. In marketing literature, the journey of every business from its birth is chronicled as PLC or 'Product Life Cycle'. Despite being from different industries or operating under varied circumstances, the concept of PLC can be traced across every organization. Its various stages mimic that of human life journey from a young baby to a ripe old age. However, no two companies or two brands are always in the same instance of the PLC journey, considering their respective environments, just like no two humans are the same. This essentially means that any actions taken from a marketing perspective for one's business may not be applicable for the other as the stages of the PLC are different, including the prevailing business conditions. For instance, Dabur, a popular FMCG (Fast Moving Consumer Goods) company in India, can afford to spend huge on its marketing actions, including onboard A-lister brand ambassadors. However, a fresh D2C (Direct to Customer) startup off the block cannot repeat the same move since its objectives are drastically different and resources are meager at that point in time.

Just because product/brand A had success with a certain move, there is no 100% guarantee that it would also work for product/brand B. Yet, brand B can still decipher the reasons why brand A went ahead with that move and tweak it accordingly to suit brand B's needs. It won't be right to presume that a baby can start consuming food like an adult does. This makes it important that one has to not only understand what is the essence of marketing, but also ensure that the right actions are taken at the right times factoring for one's circumstances. That precisely would be the difference between intelligence and wisdom. One can be called intelligent by gathering all the knowledge and facts around the world. But that person would be wise only when he knows how to apply that knowledge in their current scenario.

Even firms with enough clout, resources and market experiences still make mistakes related to marketing that prove to be costly. One quick look at the history of any company would attest to this fact. While not all mistakes could be avoided in all instances, the ones derived from fundamental negligence could definitely be avoided in hindsight. This is where PLC serves as a barometer to measure at what stage a company/brand is playing in and what sort of moves it undertook in that particular stage. This outlook serves as a fine check for marketers to not get carried away by some brand strategy's success without further investigation. PLC also provides certain key objectives that need to be fulfilled in each stage by a company/brand to survive the choppy waters of the market and ensure the growth of value for all stakeholders, thus providing the necessary gravitas for the overall strategy.

It was imperative to look at the PLC with an offbeat prism, away from the rose-tinted glasses to form a nuanced perspective on marketing and business. Being myth aficionados, the mythological stories were our first go-to reference due to their relevance in modern times. There is a reason they have survived the sands of time due to our collective consciousness, passed down from generation to generation in an oral fashion. Looking through the lens of mythology, the ebb and flow of a PLC resemble the ancient Hindu time cycle of four *yugas*. Even though time is cyclical and in a perpetual loop, our ancient sages managed to find a way to measure time. Between them, all the four yugas comprise over forty-three lakh human years. A combination of four yugas – *Satya Yuga, Treta Yuga, Dwapara Yuga, and Kali Yuga* – is known as a *Mahayuga* which chronicles the journey of time. Many such Mahayugas, in turn, form the lifetime of Lord Brahma, which also happens to be the life of the known universe. Lord Brahma is the creator of the universe and legends portray that he was born out of a lotus growing from the navel of Lord Vishnu, the protector of the universe and saviour of humanity.

These four yugas portray the rise and decline of human life from Satya to Kali Yuga, with Lord Vishnu taking on many *avatars* to save mankind from utter destruction whenever Dharma, represented by a bull was in trouble. It is said that humans used to live for thousands of years in Satya Yuga, while the average life expectancy in Kali Yuga is not even in three digits. A popular anecdote was that Dharma used to run on four legs in Satya Yuga, while in Kali Yuga it only runs on a single leg. The quality of life, the characteristics of humans (both physical and mental), and the objectives they had – all point to a declining graph, which symbolizes the journey of humans. The recurring battle between dharma and adharma is a constant across all yugas, for the wisdom of light is lost without experiencing darkness. Whenever there is an imbalance, Lord Vishnu takes an avatar to establish dharma in each life cycle. Despite having a common primary objective to restore order, the main essence of each avatar is different upon close examination. The challenges in different yugas were unique in every sense, and so were the avatars taken by Lord Vishnu to solve them. The prominent among them are popularly known as Dashavatar (the ten avatars). Re-reading of the Dashavatar always throws up new nuances that were not present earlier.

The stories of Dashavatar, part of a larger Purana *Bhagavatam* was narrated by Sukha maharshi, to King Parikshit, great grandson of Arjuna, the demi-god son of Lord Indra (the king of gods). Once during a hunt, Parikshit was passing through a forest where he found a sage Shamika in deep meditation. He tried asking the sage for directions to the lake, but he received no response. He was not aware that the sage had taken a vow of silence and was not disrespecting the king by ignoring him. In his ignorance, Parikshit placed a dead snake on the sage's shoulders. It was not an act expected out of a royal, much less than the emperor of Bharatvarsha. The moment he had done this, he regretted it and left the place in shame. However, the sage's son Shringi was not amused when he got to know of this disrespect to his father. He cursed the king to die of a snake bite within seven days. When the father got to know of the curse dished out by his son, he reminded him that sages are supposed to forgive and the king had already repented his act. But the curse was out there and there was nothing one could do about it. Parikshit wanted to make the best use of his time on earth and he decided to seek out wisdom and spiritual knowledge. He asked a profound question: what should be one's duty towards dharma when death is imminent and how to attain *moksha* (salvation). Sage Sukha Mahamuni (the son of sage Vyasa, the author of the *Mahabharata*), was roaming near the countryside when he got an invitation from sages to help Parikshit out. That was when the great sage started narrating the nuances and perspectives from *Bhagavatam*, highlighting all the avatars taken by Lord Vishnu, to establish dharma and restore order on earth in the form of stories.

Storytelling as an art is as old as the first cave paintings drawn by the homo sapiens. They did play a role in bringing humanity closer to their chosen divine beliefs. These stories set the tune for traditions and cultures that we inherited. Below the surface, those stories hold lessons for all those who wish to look. The relevance behind those lessons in modern times is a key reason for the survival of various myths. Few elements would have been lost, and few would have been adapted to suit the age, but the essence of the stories is still valid. The stories of Dashavatar across the four yugas and the mighty deeds of Lord Vishnu resemble that of a PLC where a product faces numerous challenges across *Introduction, Growth, Maturity,* and *Decline* stages. The journey is not smooth, but various brands have staved off the challenges thrown at them successfully, and many will, in the future too. But not all brands were successful and there are lessons in their journeys also for any new fledgling business to draw inspiration from.

Being a part of the marketing industry, we dashed ahead with the idea of unifying the worlds of marketing and mythology and this whole exercise resulted in this book. It is not a typical academic book. It is a simple narrative that attempts to draw similarities between two diverse worlds that have been in existence since the inception of time and pens down the common lessons from them in each stage. It presents a perspective for the readers to ponder upon the nuances of marketing and the insights from behind the scenes of crafting a brand. While our initial intent is to aim the book towards students of management and marketing, it is not limited to them. The book is also for business professionals, budding entrepreneurs, and bibliophiles who are passionate about marketing/business or mythology. It is not a solid action plan on what businesses should do in terms of marketing, but rather a playbook to act as a guide measure. We hope that it will help the readers in forming certain perspectives from multiple brands' actions, and notions on how a strategy is crafted, and have pointers to answer the question 'What is Marketing?', just as Parikshit had asked Sukha Mahamuni. We hope that from a fish who saved humanity from deluge to the fierce Kalki who is sworn to destroy Adharma, the journey of Lord Vishnu in the annals of time, juxtaposed with the voyage of a brand, would make for a fascinating read.

THE INCIPIENCE

1

Success in a Fish Scale

Vedaparaharanam kritva
Leenam somakambudhou
Hatwacharakshanam chakre
Matsyaroopam harimbhaje ||

To the basics

The common perception is that 'marketing' comes late into the game, once the business is set-up and thriving. However, from the start itself, it is an invisible hand that guides the path a new business ought to take. One can't market or create a compelling proposition for a bad product or a flawed premise!

The Hindu myths clearly demarcate the responsibilities between the divine trinity. Lord Brahma is solely in charge of creation, while Lord Shiva is tasked with destruction, and it is the onus of Lord Vishnu to preserve the known life. But there can be no preservation if there is no creation, can it? Few legends state that Lord Brahma, resides in a lotus emerging out from the *nabhi* (navel) of Lord Vishnu, which essentially symbolizes that creation and preservation go hand in hand. Lord Brahma may be in charge of creation, but without Lord Vishnu discharging his duties, the point of creation would be meaningless.

Setting up a new business is akin to a fish taking its first swim in the vast ocean. Before finding its feet on the ground, the business would have to survive the choppy waters.

Without marketing, it is impossible. Any business model has to be based on a simple idea. Special emphasis on the word 'simple', as the idea could be anything. It could be completely original like enabling people to purchase on the internet, or it could be an improvement on existing ones floating in the market, or it could be a forgotten model that can be updated to suit modern times like using salt to clean one's teeth.

Not every idea is worthy enough to start a business, but the ones eligible are formed from solid consumer insights. The words 'customer' and 'consumer' are interchangeable in most cases, but there is a subtle difference. Customer is someone who purchases the product, while consumer is the one who consumes the product. While a customer can be a consumer, not all customers are consumers. For example, in the case of crayons, the customer is the parent as they make the purchase, while the child is the consumer as they use it. For mobile phones, the customer and the consumer are the same. That's the reason why the department responsible for gathering the insights is called the Consumer Insights team.

Consumer insights are derived from daily observations on the issues faced by the common man which may look elementary. OYO, an Indian hospitality startup, is built on a basic premise to provide affordable accommodation discovery for customers while travelling. Not such an uncommon occurrence in hindsight, but none could recognize it until a business opportunity could be extracted. In a nutshell, any useful consumer insight is something that is common and can be expressed concisely without any halo. In fact, any proper insight is always simple and hidden in plain sight, till someone explicitly calls out the obvious. For instance, Dettol, the personal care brand whose famous brand is 'antiseptic liquid', found in its research that customers want something cool and soothing during summer. Now that's a simple insight that anyone could have figured out. But put it in the context of soaps, Dettol suddenly has a 'menthol cool' soap that helps consumers beat the heat.

Established companies have an ear to the pulse of the market constantly. It involves extensive studies and ultimate resources at its disposal, but a new business cannot afford such luxury. It is also something that any new business cannot do away with, for it needs to ensure that the foundation of the business is built on unerring consumer insights for appropriate future course of action.

Even in Hindu legends, the creation of the universe began with the first sentient being emerging from a golden egg in a dark space with nothingness. That sentient being Lord Brahma managed to complete the whole creation from scratch. It sounds similar to the singular insight that forms the groundwork for the business. The downside of not having a product/business focusing on the customer is not receiving enough attention from the target audience. It won't matter if the product is exceptionally well-designed and estimated to give excellent business returns, if it is not done with customer's interest at heart.

From the insight, the idea is developed into a prototype, which would then be tested multiple times before entering the production pipeline. The complexity between developing a prototype from the comfort of home and sustaining quality in mass production is a balancing act for any new entrepreneur. Any shortcomings in the product proof for customer results in failure of its marketing promise. Marketing promise is a claim by the business to the customer, that it intends to solve their problem through its product. Apple, the US based tech giant, talks about safeguarding customer privacy both through its product and its communication. Its tag line is 'Privacy! It's an iPhone'. If Apple failed to live to this line in its products, it wouldn't have had the credibility it has today.

To squash out any possibility of the marketing promise failure, capital/huge resources are required to set up systems and protocols in place to ensure product quality, irrespective of the physical or digital medium. To sustain the operations scale-up, financial resources are pooled-in through several methods such as private equity, IPO release (Initial Public Offering), loans, etc. While the method of financing is subject to the business health of the firm, their capacity and other parameters, one cannot ignore the role of marketing in generating demand and subsequently adding to the revenue. Once the production is at full steam and the inventory is out in the market, the crucial responsibility would be that of logistics to ensure robust distribution that connects the producer to the consumer.

After the product hits the stores, the main question that needs to be answered is – what would ensure a consumer purchase? The whole exercise would be futile if the potential customer is not even aware of the product's existence. Marketing plays an active role at this juncture to generate awareness and build up demand through its actions, ensuring that the top line of the business is not diminished in any scenario. An added benefit is that marketing also helps in attracting the right talent pool, which in turn would strengthen the business at all levels.

As a business takes its first steps, its core team would help in chalking out a path for further growth. The objectives of such are guided by an overarching vision that is rooted in the deep principles of marketing. As per Hindu mythology, Lord Brahma, is the first sentient being and is responsible in principle for all the creations the world has witnessed, but was not involved in the micromanagement of the process. He has appointed *Prajapatis* who helped him to flourish the world with various lifeforms, primarily human beings. The beauty of the creation is the intricate relationships, the strengths, weaknesses and countermeasures between species on the planet that is worthy of being called an ecosystem. Comparably, certain checks need to be done while the product prototype is being drafted to ensure that the business can thrive in a similar ecosystem.

The Core

Even though the product development is a silo process, the ability to bring it to the customer's doorstep cannot be done without collaboration. The fundamental task for any business is to drive a bottom line (final expenditure after all costs) that is dependent on the raw material prices, logistics expenses, and other cost overheads. The partners who enable all the above support functions could aid or break the product in the respective market it is playing that is filled with competition. Porter's five forces framework is the most basic, yet effective tool when it comes to scanning the external environment to form an initial analysis of the ecosystem the business needs to thrive. It also paves a way to gauge the initial demand the product could generate in line with the market conditions.

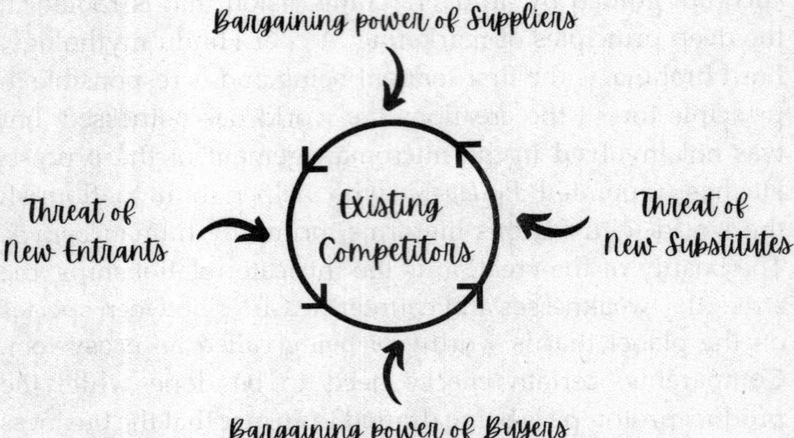

(Porter's Five Forces)

Porter's Five Forces Analysis deals with Competition, Bargaining Power of Buyers, Bargaining Power of Suppliers, Threat of New Entrants and Threat of Substitutes. These five forces applicable to a large firm with adequate resources or a boot-strapped firm, give a fair idea about whether entering an industry would make business sense or not, and whether an ecosystem could be built for a product. The first force is essentially about competition. It provides a clear picture of the existing competitors and their positioning to serve the consumers and the market. Based on the results, the target audience could be arrived at to finalize product plans or try to fit in the customer segment if the product is already ready. It's also crucial to identify the opportunity space to create a differentiation for the product.

The second force in hindsight provides how much leverage a consumer holds. Essentially a consumer would always hold leverage, what matters is the degree of leverage across segments and industries. If buyers of the product are limited, as in the case of defense systems and equipment, the buyers would be in a strong negotiating position. They would influence the price, the features of the product, and how it is being sold. The rural consumers of India revved up a silent revolution when Chik first offered shampoos in the form of sachets, which forced all other competitors to follow the same route. It could be treated as the case of competition copying competition, but where consumers are the ones who bought an integral change on how the product is sold, as sachets are present everywhere. While setting up a new restaurant, one would prefer to buy raw ingredients at the lowest price possible and on credit, if possible. However, the chosen grocery partner would not entertain the request as the restaurant is new to the market and fairly, if not this customer, he would have another buyer for his produce. The restaurant can go to another grocery partner, as the suppliers are plenty. The third force delves into the relationship with suppliers. In the case of a single supplier for multiple buyers, the supplier can demand the price and the buyers would have no choice but to take it. One such example would be crude oil, where the countries importing have no choice but to adhere to the prices set by the oil suppliers. The price increase in the raw materials would reflect in the form of reduced margins, yet the hands of the buyers are tied.

Threat of New Entrants talks about how easy it is to imitate one's business formula and derive similar success. It's not hard to replicate the business model of a popular food truck or mom and pop store. However, if a vendor possesses expertise in building metro trains, it would be hard for a new company to replicate the same technical know-how, processes, and experience to taste similar success. As the complexity of replicating the business model increases, the market slowly tends to be monopolistic. Effectively termed as Barriers of Entry, they determine how easy or tough it would be for a new player to play in that particular segment.

Threat of Substitutes deals with what kind of substitutes can overpower the value proposition of a firm. For example, OTT platforms turned out to be a substitute for normal cable and satellite tv and traditional movie theaters. IPL, a popular cricket format, stood as a threat to movies as both the entertainment formats were vying for viewers' eyeballs.

If the business is still in the introductory stage of PLC, it needs to ensure that it enters the market filled with competition on a differentiated value proposition that stands out to customers. On the other hand, if it is new to the field, it needs to constantly cultivate the ecosystem that flourishes the business. For example, OnePlus has strongly stormed Apple's smartphone market and carved a niche for itself. Epigamia, a dairy product manufacturer, was able to introduce Greek Yogurt to the Indian palate which is used to *desi ghee* (clarified butter) and *dahi* (curd).

Even though Porter's five forces framework is a tool to make strategic calls, it is related to marketing. Without a product/service in place, no business can take off and the foundation of a business is laced with the principles of marketing. All the above forces discussed help in painting a comprehensive preliminary picture, a basis on which further decisions to improve the bottom line of the firm can be taken. Let's understand it the DMart way.

DMartisation...

One of the India-based firms which tasted phenomenal success in recent times in a competitive market is DMart. High-end equipment, class apart infrastructure greet when one walks through the doors of DMart. The ambiance nails the customer's experience brief, which is different from the usual sore sight in every other retail store.

What started as a small store on the bustling roads of Mumbai, spiralled off into a behemoth and grew by leaps and bounds, ruling both the southern and western markets. It wasn't an easy task to enter into a market that is already crowded in the food and grocery retail space with players such as Future Group, Reliance, Aditya Birla's More, Spencers, etc. That too in a country like India, where food habits, cuisines, traditions and culture change every fifty kilometre. Imagine not having basic ingredients needed to make idli and dosa in the southern part and vice versa with roti in the northern parts. That's akin to failing the initial customer's preference test, where there is no product fit at all. Another source of competition, the unorganized retail space is cluttered with mom and pop stores, street vendors, flea markets, etc., which tediously cater to the diverse consumers' needs. If anything, the recent pandemic has proved its importance in the last-mile delivery to the customers. Despite their strengths, these players can never match up with the modern-day retailers in terms of offerings and services such as a wide range of product assortment, doorstep delivery and better credit opportunities.

Furthermore, due to the availability of an extensive supplier pool catering to organized players, it was easier for DMart to strike deals at the rates capable of creating a win-win situation for suppliers, end customers and itself.

Unlike its competitors who were into dealing with private labels, DMart went ahead with the philosophy of 'Give Them What They Want' by capitalizing on its efficiencies. The usual playbook that modern retailers follow is to offer their private labels, which helps them save operational costs in terms of logistics, marketing, etc., and provide increased margins. Despite being a proven strategy to an extent where Amazon has also deployed its private labels, DMart wanted to do something different. Using the huge purchase capacity, they were able to negotiate better deals for their buck and pass the benefits to the customers. They were also able to lease out retail spaces for thirty years, thus saving humongous rental costs and limiting them only to 0.2% of the total revenue. In a retail setup that runs on wafer-thin margins, the adage of money not spent is money saved stands true.

DMart has been successful in driving home the advantage for its customers through its saving proposition on various products and communicating the same. Based on the consumer insights, it has maintained a relatively limited range of offerings, enabling fast off-shelf turnover. Due to the frequent purchase cycle, DMart gets cheaper deals from its suppliers. It has always focused on operational efficiency, which ultimately led to lower costs, providing further savings for the consumers. This value proposition helped it stand out from other players in the retail space. DMart was able to cross off the checklist of Porter's five forces to make compelling changes to its product proposition to drive value to its customers. Had DMart blindly entered the retail space without understanding the ecosystem, it would have surely tasted failure. For any new business out there, Porter's five forces provide a perspective on which category to enter and how to turn that into a marketing advantage. DMart's success was recognized by the markets when its IPO was oversubscribed almost 109 times, making its founder Radhakishan K. Damani, one of the richest persons in the country.

A Mix of Blue Ocean...

DMart is a case study of making a successful foray in a sector filled with competition. Another concept that is gaining currency is the 'Blue Ocean Strategy'. It's a popular phrase that is not only evident in seminars and workshops, but is also creeping into daily conversational lingo. The blue ocean is used to express an unexplored opportunity in the market brimming with potential. It is a philosophy that states that any company must venture into uncontested market space which was previously unheard of or none bothered to pick up the opportunity at all. And once a company decides to delve into the blue ocean, it needs to strategically build advantages to survive the PLC. The rulebook on how to gain an advantage is not exactly vivid. But certain benchmarks need to be taken care of to ensure that the product/brand has some means to be a market leader in its category.

Mohit wanted to set up a food business in an area famous for making delicious parathas. He wanted to stand out, that's why he decided to sell momos instead of parathas, which is a novelty, and there are enough opportunities to grow.

It would be imperative to address a few characteristics of a blue ocean before terming everything and nothing as a part of the Blue Ocean Strategy. It deals with the idea that a company or a brand would play into an uncontested space and capture that market by creating demand through differentiation and low cost. In this whole process, it may also make the whole competition irrelevant. On the contrary, it also perceives that red ocean markets are already saturated with competition and the battle for market share is always on the go from day 1. In the previous example, DMart was not entering a blue ocean space as there were already existing players with commendable market share. It nudges brands/ companies to actively look for blue ocean markets where their efforts would have more return on the buck compared to red ocean markets. Let us check out an example of a business attempting an blue ocean play.

Battering the Way in...

Idli and dosa are staples in any south Indian household. Anyone worth their salt in the industry would claim that the key to success is in the consistency of the batter, for any south Indian housewife can make batter with one arm tied back. And this was during a time when there were no automatic wet grinders. No exaggeration, idli/dosa batter is a mammoth challenge even for the best of the best, even with all the technology at their disposal. The two main ingredients to get a batter right are ratios and fermentation time. However, for working women, it's not an easy task to keep on making batter on a day to day basis. Throw in the variations of batter between idli, dosa, uttapams, etc., and one has a challenge in the face of time crunch. This was the problem the company iD wanted to solve.

With humble beginnings to its name, iD expanded to become a company with a 400-crore turnover. And the pandemic has only given a boost to the Ready to Cook/ Ready to Eat segment in a way one couldn't even fathom. ITC has scaled up its frozen foods segment riding on the wave, as a testament to the changing behaviour.

The concept of branded batter was not exactly new. Some local players play on a marginal level. Yet they couldn't boast of high quality or better taste or natural origins of the batter. No brand could claim all of the attributes. This was the space iD wanted to venture into. Starting in a modest office space of 550 sq. ft., one wet grinder, dishwasher, and a second-hand scooter, iD grew to sell a hundred packets of batter a day within nine months. The road was not without its challenges. The consistency of the batter depends on the fermentation it is subjected to. If one overdoes it, it results in a batter-massacre and painful efforts in cleaning it up.

In a way, this segment was a blue ocean for iD when it started its operations. Its first place was Bangalore, the city of all startups. Unfortunately, no company controls the last mile distribution channels. D2C (Direct to Customer) is a concept that is gaining currency these days, for the better half of the companies are dependent on third party players to ensure that their product is delivered right to the customer's doorstep. An extrapolation of this is that neither the company has any control over the apparatus the distribution channels have in place to safeguard its goods nor the facility to provide them with it. Think of it this way – If Harini wanted to send a fresh box of batter to her aunt five km away and she employs a delivery man to deliver it for her, she can't control if the product reaches safely or not. It is totally dependent on the delivery person's behaviour. On the other hand, if she had delivered herself, she would ensure the safety of the batter. Now, extrapolate this problem to the scale of a company and imagine the consequences. For a company that deals with consumables with less shelf time, especially batter, it is a matter of scale and sunk cost. If a batter is not refrigerated properly, the fermentation process gets kicked in, leading to over-fermentation, which leads to an eventual loss.

When the founders were engulfed with this problem, they went back to the drawing board to see if anything could be done to the product itself. They tried to implement controlled fermentation technology to ensure that over-fermentation doesn't happen. They also made it a point to ensure that they distributed to stores that had the appropriate refrigeration systems in place. This way they would avoid deliberate chances of batter damage just because the store didn't have a refrigeration system in place. This led to them being the leading player in a segment that none had foreseen to grab the opportunity.

While Bangalore gave the required success to 'iD', its path to success is not over yet. It met its biggest failure in the Chennai market. After Bangalore, if anyone wanted to expand the business of packaged batter, it would logically be Chennai, for it is the land of idlis and dosas (added proximity to Bangalore operations could have been a brownie point in the initial stage). However, the market was already cluttered with local, small players who were offering their products at a price point that 'iD' couldn't hope to compete, with the promises it made on its batter. They had to maintain their leadership in the market and hence decided to expand into other major cities like Mumbai, Hyderabad, Pune and Dubai.

Using this as a template, they expanded their portfolio to include coffee decoction, Malabar parotta, wheat parotta, paneer, etc. After gaining a foothold in these segments, they have set their sights again on Chennai where they have entered with their 'Parotta' offering. After a year or so, with the confidence of building a brand presence and trust, they started pumping out their core product of 'idli/ dosa' batter. Soon enough, they won a funding round from Premji Trusts and are now looking to expand to major markets in the US also. To date, they are clocking almost 55000 kg worth of batter every day.

One thing they haven't stayed away from is their core of innovation which has always made them stand out in the market. South Indian filter coffee is also a ritual lauded with its techniques and intricacies. The delicious aroma of the coffee is not exactly conjured out of thin air. They developed the coffee decoction which makes the process much easier and at the same time ensures that the richness of the coffee is not lost. And 'iD' provided the same in unique packaging which resembles a coffee glass in a cup (the traditional way filter coffees are served with all the gymnastics elegantly performed with the coffee).

Luckily, 'iD' hasn't stopped with this. They brought something called an 'instant *vada* maker' with patented packaging. They provided an easy squeeze-out pouch that doles out perfect round vadas with holes in them, the exact way grandmothers used to make them on a Saturday afternoon. With an innovative portfolio that keeps on expanding into segments that have never been looked at as segments before, iD is making a name for itself. It still has a long journey to cover, but it has become slightly easier with the brand presence it has created for itself, especially when it goes on to explore blue ocean spaces.

Into the Sea...

While DMart's story represents the success of breaking into a market filled with competition, there is no proper blueprint for businesses trying to tap into the unexplored potential, as showcased by iD. Despite firefighting the immediate problems at hand, it is imperative for businesses (especially in the context of a startup) to have an eye on future growth and be equipped for it accordingly. One might not know at what pace the company would grow or how the demand would expand, but they need to make sure that they ramp up their capabilities to match with the supply. This forms one of the most crucial challenges at the PLC's nascent stage. Overestimating or underestimating demand would do no good to the company, for having high inventory with no takers results in financial loss and the other scenario would lead to having less turn-around time to meet the demand.

The story of creation and the starting of a business share certain similarities. The answer to the crucial challenge at the start of the PLC may be found in the story of Lord Vishnu's first avatar to save the universe - *Matsya Avatar*.

Saviour with Fins

It was the glorious Satya yuga, an age filled with dharma and prosperity. The creation willed to life by Lord Brahma, the god of creation was flourishing without any harm or fear. However, the end of time was coming, dubbed as *pralay*, the ultimate destruction, a reset of sorts for the universe. And there was only one who could save humanity from it.

Back on earth, in an ashram located near the riverbank, King Satyavrat was performing a great penance. All he wanted was to get a glimpse of Lord Vishnu, the lord protector of the known universe. As part of his morning prayers, he raised his two hands in the form of a bowl, filled it with water and began to pour it down as an offering to the Lord. After completing his morning prayers in the river, the king went back to his penance. This routine went on for quite some time. However, one fine morning, something different happened.

No sooner than he was about to release the water back into the river, he heard a voice say, "Please don't put me back into the water." The king turned to look around, trying to figure where the voice was coming from. When the voice spoke again, he managed to locate the source to a little fish present in his hands. He was surprised to find a fish, let alone a talking one. The fish had golden scales which shone brightly in the morning light.

"O great king! Please don't release me back into the water. The other predators would eat me up in a jiffy. Please take me to some place safe," requested the fish.

Moved by the fish's plea and his duty to protect the innocent, the king managed to place the fish in his *kamandal*, a special pot used by sages to hold water. In just a few hours, the fish had grown big enough to surpass the kamandal. The fish requested the king to place him in a bigger vessel so that the fish could be comfortable and have space to swim around. Perplexed, Satyavrat transferred it to a comparatively bigger pitcher than the kamandal. But he never gave a second thought on how the fish managed to speak to him or how it had grown in such a short time.

In a few hours after the transfer, the fish outgrew this big pitcher also. It requested him to change the vessel again. Satyavrat obliged gracefully and kept on transferring the fish to bigger vessels and pitchers. But it was to no avail, for the fish managed to outgrow all of them. He threw the fish into a small pond, but this action also turned out to be futile when it outgrew the pond also. He managed to take it back to the river it originally came from, but by then the fish was so huge that it seemed to dwarf the waters.

By then the king was actively pondering that this was no ordinary fish who could talk and grow at an unusual exponential rate. That was when a realization dawned on him that it is no ordinary fish and it must be Lord Vishnu, who obliged his request of *darshan* in this manner. So, he fell at the feet of the fish in reverence and began to sing the prayer to Lord Vishnu. He never questioned why the lord didn't appear in his original form and managed to come in the form of the fish. He was too happy to have a darshan of his beloved lord.

"Satyavrat! The end of time is near. In seven days, all the lifeforms would die when Lord Brahma goes to his sleep, marking the end of this yuga. That is when the pralay would begin. You come up to the highest cliff in this village, along with *sapta rishis* (the prime seven sages) and a collection of all varieties of plant seeds," said the divine fish and disappeared.

Without a second thought, he went on to follow the lord's command. On the morning of the seventh day, dark clouds loomed over the sky, giving it a black hue. What started out as a light shower began to intensify by the passing second with heavy winds. Oceans broke into the land with no respect for the boundaries, drowning all living beings, animals and plants in sight. The sun and moon were nowhere to be seen to the naked eye. Without any source of natural light, the world was engulfed in darkness with only lightning for company. The whole of humanity was in an unwinnable fight against nature.

Satyavrat reached the same point where the divine fish had asked him to stay put, along with the bundle of herbs and other plant seeds. Even sapta rishis had reached the designated point. They were glowing and emanating lights of varied colours, powered by their mediation prowess. In that light, Satyavrat could see the deluge and the carnage it was unleashing. It was unnerving to see how the whole landmass was covered in water as far as the naked eye could see. Despite his apprehensions, he had his faith in Lord Vishnu. In the distance, he saw a silhouette of a huge ship making its way towards them.

On the other hand, in Satyaloka, the abode of Lord Brahma, something unexpected was happening. A demon named Hayagreeva sought this as the perfect opportunity to steal the Vedas that were within Lord Brahma's grasp. The horse-faced demon, (not to be confused with Lord Vishnu's another avatar with a similar name) was born out of the negative energies of Lord Brahma. Without Vedas, the foundational knowledge of everything, it would be impossible to continue with the creation process after the destruction. The demon wished to stall the creation process and be the sole possessor of the Vedas.

He stole the Vedas that were dripping out of a sleeping Brahma. Hayagreeva simply believed that he could wait out the destruction in the ocean and none would be wise enough to look out for him. As soon as he reached the ocean bed, he saw a huge golden fish swimming towards him at a great speed. The demon was surprised and afraid at the same time. He didn't expect the gods to find him this soon. The huge glowing fish wasn't slowing down at all and charging with vigour. Hayagreeva also inched ahead to meet the challenge thrown by the finned animal. A fierce battle ensued between the two of them. Hayagreeva began to throw punches, to which the fish countered with its tackling. The demon tried to put up a valiant fight, but he was of no match to the divine fish. In no time, the fish vanquished Hayagreeva and took control of the Vedas.

Back on earth, Satyavrat and the seven sages safely boarded the ship that had appeared out of nowhere. The ship was sturdy enough to withstand any pressure, but it couldn't be a sitting duck against the rising waters and heavy currents. A huge fish, larger than the boat, larger than what Satyavrat had seen before, appeared near the boat. Its body extended beyond leagues, an ancient unit of measurement. Its golden scales threw a radiance that was calm and reassuring on the dark night. It used its body to protect the ship from the gigantic waves which threatened to break the ship.

After what seemed a while, Adi Sesha, the immortal serpent and the king of snakes appeared near the boat. A mount of Lord Vishnu, Adi Sesha represented the personification of time. It is peak symbolism here that 'personification of time' is helping to save life during 'end of time'. The divine fish communicated mentally to Satyavrat to tie the front of the ship to its tail using the snake as a rope. Once the arrangement was done, the divine fish began to navigate the choppy waters, deflecting the waves and standing in as a shield against howling winds that could capsize the ship.

After seven days and seven nights of incessant rain, the sky cleared up, letting the land witness the beautiful sun. With the pralay (destruction) coming to an end, it also brought forward a new dawn. A new beginning where King Satyavrat would continue the good work of creation and start afresh. For this responsibility, he was given the title 'Manu'. He was the only ordinary human being to survive a destruction and live long to tell the tale. As the future beings have descended from Manu, the name *manavas* was given in Sanskrit as a term for all human beings and his descendants.

The divine fish, also called *Matsya Murthy* is the first avatar of Lord Vishnu where he undertook the responsibility of ensuring that life continues even after destruction. He couldn't attempt to stop the destruction himself as he can't go against *Srishti dharma* (the laws of creation). The wheel of time has to keep on spinning and it stops for no one. The Lord could have taken any form as an avatar to save humanity. The form of a fish need not be his first choice. It is the humblest of all the creatures and it was cursed by Agni, the god of fire, to be hunted even in the depths of the ocean.

However, fulfilling the wish of Satyavrat for a divine darshan (appearance) as a result of his mediation, to safeguard the Vedas when Lord Brahma was asleep from demon Hayagreeva's theft attempt, and to ensure the survival of humanity during the end of time, Lord Vishnu felt that a fish form would help in tackling all the parameters. Thus, Matsya avatar was born. With the restoration of Vedas and survival of crucial knowledge, the creation and humanity survived to witness a new dawn.

Donning the Challenge

The forethought shown by Matsya Murthy and Satyavrat in gathering resources to prepare for the future, after surviving the immediate threat, is a lesson for businesses that are trying to develop new markets. It is a lesson the hyper-local delivery startup Dunzo has learnt in recent times. Starting out as a WhatsApp Group, Dunzo grew to its current position due to the efforts of Kabeer Biswas, Mukund Jha and Ankur

Agarwal. Based out of India's Silicon Valley (Bangalore), Dunzo seemed to find favour with the tech-savvy crowd which had little time to spare for mundane tasks.

To the question of what exactly Dunzo does, they deliver anything and everything from point A to point B if the customer can classify it under their catalog. 'Need medicines delivered? Forgot your purse? Need a gift to be delivered? Want to have a lip-smacking biriyani?' are some of the use-cases they cater to. Word of Mouth (WoM) helped it grow up so much that Dunzo was close to being a verb - *Just Dunzo it!*

However, it was not all sunshine for the company. As the company scaled up, they could not manage the supply side for pent-up demand. They tried to match the overgrowing demand with making slight tweaks to its supply team, but it was to no avail. The more they tried to bridge the gap, the more the demand outgrew. This caused the company to stop its operations for two months to build the necessary infrastructure to handle the exponential demand seamlessly. Imagine being a new startup and being out of business for two months. It's not an easy situation to be in. A competitor could swoop in to capture the existing customer base that one has painfully built over. As operations resumed, Dunzo was knocking doors on scores of investors before Google turned up to save the day.

Dunzo's value proposition and marketing strategy were unique through which it was acing the awareness game big time. Dunzo proved that robust operations coupled with the right marketing communication strategies make a great recipe for customer experience. Google did more than just give money to Dunzo. It made headlines and put Duzno back in the spotlight, which Dunzo made good use of. The revenue grew up from a trivial INR 0.7 lakh in FY 16 to 76.59 lakhs in FY 19.

In a true sense, Google turned out to be more than Matsya for Dunzo. Not only were the purse strings loosened for expansion, but also provided the scope of integration between Google products and Dunzo. For example, GPay lists Dunzo in the business section, allowing its users to order food and groceries from Dunzo directly. Plus, it helps to have the brand image of being backed by Google.

Had Dunzo not survived its first deluge of orders, today probably it would have joined the list of promising startups that have already shut shop. Tiny Owl is another such company which played in the hyper-local delivery space back in 2014 before the internet had overtaken the country. It expanded too fast, without building up operational efficiencies, and relied on discounts and promotions to source the demand. Ultimately it turned out to be too little, too late.

"When things grow, you need some kind of structure to make it more efficient. And when you are growing at such a crazy speed, it's very difficult to form that structure accordingly. So that's where we messed up a little," said Saurabh Goyal, co-founder of Tiny Owl in an interview.[1] Ultimately it had to shut shop by 2016, in less than two years of its inception.

Marketing communication alone wouldn't help any company that is struggling with a demand challenge in this stage of the life cycle, but it definitely would give an edge to fight out another day.

Lessons from the Fin

Most mythologies around the world have a story that features a great deluge and a boat where humanity survived to see a

1 https://economictimes.indiatimes.com/magazines/panache/the-rise-and-fall-of-tinyowl-lessons-that-startup-founder-saurabh-goyal-learnt/articleshow/60069036.cms

new dawn. Matsya avatar is the first of the Dashavatars that Lord Vishnu has undertaken to establish dharma and save lives across all four yugas. In Hindu mythology, the story of Matsya avatar is preceded by that of Lord Brahma's creation story, which collectively portrays the challenges of creating and sustaining a new creation. In the introductory phase in the PLC, a business also faces similar tribunals of forming a business from scratch and maintaining the ecosystem while dealing with varied stakeholders.

The snake Adi Shesha used to tie the boat to the rim of Matsya represents the help provided in the form of capital and additional resources to Dunzo. The theft attempt of Hayagreeva foretells the unseen, external factors that threaten to disrupt the delicate business balance. Satyavrat never asked the question of why Lord Vishnu appeared in the form of Matysa and not in his original avatar. Like the qualities of the king, it was Dunzo's solid fundamentals that attracted its saviour, Google. No matter what, as long as the business fundamentals are appropriate, the business would live to fight another day. This is evident in the cases of DMart, iD and Dunzo. Since it was the beginning of a new lease of life, Matysa was integral in navigating the choppy waters, all the while suggesting Satyavrat to gather seeds, saptarishis indicating the know-how required to rebuild life from scratch. This is essentially the concept of Blue-ocean strategy which attempts to scout out new opportunities which require businesses to start from ground zero.

Before moving on to further chapters that deal with other challenges as one progresses in the introductory phase of PLC, below is a quick summary of the learnings from the divine fish.

- Leadership and Chief Experience Officers (CXO) need to recognize the invisible role of marketing from the starting of the business setting up process to formation of the ecosystem for the business to thrive and take decisions going forward.
- Customer insights are simple in nature, and in hindsight, obvious to recognize. Appropriate customer insight needs to be chosen as the basis for the formulation of any business model starting from product design to customer delivery.
- Before taking a decision to enter into an existing market space, preliminary understanding of the market can be formed using Porter's five forces model (Competition, Bargaining Power of Buyers, Bargaining Power of Suppliers, Threat of New Entrants, and Threat of Substitutes) to craft the market/segment entry strategy accordingly.
- In case of looking to enter brand new markets, one can use Blue Ocean Strategy as a mechanism to scout for untapped markets and build the new category accordingly.
- While the to-do list is plenty for any new business, the main objective in the starting phase of the PLC is generating enough demand through market awareness and its actions need to reflect that.
- The product/business needs to ensure that proper systems are in place. Constant evaluation of demand is required to not lose out on market opportunities in extreme scenarios and create a negative dent in the consumer mind space.

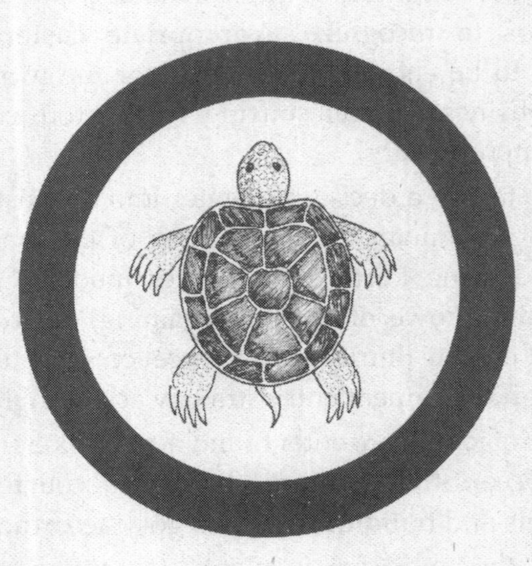

2

Ace in the Tortoise Shell

Ksheerabdhimadhanesastram
Mandaradrim samuhdvahan |
Swayam kurmataam praptastam
Vande harimachyutam | |

The Mantra of Awareness

The decision to enter a market of one's choice has been taken. The product has been developed according to customer's preference, perfect business model has been set up within the available limitations and existential threat to the business has been successfully staved off. This is just the start and it is a long way in the journey before the business could realize any profits on the investments made.

While immediate problems plaguing the business like solving financial concerns, product-related changes, setting up supply chain logistics will be solved eventually, the primary concern throughout the introductory stage of the PLC would be to create market awareness, which in turn would lead to demand generation. One should be in a position to attract customers.

For example, if Koushik had set up a new variety of snacks stall, it would be tough to attract customers since they don't know anything about him. However, if he manages to get some customers to try out the snacks, they are called 'Innovators'.

"Innovators" are defined as an early set of customers who would be experimental enough to try out new offerings. Attracting Innovators towards the product would be a crucial task with appropriate communication.

While we are still in the introductory phase, we will address product/offering as a separate entity from the term brand. At this juncture, the entity of a brand would germinate alongside the offering, but it would be in a very nascent stage. The concept of a brand would be dealt with in further chapters as the business continues to grow alongside the PLC journey. The subtle difference between a product and a brand is that a product solves the immediate need of a customer. For instance, if a customer requires a tool for writing, a pen or pencil would do the trick. On the other hand, if the pen carries the sticker of 'Mont Blanc', it adds an extra value for the customer as a brand is a sort of living entity in the customer's mind space.

In the journey of creating market awareness, the cost of customer acquisition would be high, for one has to educate a customer about their presence in the market. Customer acquisition cost (CAC) is a term used to define the monetary efforts required to make the customer try out the product or offering for at least once.

Rahul had opened a saree shop. He employs an auto with a microphone to ride along the streets, broadcasting about the new shop. If one customer walks in after listening to the microphone and makes a first purchase, then a customer has been acquired. If the cost of the microphone is Rs 1000/-, then the customer acquisition cost is defined as Rs 1000/-. If it was two customers, then the acquisition cost is Rs 500/- per customer.

The definition of CAC is dependent on the marketing

channel used and the number of customers who made the first transaction through that marketing channel. If the same customer comes back to make another purchase, that is called a repeat purchase. And if the same customer tells her friends about the saree shop and the experience she had, that is word of mouth.

Once the innovators check out the product, then comes the process of inducing repeat purchases for sustenance and enough word of mouth to attract other customers towards the sales funnel. Sales funnel is an elaborate journey that a customer goes from 'Awareness' (Knowing about the product) to 'Interest' (Actively looking out for solutions) to 'Desire' (Researching more about the solution) to 'Action' (Making the purchase). Getting customers into the sales funnel is a task in itself.

Amazon and Flipkart would know the struggle of the introductory phase a bit too well. Both started as book delivery businesses before turning into present-day behemoths. Flipkart was formed by ex-Amazon employees who decided to bring the e-commerce bug to Indian customers. VVK Chandra, whose love for books was unparalleled, happened to be the first customer of Flipkart. He started scouting for a book named *Leaving Microsoft to Change the World*, written by John Wood. But to no avail, for it wasn't available in any offline stores. That customer used to blog about technology and stuff, where Sachin Bansal, co-founder of Flipkart, left out a comment on the blog about the availability of the particular book in their inventory. Curious, the customer went in, checked out the book he wanted, and made the first order of Flipkart. Once the order was placed, it was not a smooth journey. After a lot of tribunals, Flipkart made through on its first order and the rest they say is history. This happened during a time when the internet was still booming or the word 'online shopping' was not uttered every second. VVK Chandra was an innovator who was willing to try out a new offering just on the product promise, and such innovators are crucial in fine-tuning the whole value chain of the offering as time progresses.

At a nascent stage, any business struggles out for awareness, which ultimately leads to sales conversion in the end. If the customer doesn't know that an offering exists to solve his need, he would not be in a position to avail the solution. And if the offering is playing into a new category, then the onus of educating the customer is on the business. It is an added effort for the organization to educate the customer of the new category that intends to solve the problem and then emphasize the benefits provided by the business. The concept of awareness can range from simple recognition of existence to granular demonstration of the offering.

In an apartment complex of over five hundred residents, Kalyani decided to start a grocery service that caters instant groceries at a bargain price. However, she has not communicated to the residents about her new venture. If they don't know about this venture, then they wouldn't be in a position to make any purchases. So, Kalyani has to make efforts to educate the residents about her new venture and how it solves their problem.

One major risk associated with this approach is that any viable competitor could just swoop in to utilize the awareness capital painstakingly built by the first mover. It's not an easy position to be in. Imagine getting the product right, crafting the right communication strategy, employing various methods to develop the new category, only to see a competitor just piggy-riding on the success created by the first mover. This was witnessed when Swiggy (a food delivery startup in India) introduced an offering of 'Swiggy Genie' while Dunzo has struggled to put up a business model surrounding hyperlocal delivery from scratch. It is witnessed even in industries that have enough players but are venturing into new product propositions. Sunfeast - Dark Fantasy is a molten chocolate-filled cookie introduced by ITC which turned out to resonate with the audience back in 2010. A decade later, it still commands a premium in its chocolate-filled cookie subsegment. After Sunfeast's success, Britannia and Mondelez launched their versions of this biscuit to not let ITC have a free run in the chocolate-filled cookie subsegment. The jury is still out on how much market share could they capture, but the two companies have enough resources to fight a prolonged battle with ITC, effectively nullifying ITC's first mover advantage.

Apart from the strategic risks associated with a first mover, the customer acquisition cost is also high (in a traditional setup like newspapers or TV advertisements) as it is a consequence of creating awareness. In its initial days, Nirma's founder Karsanbhai Patel used to sell detergents from door to door on a bicycle because he didn't have enough resources to splash on expensive advertisements. That amplified the word of mouth and increased the initial trials, which helped in Nirma gaining currency amongst housewives.

Generating awareness is not a one-time activity. It needs to be repeated at a frequency so that the customer registers the offering or the brand name and is at his top-of-the-mind recall when he is about to make a purchase. In today's world, the frequency needs to be increased over existing levels for the average attention span of a customer has reduced to less than ten seconds. Simply talking about the benefits of the product, providing any discount, using influencers, etc., are some of the ways to generate awareness and bring on initial trials. Cut back to today's scenario, even though the cost of digital marketing is a fraction of what a traditional medium is, the CAC has skyrocketed in general. This could be attributed to different reasons – lack of attention span, superior offerings in the market, product price viability, etc. Zomato, a player in the food-tech space, has the experience in generating awareness through its marketing strategies.

Zomato and the way of Red

If one had to put a start to the Zomato story, it was not even a food delivery business, to begin with. It started its humble roots as a dining catalogue in 2008, in the avatar of Foodiebay.com. Starting out as a brainchild of Deepinder Goyal and Prasoon Jain, Zomato did grow out of the dining menu catalog avatar and ventured into other verticals such as HyperPure, Zomato Gold (now known as Zomato Pro), Fitso, Blinkit, etc. Foodiebay eventually turned into Zomato – which suspiciously rhymed with the vegetable tomato – within six weeks of launch and expansion into other cities apart from the NCR region.

On the other hand, Swiggy was leading the food delivery business in India. Swiggy in its defense was first a logistics company before it could be deemed as a competitor in the food tech space. Its robust delivery fleet and operational capabilities helped it shape up its growth from the time in 2016 when the food delivery business was still in its nascent phase. Up until then, Zomato was supposed to be a restaurant finder and diner catalog, but it decided to utilize that strength to venture into the food delivery business. Zomato did have a significant user base that it could leverage to the fullest. It was the logical step for Zomato. From a modest thirty thousand orders per day in 2016, Zomato grew to 1.3 million orders per day in 2019. But all this was not without a cost. It had locked horns with Swiggy in a heavy discount battle for market-share supremacy. The discounts spiraled into heavy customer acquisition costs which either companies are not able to come back from. Eventually, the customer was the winner of this battle as both the startups were bleeding money in the name of awareness and customer acquisition. From the customer perspective, the core offering of either Swiggy or Zomato was delivery of the food, since neither of them upfront had any food brands of their own (though Swiggy started to experiment with private labels in cloud kitchens) nor did they create food in the first place. So, it doesn't matter to the customer if he is getting the food from Zomato or Swiggy as long as he is getting it from his favorite restaurant 'XYZ'.

On a closer inspection, the battle is not merely about which startup would have the higher customer base. It is also about inducing a new habit to the populace that couldn't put together the words 'food delivery' a couple of years back. Imagine, a couple of years back, going out to eat was a ritual. Now, if one doesn't feel like cooking or doesn't have any food, it simply means 'Let's order food online'.

As marketers, the known conviction is that it is hard to generate a habit from scratch, but it is slightly easy to point the customer in a certain direction when there is enough intuition displayed already. It is tough to get someone to try out chocolate; but if they already eat chocolate, then it wouldn't be too much of a stretch to make them try a chocolate cake. Today, it would be unimaginable to witness a world without food delivery. Convenience has been introduced in customer's lives and it would be a challenge to go back to an era where a click of a button doesn't bring food to the doorstep. 'Let's order from Zomato today' is a testament to Zomato's marketing team's efforts in building a new habit and generating awareness about food delivery in the consumer's mind space. From running creative billboards to quirky advertisements on social media to offering discounts, Zomato has tried every trick in the book to increase its customer base and in turn, develop awareness for food delivery as a space.

However, the success of inducing the habit is not that of Zomato alone, even though it is one of the pioneers in the food tech segment. Swiggy was also equally instrumental in inciting the habit of ordering food online in customers. The aggressive battle between Zomato and Swiggy has caused the habit to change in a rapid timeline. What was supposed to take almost five to seven years in an ideal scenario, was completed in less than four years. Zomato and Swiggy had spent humongous resources educating the customer about the food delivery business and in turn, spread their reach in the process. While the first mover is responsible for creating awareness of a new product/segment, having a competitor accelerates the process. Once the category awareness is created, it would be easier for companies or brands to communicate their proposition without too much of an effort. For example, earlier Zomato had to talk on the lines that 'We deliver food'. Today, Zomato has an option to say 'We deliver food in thirty minutes'. The words 'We deliver food' is to educate the customer about the whole food delivery category. And the words 'in thirty minutes' represents Zomato's promise to the customer. This phenomenon of joining hands with rivals for the greater good has been witnessed in the story of *Kurmavatar* of Lord Vishnu.

On the Tortoise Shell

The creation was saved from destruction and it was flourishing into a new era. Sage Kashyapa, one of the Saptarishis had two wives – Aditi and Diti – daughters of Dakshaprajapati. Aditi was the mother of *Devas*, while Diti was the mother of *Asuras*. Devas and Asuras were in constant war for one-upmanship in wealth and glory. Countless have lost their lives on either side. Devas were guided by rishi Bhrispati as their guru, while the Asuras had rishi Shukracharya. At that moment, Devas had the upper hand. Amaravati, the capital city of Devas, looked flamboyant and fabulous with all their grandeur and wealth. But they were not immortal. Once sage Durvasa was just returning after visiting the divine realms that hosted the holy trinity (Lords Brahma, Vishnu and Shiva). He was carrying with him a garland that he had received as a gift. He wanted to find someone worthy to partake in the *prasad* of the garland. He came across Indra, the king of Devas who was atop a white elephant, Airavat.

After necessary greetings were extended, sage Durvasa as a mark of respect furnished the flower garland to Indra, who in turn, accepted it and immediately placed the garland on the elephant's forehead. The sweet smell of the flowers attracted bumble bees which riled up the elephant. It lifted its trunk and threw the garland on the ground and trampled it with its foot. Durvasa was not pleased. Indra could have apologized or done something . Yet, he sat silently. The sage took this to be an insult and cursed that the Devas would lose everything that made them so proud in the first place. In an instant, the grandeur, wealth, and all of Amaravati was lost into the milk ocean. It resembled a ghost town more than a thriving city in mere seconds.

Devas were aghast with the turn of events. Now they were more vulnerable to attacks from Asuras and there was nothing they can do to defend themselves. Upon their guru sage Bhrispathi's suggestion, they rushed to Lord Brahma residing in Satyalok for deliverance. The Lord with his four faces looking in either direction, sat peacefully upon a white lotus, holding a kamandal, a flower, and vedas in his four hands. He suggested that Lord Vishnu would be the right person to help out with their crisis. Devas didn't know that Lord Vishnu could help. Lord Vishnu always took an avatar whenever Dharma was in trouble or any being asked for help and they had a just cause. They raced to Vaikuntha, the humble abode of Lord Vishnu.

Lord Vishnu looked regal upon the bed of Adi Sesha, the eternal serpent. Upon listening to their problem, the lord realized that Devas were already repentant for their mistakes through their words. Lord Vishnu decided to give Devas another chance to redeem themselves. He suggested that they churn the milk ocean for the nectar of immortality. That would solve the problem of being in constant war with the Asuras. The milk ocean has a lot of treasures that can be unearthed in the process. Yet the milk ocean was vast enough that only the strength of Devas wouldn't be sufficient for churning it. Upon Vishnu's suggestion, Devas reached out to their mortal enemies, Asuras, for a truce to help them with the milk ocean churning. Asuras only agreed to help as long they were promised a share in *amrita*, the nectar of immortality.

To churn the vast milk ocean, an equivalent churning apparatus would be required. The lord suggested they use mountain Mandara as the churning apparatus, while Vasuki, the serpent king, would form a replacement for the rope. Devas and Asuras struggled to lift the mountain and place it in the middle of the ocean. Thousands of them lost their lives in the process, but they didn't falter in the light of adversity. When it came to the case of Vasuki, both parties fought like squabbling children. Asuras were adamant they were superior and had to be on the head side of the snake, while Devas were unrelenting to be on the tail side of the snake in the churning process. Lord Vishnu brokered peace between the parties.

Everything was set in place, Asuras took the head side of the snake, while Devas contented with the tail side, as none of them were immortal. The reason is, Asuras have a secret of pseudo-immortality through their guru Shukracharya who knew the *Mritsanjeevani* mantra which is used to bring back people from the jaws of death. Yet it was not sustainable as only Shukracharya knew about it and was supposed to be administered in a limited time frame. Shukracharya never tried to misuse this for nefarious gains. Even then the Devas had no such aces up their sleeves. Hence, they took the safer tail side for the churning process.

The apparatus was in place. Both the parties were on either side and they started churning out. The force from them was not enough to keep the mountain afloat. It was to no avail. The mountain began to sink into the milk ocean with the Devas helplessly watching on the sidelines. In the exercise of ironing out larger issues of getting the churning process started, this particular teeny tiny problem was missed out. The milk ocean was an impartial celestial body that was exactly not under anyone's jurisdiction of powers. Like how Lord Varuna, god of seas, would allow Lord Ram to build a stone bridge by making the stones afloat, or Goddess Yamuna would part the river to facilitate Krishna's escape from Kansa's clutches. However, that wasn't the case here and someone had to do something before everything was lost. If the operation didn't work out, Asuras didn't have any qualms over giving up the truce and taking advantage of the Devas' weakened position.

Even in such a bleak situation, Devas didn't lose their faith in Lord Vishnu. Out of the blue, the Mandara mountain started rising up. Upon closer inspection, the Devas found that the mountain was resting upon a huge tortoise that extended beyond the length and breadth of the mountain. That tortoise was Kurmavatar, Lord Vishnu's second avatar. With the tortoise shell acting as a base for the mountain to take support on, the churning apparatus was complete.

Once the system was stable, both the groups – Asuras and Devas – started churning the milk ocean with rigour, like never before. Devas also threw in some medicinal herbs to aid in the churning process. It was for a while before anything started to emerge. The first to emerge from the churning was Goddess Lakshmi. She consented to stay on Devas' side as a consort to Lord Vishnu. After that, many beings such as Airavat - white elephant, Ucchaishravas - divine horse, Kalapavriksh - the wish granting tree, Moon god Chandra, etc., came into existence out of the churning.

Both the parties kept on churning without taking any breaks till the goal was reached. All this time, Kurma Murthy bore the brunt of the mountain without any complaint. Earlier he had advised the Devas, patience is the key to achieve something. Here he was showing it in practice. But it was a while before the nectar of immortality surfaced out. After most of the known treasures surfaced, something different started to happen.

The milk ocean turned into a shade of green with poisonous fumes rising which started knocking everyone into a frenzied state. It was the emergence of *Halahal*, the poison potent enough to succumb the very existence into ashes. Scores of Devas and Asuras fell down unconscious. The remaining ones scrambled around to find a solution. If the Halahal crossed the boundaries of the milk ocean, all the fourteen worlds were at risk. No living being would survive the poisonous fumes and live to tell the tale.

Lord Vishnu was already bearing the weight of the mountain and maintaining stability of the churning apparatus against the currents of the milk ocean. They couldn't stop churning within inches away from the finish line. They didn't have the resources to repeat the whole churning process again. It was a now or never situation and Lord Vishnu suggested the Devas reach out to Lord Shiva to save them from the poison.

Only Lord Shiva was capable of containing the poison before it caused any permanent damage. Devas reached Kailasa and made a plea to Lord Shiva to save them from absolute destruction.

Lord Shiva obliged and started sucking out all the poisonous fumes into his palms where it began to solidify. In no time, the whole Halahal was in his hands. He began to drink the poison. His body shuddered for a minute because the poison was potent, but he couldn't let it reach his stomach because the whole of existence lives within him. Before any further damage, he stopped the poison just at his throat which turned blue and earned him the name Neelkanth. As a safety measure, lady Parvati, the mother goddess and wife of Lord Shiva placed a garland of a snake on his neck. Few regional variants of this story are present.

With the threat of Halahal averted, the churning continued with renewed efforts. The ocean turned back to the shade of white and started bubbling with nervous energy. The tension in the air was palpable. The only thing left to emerge out was amrit, the nectar of immortality. In a few minutes, a being emerged out with a golden pot in hand; the nectar had finally emerged from the depths of the milk ocean. Once the amrit was out, the task was not completed yet. The Devas had to consume it, but there is a tiny problem with Asuras. Making the race of Asuras immortal would have been inviting trouble for eternity. A brawl broke out between either party on who should get to consume the nectar first. Asuras' side was right to be suspicious that Devas would consume it first and never honour their promise. Similar mistrust was displayed by the Devas too. Kurmavatar was nowhere to be seen. In the fight, Asuras managed to get hold of a golden pot and they scrambled to consume it first.

Suddenly, there was a bright light on the shore where the fight was going on. Out of it emerged a beautiful maiden that the world had never seen. Asuras paused to look at her and forgot momentarily what they were doing. She called herself Mohini and suggested that she would be an impartial judge to ration out the nectar without any further violence. Enticed by her beauty, Asuras agreed to the deal and handed over the pot to her. She called the Devas first and started giving them a share of immortality. None of the Asuras objected to anything, for they were mesmerized by her. However, one Asura, Rahu, felt that something was not right. He joined the Devas' queue and took his share of amrit. It was Surya and Chandra, the gods of sun and moon, who indirectly indicated to Mohini that Rahu was not a Deva. Mohini instantly unleashed *Sudarshan Chakra,* the divine discus of Lord Vishnu upon the Asura and cut off his head. Yet, since he partook the nectar, he was immortal and couldn't die. The separated head came to be known as Rahu and the body turned into Ketu. Every year, Rahu and Ketu get their revenge on Surya and Chanda. That is how solar and lunar eclipses occur.

Once all the Devas got their share of nectar, they fought bravely with the Asuras present, who realized a bit late that they had been tricked. They restored their capital city, Amarvati to its former glory with the treasures from the milk ocean. Lord Vishnu had undertaken two avatars – Kurmavatar and Mohini avatar to aid in the milk ocean churning process. In the previous avatar as Matsya, he actively involved himself, while as Kurma he got into the field upon the request of his devotees – Devas, who are also a part of the creation. Had Lord Vishnu not intervened, probably the contours of the creation would have been different and unimaginable.

Know Thy Name

One of the key lessons for a business from the whole exercise of the churning is that one might have to join hands with rivals to ensure survival for the greater good. The efforts of Zomato and Swiggy towards creating a habit of food delivery to a populace that earlier loved to go out and dine is a testament to this. As they had pointed out, the marketing challenges for any nascent company are dissimilar to that of traditional companies with considerable muscle power. The playfield is never the same.

Taking a step back, before reaching the stage of building a new category, one must ensure the right product mix or it would lead to undesirable results. Entering a new category without the right product is a sure shot way to take back the company/business into the decline stage of the PLC in an accelerated manner. Not having the appropriate churning apparatus almost thwarted the manthan process and not every company has resources in the form of a Kurma avatar that can come to its rescue at lightning speed. Any misreading of the market and the company/brand would sink into the ocean without any trace. The difference between a blue-chip company like Nestle launching a brand-new plant protein snack bar and an off-the-block new startup offering the same is not too subtle. An established company would have the resources and the brand name to cushion the initial challenges while playing into a new category, which the startup won't have access to.

Here is where the concepts of 4Ps come into significant play. 4Ps or classically known as Marketing Mix is the basic framework that any B-school graduate would swear by. But it's a classic as far as frameworks go. Any misconceptions or illusions in this would lead to not-so-desirable results for the business.

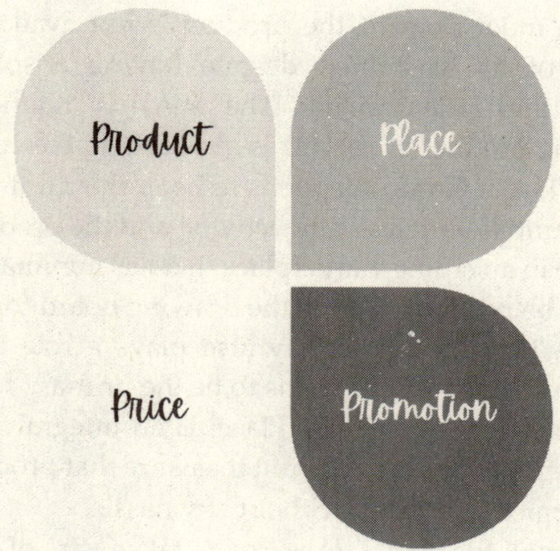

'Product', the first 'P', is essentially a solution that solves the customer's need around which the whole business model revolves. It deals with having a quality offering with all the requisite features, the right set of packaging, sizes, etc. The key outcome of a solid consumer insight happens to be the product which serves as the dominant proof of marketing promise to the customer.

Second 'P' refers to the price that one intends to offer to the customer. The pricing strategy is usually in sync with the target base and the business objective to be achieved. It could be preferring higher pricing to play on higher margins, or to go for lower pricing to capitalize on higher volume levels. Pricing is dependent on internal and external factors which one has no control over. Only with an outlook of the short-term objectives and long-term vision should one arrive at pricing decisions.

It's a moot point if the product is not available in the vicinity of the customer, despite having a solid design promise and killer pricing. The third 'P' refers to Place, where the product or service is available to the customer. If the TG (Target Group) happens to be in the rural hinterland of the country, with less connectivity, and the product is only available in an online marketplace that has minimal presence, it would be prudent to go to the drawing board for a revamp in plans. Place of availability also plays a role in creating awareness which still happens to be the primary focus of the Introductory stage of PLC. 'Place' is an integral part of the ecosystem that needs to be built to ensure that products reach the customer's doorstep without any hassle.

While all the above three Ps are taken care of in the first stage itself (they are not set in stone and can be tweaked later in line with the business context), the last and the crucial 'P' is Promotion, which is a key tool in ensuring that one could reach a wider customer base along with the innovators. Promotions could be of various forms – sales promotions in the form of discounts as Zomato and Swiggy have done for a considerable amount of time, or in the form of providing in-kind offerings (cash backs, coupons, etc.) or the awareness-creating advertising that would involve both offline and online mediums, public relations, etc. A practical aspect of it to consider is that the results of any promotions are not instantaneous and are dependent on the intended objective in the sales funnel. There are proxy workarounds to estimate the impact of the promotions as no business decision should be a shot in the dark, but they are not entirely foolproof. It could also explain why there is a sudden surge for the field of Data Science as they help in presenting sharper insights for the management to base the decisions. For instance, if any social media campaign is being run, the statistics could throw some light on the performance. In the case of offline mediums such as newspaper or radio ad, one way to gauge the impact is to monitor any change in the sales during the defined period.

Surya wanted to start a customized merchandise business. Since his customers are young and tech savvy, he opted for online selling as the place of purchase. As he would be selling it for the first time, he wanted to price it at a low level to attract customers. In order to generate interest in the stickers, he decided to use social media channels for a promotion of an early bird discount.

4Ps are a crucial aspect that any business needs to get right before venturing into new or existing markets. Without the complete apparatus of Mandara mountain as the churning machine, Vasuki snake as a rope, and Kurma avatar as the base, the manthan wouldn't have been possible. Similarly, without having the right product at an optimum price available within the customer vicinity and astounding promotions, it would be near impossible to play in the market. The story of Pulse is an appropriate example of getting the marketing mix right and creating a whole new category from scratch.

Catching the Pulse

It's easy to say that a successful venture has been due to the right marketing mix in retrospect, but it would be impossible to know if the product would succeed or not before one enters the market. This level of uncertainty could be reduced through a deep-rooted understanding of the customer which minimizes the risks associated with the 4Ps. If the DS Group told anyone before the launch of Pulse that they would revolutionize and take the confectionery market by storm, no one would have believed them. The market was already crowded with players like Perfetti, Parle, ITC, etc., and the margins in the industry were razor-thin. Chocolate, gum, and sugar candies are the major categories in this market. Hard-boiled sugar candies form a major chunk of the candies segment with players like Parle Mango Bite, Kacha aam, etc.

One peculiarity with the DS Group is that they claim to not launch a product unless and until they are sure of it. It's hard to guarantee the success of a new product launch. They might even take their own sweet time for the launch, which was reflected in their two years to study the confectionary market. They observed that while raw mango as a candy flavour was liked by all age groups, Indians tend to sprinkle salt and chili powder before consuming raw mango in usual practice. This tends to bring out a perfect combination of sweet and sour. Rajeev Kumar, DS Group chairman, was quoted saying to his research and development team, "Your eyes should close immediately while relishing it." The result was a hard-boiled sugar candy with a filling of salt and spices at its center, in line with what the market research had concluded and the brief from their chairman.

While the product Pulse was ready, they decided to test it in a couple of test markets such as Gujarat, Rajasthan, and NCR before going for a full-fledged launch as these regions favour sweet and sour combo in their cuisines. Saying the test launch was a success is an understatement. People loved the candy and started buying out in bulk like five to six candies instead of the usual one candy, resulting in demand outplaying supply.

Pulse candy was priced at Rs.1, against the market normal of Rs. 0.5 due to higher grammage. Plus, it had a glossy black and green packing under the umbrella brand Pass Pass, giving it a new look. It decided to leverage the distribution network DS Group had with various small-scale retailers, paan shops, etc., with whom they have connections through its other products such as Rajanigandha, etc.

Initially, Pulse didn't engage in any form of promotion. Its early adopters gave the big break for it on social media, generating positive word of mouth, in turn increasing its demand. So much so that the DS Group had to rope in contract manufacturers to meet the country's demand. After a year or so, it began to engage in BTL activities, even released a television commercial with the tagline - *Jaan jaye, par Pulse na jaye.*

Had Pulse not engaged in any form of promotional activity that would have generated awareness for itself nor had the word of mouth happened which was due to getting the marketing mix right, Pulse would not have been a sensation today.

Wisdom from the Tortoise

The churning of the milk ocean is a turning point in Hindu mythology as it restored the creation to its former glory and gave us the known world. A deeper focus of the story reveals the necessity of working with rivals for the greater good (i.e. building category awareness), not losing hope in the face of obstacles, and the importance of patience while doing one's duty. Kurmavatar also happens to be one of the only avatars apart from Buddha which didn't require vanquishing of any demon to fulfill the objective. This is even reflected in the truce formed between Asuras and Devas for finding the nectar of immortality. The unofficial understanding between Zomato and Swiggy had accelerated the awareness of food delivery to a $2.3 billion dollar industry in 2020, with an estimated Compound Annual Growth Rate (CAGR) of 28%. The tactics behind building Pulse by having an optimum Marketing Mix represents getting the churning apparatus right, from the Mandara mountain to Vasuki snake to Kurma tortoise base to Devas and Asuras as the churners to complete the churning process.

While the next chapter deals with the impact of the Varaha avatar as the business enters the last stage of the introductory phase in the PLC, below is a quick summary of the wisdom from the tortoise.

- ✧ Building awareness is crucial for the introductory phase and double efforts are required to generate awareness amongst potential customers if the product is playing in a completely new and unknown category.
- ✧ Having multiple competing players may induce a quicker adoption for the new category amongst customers as the effort of educating the customer is split between the players.
- ✧ Before embarking on a category building exercise or playing into an existing category, it is important to get the marketing mix (Product, Price, Place and Promotion) right.

3

Power of a Boar Tusk

Bhuvamsamveshytasamleenam
Tadaityam sagaravaarini
Jaghuna krodaroopaena
Tamvande loka rakshakam ||

To be or not to be a Pioneer

It's the journey that matters, not the destination. This statement is profoundly true, not only for humans, but also for brands and businesses alike. While the initial journey starts out as a product, it slowly morphs itself into a brand whose subset happens to the physical product or service. Before a brand is born and is sent off into the wind through metaphorical ashes, it has to undergo numerous tribunals. As discussed in the previous chapters, the decision to enter into a new market, build the necessary ecosystem for the product to thrive, craft the right product mix, and generate awareness is being done. The whole process is extremely capital intensive and it could be a while before one could even utter the word 'profits'.

Unfortunately, when one is in the business of building brands or businesses, timing the market is extremely crucial. If one happens to be the first in the market, a huge chunk of resources is directed towards building the market, which is laced with risk. On the other hand, if one happens to be a firm with superior technology or enough leverage to create strong market advantage, it would be prudent to enter at a later stage when the conditions are favourable. Taking this decision or not would make the new brand/product the pioneer in the new market, irrespective of whether the firm is an established one or a budding new startup.

For starters, being the pioneers in the market or the first ones in the market, one could set down the ground rules on what attributes the product in the new category could have or should possess. This might help in largely limiting the scope of debate for future competitors who would want to play in the same category. Another factor of the pioneering advantage is the quantum of innovation. Brands with completely new products in the market may have a tough time in comparison with incremental innovators who switch from one technology to another as time progresses. For example, companies making normal television would have an effortless transition to LED smart TVs while talking to the customers. In comparison, startups with a brand new IoT-powered television would have a tricky time convincing the customers to give them a chance.

Secondly, pioneers can gain from the early base who would flock to them due to the loyalty created by the satisfied product and initial customer base. Once enough early innovators are attracted, pioneers can chalk up strategies to attract the middle of the market by enhancing the product for them and adding more users in the process. Even after 60 years of market presence, 19 out of the 25 market leaders established in 1923 have continued dominance in the market. Being the first one also helps with customer inertia drawing a slight advantage in higher brand recall or occupying customer mind space. From another perspective, being the first to enter a market also helps in gaining economies of scale as the business galvanizes to move from the introductory stage to the growth stage to the maturity stage in the PLC cycle in a short timeframe. It can claim leadership in technology, apply for valuable patents (especially in the medical or pharma sector, which would help in significant first-mover advantage and prime access to the market). It would also provide an opportunity for a business to own scarce resources which are critical to making the product. This in turn would help them in erecting barriers of entry if any competitors came knocking on the door hoping for an easy run. Starting a bit early on the timeline would allow brands to allocate marketing spend effectively and ensure that they are being spent to draw out repeat purchases. Not to mention, it would put the brands on a watchtower on a lookout for any competitors who would be planning to enter the same category. It is a different discussion altogether if a brand can utilize this watchtower effectively or not at a later stage.

Ram Chaitanya had opened a brand-new tiffin center at a hotspot location in Hyderabad. His major advantage was that he was the first one to do so and he knew his audience well. His customized menu created a loyalty to his hotel so much so that around four tiffin centers that opened up as a competition had to shut shop in less than a year. No one was able to break the monopoly of Ram Chaitanya's tiffin business in that particular area.

Seldom is anything without certain drawbacks or disadvantages, since the market doesn't operate in a utopian setup. The second-mover advantage is a phenomenon where any brand that intends to be a first-mover should be cautioned against. In layman's terms, while one does all the hard work of creating a market for a new category from scratch and if there is no point of differentiation between one's product and that of a competitor, nothing is stopping them from hitting a home run. They would overtake one's position as the market leader, making the most of the second-mover advantage. One thing that works for the second-mover is that they need not scream from rooftops on why the category their product is playing in should be of substance to the customer. Case in point being, in an era of fountain ink pens, the first ballpoint makers had enough trouble to find suitors for their product. But once they got their big breakthrough, it attracted every pen maker to the new enterprise and thus effectively killed their first-mover advantage. Milton Reynolds was the first one to bring out a viable ballpoint pen under the name Reynolds Point. In time with its success, it also brought enough players that the market became saturated and Reynolds company had to look for other options by the 1950s. First-mover advantage is a double-edged sword that needs to be wielded with care.

Kiran managed to set up a stationery shop in a residential area in a bid to cater to the school going students' needs. It took time to witness certain results However, one fine day he found a competitor offering stationery services along with a copy machine. It was something Kiran couldn't afford. He lost his first-mover advantage and could never recover his business again.

Fine Notes of the Product

If a company brings out a new product and develops patents in a new product category, they are treated as innovators (not to be confused with the other definition of innovators, the early set of customers willing to try one's product as highlighted in the previous chapter). Apple could be one such innovator who strives to bring out new technological products every now and then. On the other hand, if any competitors develop on the same premise with an additional benefit or tangible point of differentiation, they are called imitators. Local potato chip manufacturers like Balaji, Diamond, etc., are imitators as they managed to imitate Lay's flavour portfolio and packaging theme to their needs. The perpetual battle between innovators and imitators rages across all product categories. Even though innovators have a slight upper hand, that should not lead to ignoring one's chinks in the armour. The product being crude enough with only a core solution and not matching up to customer expectations is one of the chinks. This leads to an opening for an imitator to turn up with a superior product. Whilst some of the key brands that rule the day are accidental innovations, certain products within them did not meet their objectives causing customer dissatisfaction. This is quite evident in modern-day startups who promise the moon and do not even come close to the ground reality. This would be further explored in the forthcoming chapters in detail.

Wrong positioning of the product/brand is one issue every marketer needs to be aware of. Imagine spending crores of rupees on getting the product right, only to realize that it is not being appropriately communicated to the target audience, resulting in complete failure. Product/brand coming into the market before there is enough need for its existence is also one reason why imitators have an advantage over innovators. TikTok happens to be a good illustration of this phenomenon. There is nothing unique about TikTok at its core, for it is a short video-sharing application. It is not the first one in its field, nor would it be the last. There are plethora of applications that have seamlessly integrated the same offerings into their existing system with Instagram being one of them. TikTok's lucky break happened as it entered the market when there was democratization in terms of smartphones and the internet which made its growth viable without any major hiccups. The same could have happened for Dubsmash (a short video sharing application that enables its customers to lip-sync to dialogues/scenes/songs from popular movies), but it was launched at a different time before there was strong demand or need for it.

The third avatar of Vishnu, the story of Varaha, sheds some light on how to safeguard against the threat of the second-mover.

The Curse of Ignorance

Ignorance is bliss. But unfortunately, Jaya and Vijaya, the doorkeepers of Vaikuntha – the abode of Lord Vishnu in the milk ocean, the highest place in all of creation – would say otherwise. They are arrogant upon their proximity to Lord Vishnu. Since they were the doorkeepers, they controlled the access to the blue lord and thus assumed themselves to be powerful.

Once the lord and the goddess had a mild altercation, quite natural in a normal, healthy marriage. This was somewhere during the Satya Yuga when the creation was still finding its feet in the universe. In a bid of anger, Goddess Lakshmi stepped out of the seventh door to collect her thoughts. When she finally calmed down and decided to go back, she was stopped by Jaya and Vijaya.

They wouldn't let her go inside at all. She argued that she is the lord's better half and the he himself gave her a place in his heart. The doorkeeper's counter was dripping with arrogance. They replied that she only has the right to come out of Vaikuntha whenever she wants, but not to go in without permission at any time. It is an understatement that goddess's anger knew no bounds. She cursed that doorkeepers would lose the very thing that was the root cause of their arrogance.

Now that Goddess Lakshmi uttered the curse, it had been set in motion and it was to be fulfilled in the most unusual manner. Four dwarfs, naked except for white loincloths, decided to visit Vaikuntha and pay their respects to the great Lord. Upon approaching the fabled seven golden doors, they requested the duo (Jaya and Vijaya) for an audience with Lord Vishnu. Unaware about the four dwarfs, they both made fun of them for their appearance. At first, the dwarfs were surprised at why the doorkeepers were behaving in this manner. As the duo questioned how people of their stature could even wonder to meet Lord Vishnu himself in a mocking tone, their surprise turned into anger. In their arrogance, Jaya and Vijaya chided the dwarfs to go and try their luck somewhere else as they were not going to meet the lord. In the end, the dwarfs were not granted permission to walk through the seven golden doors to meet Lord Vishnu.

Enraged by this attitude, the four dwarfs cursed that they both would be born on earth, away from Vaikuntha, as the proximity was the reason for their arrogance, thus fulfilling Goddess Lakshmi's curse. No sooner did they utter the curse, the four dwarfs vanished from that place without a trace. They were not any ordinary dwarfs. Born from the pure thought of Lord Brahma, they are known as Sanath Kumaras who can take on any form they wish to take and are blessed with divine powers to travel around the divine worlds in search of knowledge.

Despite their arrogance, they knew that curses have power, dwarfs or not. Alarmed at the situation, Jaya and Vijaya scurried to Lord Vishnu for mercy. Irony was that there was no one to stop them from entering the doors and meeting Lord Vishnu without permission. Lord Vishnu, being omnipresent, already knew what had transpired outside his own doors, but he still gave a chance for his doorkeepers to explain their story.

When the story was finished, Lord Vishnu's expression turned grave. They pleaded with their overlord to save them and accepted their mistake without any arguments. However, the lord declared that he would not be in a position to help them out. He suggested that they live out the curse without any delay. The feeling of dejection and remorse was clear in Jaya's and Vijaya's pained expressions. But there was nothing that could be done. The duo began to walk away in expectation of being taken away from their beloved Vaikuntha.

All this time, Lord Vishnu was testing if his doorkeepers would tell him the absolute truth or not and secondly if they had learnt from their mistake. After comprehending that the doorkeepers were genuinely intending to make amends, the lord decided to tweak the sentence dished out by the Kumaras. A curse once given cannot be taken back. It is probably one of the reasons why the notion to hold one's thoughts pure is propagated across generations. Any harm that one wishes for others cannot be taken back.

He asked the duo to stop. Since they were only repenting their actions, the lord declared that they can either live seven lifetimes as devotees of Lord Vishnu or three lifetimes as enemies of the lord as a part of their penance and return to Vaikuntha. They both instantly understood what the lord was suggesting. Either have a very long life in lord's devotion, which could be an eternity, as seven lifetime is a very long time. Or live a very short life warring against the lord without any good intentions. They declared that they would prefer three lifetimes as enemies of the lord as that would mean they could return to his service in less time compared to the other option. Since the duo accepted the amendment in the curse, the lord blessed it into action. So, Jaya and Vijaya would be born as Hiranyakshya and Hiranyakashyapa, Ravana and Kumbhakarna, and Shishupala and Dantavakra in different yugas to challenge the avatar of Vishnu respectively, and thus fulfilling the curse of Goddess Lakshmi and the Kumaras.

After a couple of years or a couple of minutes, depending on the time perspective one is looking at, the story of Varaha avatar begins (time works differently in Human terms and Vaikuntha). Sage Kashyapa prajapati and his wife Diti were blessed with dizygotic twins - Hiranyakshya and Hiranyakashyapa. Diti was so happy that finally her children would be revered as the Devas, the children of Aditi. However sage Kashyapa using his powers of mediation looked to see a glimpse of the future and was shocked to see what it foretold. He didn't have it in him to break his wife's heart, but he still told her what might happen. Diti was crestfallen that her children would always go to war with the Devas, but there was only so much she could do.

Hiranyakshya grew up hearing tales on how Lord Vishnu cheated Asuras of their rightful share of the divine nectar of immortality. His rage only grew exponentially at the blatant deception by the Devas over time in multiple encounters. He decided that he must embark on a conquest of all the three worlds, starting with earth. He performed penance for a very long time to invoke Lord Brahma to grant him boons. Satisfied with his penance, when Lord Brahma appeared, Hiranyakshya asked for superior strength and invincibility that would make him capable of a conquest of all the three worlds - heaven, earth and the nether world. Surprisingly, he never sought out immortality.

After he got the powers he requested for, the first thing he did was to kidnap Bhoomi Devi or Bhu Devi as she is known in certain parts of the country, the goddess personification of planet earth. He was able to transform her into that of a globe, the one which we are familiar with in the atlas books, and hid her in the depths of primordial waters, an ocean different from the milk ocean witnessed during the churning process.

People on earth were desperately praying to their gods for deliverance. Alarmed at this audacity and the threat of absolute destruction for all living beings on earth looming in and possibility of other worlds if Hiranyakshya was not reined in, all the gods ran to Vaikuntha, the abode of Lord Vishnu for salvation. The lord had specific rules on when he had to take an avatar. Couple of them are when the whole universe is in distress and there is a tangible threat to Dharma, or when a devotee sincerely asks for help out of their troubles, etc. Lord Vishnu decided that it was the time for an avatar again for the preservation of the universe before it was too late.

Cut back to Hiranyakshya – the primordial waters were brimming with ancient energy, the very powers that were responsible for creation. It was only the boons obtained from gods that were saving him from becoming a demon mess. He had placed planet earth at the bottom of the seafloor and was on the surface, standing on guard, knowing well that the armies of Devas would rush in to save their beloved Bhoomi

Devi. He could defeat them all in one place single-handedly instead of engaging in a proper conquest to rule all the three worlds. Devas had consumed the nectar of immortality. They were invincible. So why should they even fear an upstart Asura who was not immortal? Lord Vishnu has shown in his Mohini avatar that it was possible to hurt divine beings (Rahu and Ketu) in an irreparable manner, despite having partaken amrit. Even though they are immortal, they could still be harmed physically and some wounds will never heal for perpetuity.

While Hiranyakshya was gazing at the horizon, lost in his thoughts, a huge white figure shot past him into the water. Hiranyakshya wondered who would be a fool enough to challenge him in a suicidal mission. He sought to destroy whoever came once they emerged from the waters and send a message to his cousins to not play tricks with him.

After a few seconds, which seemed an eternity, a wild white boar emerged out of the primordial waters, with its tusks supporting the planet earth. Larger than the usual size for a boar, it was leagues ahead in dimensions and it was quite capable to bear the weight of the whole earth on its tusks with ease. It was the emergence of Varaha, the third avatar of Lord Vishnu.

On witnessing this image, Hiranyakshya's rage knew no bounds. He threw his mace at the boar that was attempting to restore the earth to the heavens. The mace hit its target and managed to topple the planet earth from the boar's tusks. The boar simply realigned its path to stop the planet from falling down. A fierce battle ensued between the boar and the demon. The boar was balancing planet earth on its tusks all this while. Hiranyakshya managed to hold on his own against the raw strength of Varaha.

The Asura prince struck at its tusks, which made the boar lose balance and the earth fell right back into the primordial waters. With a fresh purge of strength, Varaha used its tusks to tear into Hiranyakshya, bringing an end to his failed conquest and to him.

Once the boar took care of Hiranyakshya, it dived right into the water and swam as fast as it could possibly do divinely before the planet hit the ocean floor. Varaha, the white mammoth boar, emerged out of the waters with the planet placed firmly between its tusks. This was the third avatar of Lord Vishnu, where he had taken the form of a ferocious boar to save the nascent creation from destruction that could have devastated the fabric of the universe. Alongside also fulfilling the curse of Jaya and Vijaya where they play the role of his enemies.

Barriers of Entry and Point of Differentiation

Even though the whole legwork was done by Lord Brahma, Devas and Prajapatis in particular in setting up the creation, it took just an instant for Hiranyaksha to threaten it. It was foresight on the part of Lord Vishnu to have contingency against such threats and the absolute role of preservation in it. Lord Vishnu's Varaha avatar has shown that even though nascent creation is flourishing, it needs to prepare itself for unforeseen challenges to its very core without being complacent. Similarly, one card first-movers use as a defense mechanism is to leverage the barriers of entry against any potential competition during the process of creating the category from scratch. As demonstrated by Jaya and Vijaya, those who control the doors, control the access to Lord Vishnu.

For certain industries, statements like 'The barriers of entry are too high for any competitor to play in that market' or 'The toll price a company has to pay would be too steep for the potential ROI it gains from the whole endeavour' are heard. The good folks at strategy consider that there are four possible barriers of entry into any industry – economies of scale, product differentiation, cost advantages independent of scale, and government regulation of entry. Amongst them, product differentiation is the most primal and fundamental barrier of entry.

There's a running gag that a marketer would be able to market anything as long as he/she is equipped with their wits. Imagine for a product like steel or water, it's a bit hard to differentiate what makes one's product different from that of competitors. One can always say that Steel A has 50% carbon, while Steel B has 80% carbon. But that would go into the realm of technical terms, easily losing out the customer in the process. In such industries, a huge scale of investment is involved where private players may balk at playing a key role. There's also a high possibility that in industries such as steel, chemicals, auxiliaries, etc., the numerical superiority of users/buyers is not intense as in sectors like FMCG, Automotive, etc. This leads to major heavy industries having state involvement and scarce private participation, which was essentially what was witnessed during independence when the government had to set up multiple PSUs to produce the necessary goods.

On the other hand, where there is scope enough to create differentiation between products, the barriers are not extravagant. In the telecom sector, the differentiation earlier was in terms of data speed and signal connectivity. Now the conversation has moved a bit forward to the bundling programs offered with a data pack and the serviceable capacity. In the FMCG sector, it is easy to create a perception, identify a gap, and turn that into a potential point of differentiation for the product. In the case of body lotions, one can say product A provides moisture and smoothens the skin, while product B avoids the aging of the skin. This also ties in with other factors such as economies of scale, cost advantage, etc., thus adding strength to the first-mover advantage. In the field of cosmetics, there are enough boutique brands that cater to niche segments even in the light of major players as they have the scope to create differentiation. A similar story doesn't hold for products like cement or metals, etc., where the product is ubiquitous.

A group of friends decided to open a pani-puri stall in Indore. However, they disagreed on what strategy needs to be employed. So, they made a pact to pursue individual ideas for a month and continue the idea that works out for the best. The first one claimed that he would provide unlimited pani-puri only for Rs. 50. The second one managed to crack a deal with his suppliers and has priced a plate of ten puris for only Rs. 5. The third friend said that he would provide the highest quality possible, even using mineral water and organic products. And the fourth friend wanted to provide different flavours of the water with the puris in a single plate as a part of gastronomical experience.

Unbreakable Bond

It is easier and viable to create points of differentiation in a category that is feasible to do. In a tough and traditional industry, the challenge never gets easier by the second. But one brand has managed to crack the code and that happens to be Fevicol. It has provided iconic taglines such as *zor lagake haisha, mazbhoot jod, tootega nahi,* etc. Fevicol is a synthetic resin-based adhesive that is primarily used in furniture, shoemaking, etc., from the house of Pidilite.

Close to 85% of the furniture market is in the unorganized sector, where carpenters play a key role in deciding what sort of adhesive, he/she uses in making the wood piecework. While this is a given, it is also plausible that the end customer (who in this case is the furniture owner) would not fret too much about the sort of adhesive that went into the making of furniture. Yet Fevicol went ahead to build out a whole brand out of it and ensured that it has high recall value to date. At a later point after inception, Fevicol embarked on a brand extension spree and today it boasts of around seventy-five products that are product leaders in their respective categories and have a strong presence in more than seventy countries.

Most of its iconic advertisements revolve around the idea that anything attached with Fevicol is unbreakable. One of its advertisements features a small hotelier trying to break an egg for an omelet. Translated from the cartoon world to reality, the egg does everything, even making a hole in a metal pot, except for breaking it into two for making the omelet. The advertisement ends with a frame where the hen is shown to be eating out of a Fevicol container before laying the egg. In recent times, there was an advertisement where the hero of the story was a chair that was gifted during the wedding to the bride and it continues its journey over time to her great-grandchildren. They happen to use the chair and there are few instances where Fevicol was used to repair or revamp the chair according to the taste of that family, underlying the idea that time might change, people might come and go, but anything made with Fevicol stays strong till times immemorial. This cleverly ties in with its tagline - *Fevicol ka mazboot jod.*

In layman terms, Pidilite falls into industrial adhesives where the difference between customer and consumer is starkly different. The purchase decision of Fevicol lies with the carpenters, even if the actual purchase is done by the client. And it is the carpenters who use the Fevicol while assembling the furniture, while the end customers use the finished furniture. If the furniture is not assembled properly, the customer would question the carpenter, not on what adhesive is being used. This makes the carpenter a crucial piece for Fevicol in its strategy puzzle. So, the company embarked on various initiatives so that their relationship with carpenters is unbreakable and they managed to extend this to other purchase decision makers on some level for other products also. With this move, there was no need for Pidilite or rather less scope for Fevicol to build a brand presence with an audience who may not even be their purchase makers.

Still, Fevicol went ahead and managed to make quirky, memorable advertisements that made a mark on the end customer. If the carpenter does not wish to use Fevicol products, customers insist on using it thanks to the marketing campaigns. This resulted in popularity for Fevicol that turned into a huge barrier of entry for other competitors to enter into adhesive space. Even if they did, they would have a tough time removing Fevicol from the market leader position. The result for everyone to see is that Fevicol is synonymous with unbreakable. Over the years, their marketing team manages to bring out a fresh perspective on unbreakable in its campaigns. This double-pronged strategy helped Fevicol, and Pidilite industries in extension, to create a point of differentiation which strengthened its leadership position in the market. The icing on the cake in this whole Pidilite saga is that it was not an easy category to play on the differentiation factors due to the nature of the industry and business model, yet managed to use marketing to its favour.

The Other Side

Pidilite is a classic example of how a brand went to build its competitive advantage through marketing actions in a way that was never explored before. While the point of differentiation plays a key role in ensuring that enough barriers of entry are deployed to maintain the leadership position in the market, the converse is also true. Having no differentiation is a sure-shot way to invite second-movers to enter the market and capture the market leadership position without any fight. Micromax's failure to deliver a proper point of differentiation is a testament to losing market share.

Micromax is an Indian mobile manufacturer which introduced budget smartphones to the Indian audience. It entered into the mobile handset business in 2008 and since then has expanded into various product categories, catering to a diverse audience with a common thread being affordability. By 2014, it turned out to be the tenth largest global handset maker, even dethroning Samsung from its first position. It would be an understatement to say that back in the hay day, most of the eligible Indian population had interacted with a Micromax handset in one way or the other.

Micromax had outsourced its manufacturing to Chinese companies, enabling it to provide its products at a budget price. Micromax went aggressive on marketing, even to the point of hiring Hugh Jackman as the brand ambassador with only competitive pricing as its key USP. It never talked about how its phones have a higher battery life or are durable or have the latest technology features within them. It was about giving the phone at the lowest price possible. These strategies helped Micromax beat Samsung for a while to claim the market share crown. However, Samsung also began to bring in affordable products using a similar playbook of outsourcing manufacturing along with its flagship premium products. It simply saw what Micromax was doing and expanded its product portfolio to cater to all price points. On the other hand, Chinese manufacturers began to enter the country playing on the advantage of the supply chain and expertise they had due to being third party contract manufacturers. When competitors with similar price points and better features came knocking, Micromax couldn't do anything except to watch its market share sink to rock bottom.

Assertive marketing spending would eventually result in craved awareness in the introductory stage of the PLC, but would not result in long-term gains if 'Point of Differentiation' is not built. As that would lead to a second-mover building on the efforts taken by one's brand in shaping the new category from scratch and the first-mover advantage is essentially nullified.

Wind Up the Tusk

Varaha avatar is a crucial turning point in the Dashavatar saga, for it was responsible for creating the next obstacles in the form of Jaya and Vijay's villainous incarnations and how Lord Vishnu had to face them across the time of four yugas. The saga of Hiranyaksha and Varaha emphasizes the fact that it needs incredible resources to gain a competitive advantage over entry barriers. Lord Vishnu had to take the form of a wild boar capable of swimming through the primordial waters with strong tusks to bear the weight of the earth.

One thing to notice is that all the first three avatars of Lord Vishnu are essentially animals, indicating that the challenges involved were too brutal and required a response of a similar kind. They are insignia for tests of strength, power, and aggressiveness in action which is in contrast to the sophisticated methods used by the other avatars in the later stages of time. Another interesting thing to note is that all the three avatars – Matsya, Kurma and Varaha – are related to some or the other ocean setting representing the brutal power of nature and the unmounting challenge a new business/ product has to overcome. The gradual introduction of sophistication in the processes is what transforms a fledgling product into a brand powerhouse in the coming days.

Before moving on to the other stages of PLC in the next stage, below is a quick summary of learnings of the warrior boar for the last stages of the introduction stage.

- ✧ Generating awareness to build demand is a primary objective in the introductory stage rather than focusing blindly only on the ROI.
- ✧ Being a pioneer (first-mover) in any category is for naught if a proper foundation is not built to capitalize on the advantage. That would open up an opportunity for second movers to ride along.

- ✧ Barriers of Entry (Economies of Scale, product differentiation, cost advantages independent of scale, and government regulation of entry) of any industry provide a means for strengthening competitive advantage against second-movers and building a 'Point of Differentiation' as a strategic advantage.
- ✧ Marketing can be used as a strong Barrier of Entry in industries/categories where it is difficult to create a point of differentiation.

THE FLOURISH

4

All in the Name of Mane

Reremurkha harikvaste
Darshayonam tvamadyame
Vadamtamevamdytyam
Tam nriharetvamavadheepuraa ||

Transformational Conundrum

The transition of any form is herculean, but it is quite necessary. A pot doesn't take shape if it can't brave the fires of the kiln. But if someone were to interfere with the process or falter in the process, there would be no progression to the next phase – the pot would crumble at the slightest touch. The lifecycle of a butterfly terms this transformation as metamorphosis, the journey from a puny larva to a beautiful butterfly. The main struggle is to break out of the cocoon on its own. If it doesn't break out, the young larvae would be kissing goodbye to a whole new life altogether.

On a similar note, in the PLC there is an inappreciable gap that one needs to cross between the introduction phase and growth phase. This gap is ascertained as 'Chasm' and the very act of navigating it is termed as 'Crossing the Chasm'. Crossing the chasm is crucial for a brand as it goes on a trajectory where the user base increases from innovators to early adopters. This would give the brand wider access to a market which would help in spreading the marketing costs over the large volume comparatively and move an inch closer towards profitability. For instance, if Rs 1000 spent on marketing results in two customers, the customer acquisition cost is Rs 500 per customer. However, the brand continues to grow, the same Rs 1000 may result in ten customers, thus resulting in a new customer acquisition cost of Rs 100 per customer.

In the unlikely case, if a brand fails to cross the chasm, it would reach the decline phase of the PLC pretty quickly without even navigating the phases of 'Growth' and 'Maturity'. Particularly in FMCG, a sector which is aplenty with new launches and new brands being bought out every other day, around 85% of the products are bound to bite the dust and fail to take off the shelves, as per a study conducted by Nielsen (a popular market research agency). It is daunting as new launches are a costly affair, for it involves crafting a product from scratch, building up the demand for the product by generating product awareness amongst early innovators. For instance, if a new product managed to go from 0 to 10, those 10 users are innovators who were willing to try out something new without any proof that the product would work. But going from ten to a thousand is not a cakewalk and that's where the majority of the bets fail. In this journey, the management needs to enhance its product, boost its marketing spend and improve its efficiency across the value chain. Despite doing all this, there is a high chance of courting failure due to factors beyond the management control. While an established company may write off such failed launches as a sunk cost on its balance sheet, new startups or small businesses may not have such a luxury. They would have no option but to toil ahead to cross the chasm so that they can reach into the next phase, i.e. 'Growth phase'.

One Problem, Multiple Solutions

Starting the growth engine and increasing the market share is the only way a brand/product might be able to avoid its fate in the chasm. Its top line of the balance sheet (i.e. revenues) should be growing at par or at a higher proportion to its bottom line of the balance sheet (i.e. profits). Going forward, we would be addressing the brand in a few instances as a separate entity apart from the product, as by this time in the PLC cycle, it is poised to grow on an independent basis. In this phase, all the multifaceted strategies – ranging from product to place of the marketing mix, from sales and marketing functions to operations are aligned in this direction of increasing market share of the particular brand/product.

While one may have tasted success with the early innovators with a basic product, it won't suffice when positioning the same for the masses. Tinkering of the basic product is required as it only offers core benefits and the expectations of the early majority would be higher. Marketers need to create something called an 'Expected Product', which is a finished product containing additional attributes and values, a customer inherently expects while making a purchase decision regarding the product.

When moving further down in the PLC cycle, 'Augmented Product' is created from expected product by adding attributes that exceed customer expectations and go beyond what he/she regularly asks. This usually is a phenomenon in developed countries where there is enough disposable income to drive the crafting of brand positioning and playing the competition at the expected product level. A 'Potential Product' is born out of expected product which compasses all possible transformations or any potential attributes that can be added in the future. This is usually taken up at a future level when growth needs to be induced to a mature brand that has already been in the market for a while. The point of discussion is that a brand needs to create an expected product out of the 'Basic Product' it offered to its early innovators. These could range from extra attributes to additional benefits such as warranty, services, etc. In crude terms, a basic function of a mobile phone is to enable communication. Additional benefits of a camera, radio are added to make the expected product.

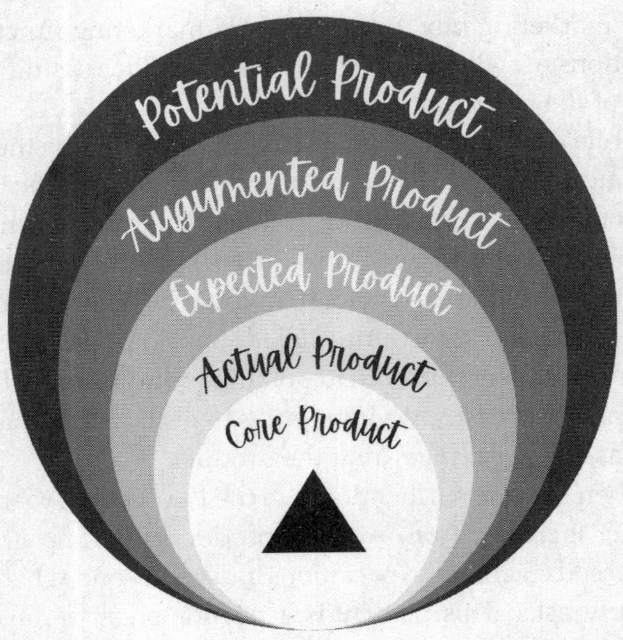

Raghav owns a dosa food truck at the corner of the street. Initially, he only offered a couple of basic dosas to his early customers. Churning out dosas was his core product. However, as the business

grew, he wanted to ensure that customers keep coming back. He sold dosas with free vadas, making it as the expected product. Along with proper hygiene and good quality ingredients, this combination became his expected product. As the business further grew, he started to make different varieties of dosas, experimenting with the batter and the filling, thus creating an exclusive menu. This became the augmented product for Raghav's business. Way into the future, if Raghav could figure out a way to cut down calories while making dosas, that would be the potential product that witnesses future use, but not suitable for the current scenario.

There are multifold pricing strategies to choose from. The concept of penetration pricing or introductory pricing gained more prominence as a proven strategy to attract sales with low prices due to the results of Jio, an Indian telecom operator. Penetration pricing essentially is a tactic where the company reduces its prices to a lower figure in comparison with its competition to bring in new customers to its fold. Jio is not the first brand that was able to use this penetration pricing strategy to the fullest, nor would it be the last. Netflix has been sneakily deploying the same over the years. It usually offers free or near-free subscriptions at the start and hikes the prices gradually. The strategy attracts a user base at larger numbers and when enough time has passed, Netflix is left with an optimum number of a sticky consumer base who would keep the party rolling with the higher subscriptions. The main challenge with penetration price is if the product/service is not up to the level of customer expectation, no amount of lower price would salvage that.

Since Raghav was new in business, he wanted to have competitive pricing. If others were selling dosas priced at Rs 100/-, Raghav decided to price his dosas at Rs 50 which increased his customers from ten to sixty per day. After a while, as the sales volumes kept on increasing, Raghav hiked his dosa price from Rs 50 to Rs 120 in a gradual manner, which resulted in a fall to thirty-five customers per day. However, the customer decline was made up for by the increase in margin.

'Place' happens to be an integral part of the marketing place. After all, if one's product is not available in a place from where the customer usually makes their purchases, then all the efforts of creating awareness and interest would be for naught. Usually, before launching a new product, especially in the FMCG sector, pilot tests are done in select markets and cities. Based on the results, the decision is taken on whether to expand the scope of distribution or not. When Lays was looking for QSR (Quick Service Restaurant) to partner with to shore up a portion of its institutional sales, it made a pilot in select stores of Subway in New Delhi, which it thought would represent the demographic mix of the country. Pilot is essentially a real time experiment to be run in small-scale conditions that usually are a representation of the larger variables. They are usually sanctioned to determine the validity of an idea or a hypothesis. The pilot successfully worked, showing an uptick in the sales of Lays, whenever a customer walked to order from Subway. Based on these results, Subway won the contract with Lays for three years that could be negotiated over time based on the performance. Lays may not have been in its growth phase stage of the PLC at the time when this deal happened, but it does remind the fact that new avenues to reach out to the customer from the start itself would be helpful in making a brand's case. Having a hypothesis that customers would only purchase from one avenue and would never move to another avenue is only detrimental to your business from both a short-term and a long-term perspective.

After a while, Raghav used to get calls from some customers to keep their order ready while they pick it up. When such repeated requests started coming in, Raghav decided to provide a home delivery option by hiring an extra person. Over time, he noticed that the customers who never even turned up at this shop, have started to order via the home delivery option.

For instance, when Epigamia (the Greek yogurt brand) was launched in India, it made a pilot in Bangalore. Kirana store owners were skeptical if such a product would work or not, for no one knew what Greek yogurt was, let alone taste it. In order to overcome that, a deal was made to ensure that Epigamia got maximum visibility in any store set-up on a credit basis. This visibility in turn generated intrigue and led to sales. Since then there was no looking back for Epigamia. Today, the brand Epigamia has branched out into multiple products ranging from Greek yogurt to curd to smoothies to paneer (cottage cheese). All this growth was because they managed to crack a crucial piece in the distribution puzzle. If the product was half the game, availability ensures that a home run is scored. Usually if one notices, most of the pilot runs are conducted in metro cities like Delhi, Bangalore, etc., which represent the demographic mix of the country to an extent. Bangalore has a certain skewness as the majority of the popular startups in the country have origins from the streets of this city. An additional factor is that the supermarkets and grocery chains in Bangalore would be drastically different from others in the country due to the presence of various new brands and products in the shelves.

Sales promotion is a slightly different concept in comparison with advertising. While both increase the marketing expenditure, sales promotion is more in the line of providing incentives to the buyers to ensure sales on a short-term basis. It could be in the range of providing free samples to direct and indirect coupons to rebates to prizes. Anything which offers short-term incentives falls under the bracket of sales promotion. They form a great tool to capture the market share. When Google Pay was launched in India, UPI payments (developed by NPCI - National Payments Corporation of India) were still in their nascent stage. Google had to find out a way where it would be in a position to easily acquire customers. No one said it was going to be effortless. It started a referral promotion where any user who signed up on a referral code would receive Rs 51. That worked wonders for users who were sending out referrals left and right, adding numbers for the search giant. This run had to end somewhere and customers would have needed an incentive to stick along. That was when GPay came up with the scratch card scheme, a sort of hidden, unknown reward awaiting the user who made a transaction. This cost would be spread over the large user base that was obtained in the process, instead of the expense promotion of Rs. 51 to acquire a customer. One must also be prudent enough to understand when to stop the discounts before it starts becoming a constant expectation from the customer end. While sales promotions are a great scheme to attract sales, it is not a great idea when the customer doesn't come back for a return purchase, or worse, there are not enough customers sticking around. A customer who came in just because the brand was offering a discount, would not stick around the moment the prices are increased.

After the success of one dosa truck, Raghav wanted to add to another food truck. He was not starting completely from zero for his brand is recognizable, but getting high sales numbers for the new truck too was a challenge. So Raghav thought of offering a 'Buy one, get one' scheme to increase sales for just one week. The promotion worked quite well and he clocked in more than 150 customers per day. However, the moment the promotion ended; the sales figures fell down to sixty customers per day.

One way to stand out from the crowd without any of the usual discounts or price tricks is to genuinely try something that piques the customer's interest. Building exclusive campaigns exactly fit this bill and it has been adopted by One Plus, a premier smartphone brand in the country. It has started out an invite-only system where a select few customers were offered the option of signing up to purchase a One Plus device. This not only confirmed the exclusivity of the product, but also ensured that they turned into ambassadors for the product. The whole process resulted in generating a massive word of mouth, which propelled One Plus into one of the top-selling brands in the smartphone segment, threatening to eat away market share from established players. It didn't hurt that it was offering high-end technology and features at a value price. On top of it, the tagline 'Never Settle' just alludes to the same. This is one unique way of generating interest and creating awareness of the product, taking the exclusivity route to generate interest and slowly expand the scope of exclusivity as the customer base grows.

While we are still talking about the marketing examples in the smartphone segment, it would be hard to ignore what Samsung had done to promote its Galaxy Note 10 and Note 10+. According to Statista 2021, around 695,000 stories were shared on Instagram in just a minute. In an age where everything is moving digital, it was quite a challenge to break out of the clutter. Inspired by the film *Bandersnatch* where the viewer could select what happens to the characters in the story, Samsung attempted to create a similar experience over Instagram stories, by highlighting the phone's key features in an interactive format that followed a storyline. The success of the campaign could be visible vividly in the reach it generated and the sales numbers clocked for the new product.

The above illustrations depict a manner in which one variable within the marketing mix (Product/Place/Price/Promotion) could be manipulated to avoid the chasm and sail into the growth phase. Let us explore the story of how HPCL managed to use all means to overcome a similar challenge.

Cleaning Away the Firewood

Cooking gas is still a phenomenon that needs to be adopted largely in the subcontinent, especially in rural areas. In order to serve this market, HPCL has introduced a five kg cylinder priced at Rs 95 and an introductory price of Rs 800 for the connection, making it affordable for the customers. While it was able to attract initial customers, who were curious on how a gas cylinder works, it couldn't take off as exponentially as they had expected. They couldn't fathom what was the issue even after having an attractively priced product and promise of ample demand without any obstacles. Distribution in rural areas could be a challenge, as we will explore in Chapter 8. Despite doing all the right things when it came to marketing mix, the results were not what HPCL had envisioned. When things didn't go in their favour, they decided to go back to the drawing board to analyze what had gone wrong. HPCL constituted a study to find out the root cause of the issue. In the study, it was found that the women were apprehensive about the safety concerns of the cylinder. Few were worried that it could explode at any point, while few were concerned about potential gas leaks which could damage their body and their family's upon inhalation.

With a mission to educate the women about the benefits of using a cylinder over firewood, HPCL also sought to generate awareness concerning the safety issues. To achieve the same, they constituted *Ghar Rasoi* on the lines of community kitchens in selected villages as a pilot. All they needed was a space provided by the local panchayat as a part of the partnership, while HPCL provided the cylinder set up and appointed a woman from a self-help group (SHG) who would don the role of a caretaker. This community kitchen ensured that women could come up with their raw material and cook in the setup already done without any inhibition. They were asked to pay a nominal token fee of Rs 2 to use the equipment which would be used for refilling the cylinder and the expenses of the caretaker. In this way, womenfolk learnt how to handle a cylinder, developing a certain trust towards the safety of the apparatus. By asking them to pay a nominal fee, HPCL was ensuring to attract the customers who were genuinely interested in learning more about the product. After using the community kitchen apparatus for a while, the women become more comfortable in using a gas cylinder setup. When they are ready, HPCL engages with them to purchase their own cooking apparatus. Once all or most of the eligible women make a purchase, the community kitchen apparatus would be successfully transferred to a neighboring village to provide for the next twenty family dependents over there. It not only helped the women in moving away from harmful firewood which is dangerous for their health, but also to the environment in the form of deforestation. HPCL to date has developed around 1600 such community kitchens with an average cost of Rs 8000 for every twenty family communities. Buoyed by its success of the pilot, the government has directed other oil companies to also look into programs of this kind.

HPCL's Ghar Rasoi has proved that even with the right pricing and promotional strategies, a product would fall flat in their face without any means to create awareness or induce interest in the product as that sustains the demand generated. As a company is in the transition phase, it would be plagued by issues that may remove its attention from the primary objective of sustaining the growth. The story of *Narasimha* avatar faces a similar dilemma that is explored below in detail.

Tale of the Claw

In the previous avatar we have learnt that Lord Vishnu took on the avatar of Varaha to vanquish Hiranyaksha and save the earth from being submerged in primordial waters. Before he died, the Asuran king had painstakingly built an empire that was supposed to last for generations. Unfortunately, the throne of the Asura empire went to Hiranyakashyapa. Being well versed in the religious texts and philosophical teachings, he consoled his mother and sister-in-law to not ponder too much on his brother's death. Yet he never aimed to follow the same preachings he had advised to his relatives. He was too angry at the fact that Lord Vishnu and in turn Devas had killed his brother through their treachery. He made it his life's mission to hate Vishnu with his very breath.

Hiranyakashyapa was much smarter than his brother and to overcome his shortcomings, he began a penance to bring the supreme gods down to earth. Neither the deafening thunder clouds, nor the frantic cold gales, nor the incessant heat bothered Hiranyakashyapa from his penance. He was surviving purely on air and resembled a skeleton corpse who was on the verge of death. Huge anthills formed around him to protect him from the harsh strokes of nature. Soon after, smoke started emerging out of his body that started making its way to the abode of Devas and all the living creatures across the fourteen worlds. It threatened to burn everything in its path without mercy. There was nothing Devas could do to stop the smoke as it was a result of pure meditation and the intensity of focus.

While this was happening, the Asuras surrendered to the Devas without putting up too much of a fight. Indra, the king of Devas wanted to capture Leelavathi, the queen of Hiranyakashyapa. The queen was pregnant with the Asuran king's child whom Indra wanted to kill to end the threat. But sage Narada, an ardent devotee of Lord Vishnu and son of Lord Brahma intervened. He stopped Indra from carrying out his act and took the queen under his personal protection.

The fumes emerging out from the Hiranyakashyapa's penance were becoming unbearable for everyone. Only a divine appearance from one of the supreme gods could have done to stop Hirayakashyapa's penance. Moved by the plea of the Devas and pleased by the efforts made by Hiranyakashyapa, Lord Brahma appeared before him in all his glory. The Hiranyakashyapa who greeted Brahma resembled a malnourished figure on the verge of death.

The first thing the lord had done was to restore Hiranyakashyapa to his former self with complete health. As a result of his penance, Lord Brahma offered him a boon of his choice. The king wasted no time in asking for immortality, the ability to live on forever. Lord Brahma refused to grant the boon, citing it is against nature's laws to grant immortality on just a whim. The Asura king fully anticipated this scenario and had an ace up his sleeve. He requested for a boon as follows - "I shouldn't be killed by a man or a beast or anything that is born out of a living womb. I shall not die during the daytime or the night time. I couldn't be killed in air or fire or water or land. No man-made weapons or poisons or divine *astras* by the gods should harm me." It was an impossible way of saying that Hiranyakashyapa can't die. Lord Brahma granted the boon, without any protest, despite knowing the fact that he would be using the boon for nefarious purposes. Armed with the boon of invincibility, Hiranyakashyapa began the conquest of all the three worlds. Despite receiving a boon, he never stopped hating Lord Vishnu for a second. In no time, Hiranyakashyapa established the Asura empire to its former glory. He made Devas and their king Indra flee their capital city Amaravati.

In the meantime, Queen Leelavati was spending the remainder of her exile in sage Narada's hermitage. He used to religiously speak about the virtues of Lord Vishnu or commonly called *Hari* to the pregnant queen. Leelavati was always an ardent listener to the sage's teachings. However, there were few instances when Leelavati herself fell asleep due to fatigue, but the fetus inside used to listen intently to sage Narada's stories.

When the king returned triumphant from his conquest, his queen was welcomed to the capital of the Asura empire with a son named Prahalad. The empire rejoiced at the return of their king and the birth of his heir. Everything was going smoothly, until one of his advisors suggested Hiranyakashyapa to proclaim himself as god.

Hiranyakashyapa agreed with this suggestion as it was inherently in line with his hatred towards Lord Vishnu. All the arrangements were done, proclamations were made across all the three worlds (Earth, Heaven and Netherlands) that only Hiranyakashyapa should be worshiped from that point onwards. Multiple temples with his statues were built in a whiffy manner. None of his subjects dared to object to this proclamation. All the sages and rishis who worshiped the gods were disturbed by this order, but didn't do anything. What could they possibly do? They were weaker in every aspect to the empire's forces! They only prayed for deliverance. Time went on, but there was no stop to the Asura rule in all the three worlds. Hiranyakashyapa summoned the best of the best teachers in the land to educate his son in the ways of Asura culture.

Things were going on smoothly with no hiccups. It was almost as if the entire world was getting used to the Asura empire under king Hiranyakashyapa. One fine day, the king woke up to hear the chant of 'Hari' being taken up in his palace. Leave alone uttering the word Hari, the mere thought was considered a treason, punishable by death. Baffled on who would dare such impunity, he went on to investigate the source of the chant in the palace. When he found who was uttering the chant, he couldn't hide his shock for it was his own son, Prahalad, who was worshiping his arch enemy.

Believing that his son was misguided in an attempt to hurt him where it hurts the most, Hiranyakashyapa tried to cajole Prahalad out of the chant using love. Imagine the political consequences when the crown prince himself challenges the emperor's godly declaration. He immediately summoned the teachers and tried to find out who was teaching rubbish to his son. The teachers pleaded innocence and requested for a fifteen-day time to set things right. Back in the *gurukul* (an ancient residential school), the teachers failed to get a response from the prince on where he had learned about the word Hari. They left Prahalad in the classroom full of other students as they had to attend to some urgent duties. By the time the teachers came back, the whole classroom was chanting the word Hari. Alarmed at this turn of events, the teachers quickly went to meet the king in his court. They pleaded that nothing can be done to cure the prince of his Hari disease and they asked him to relieve the teachers from the duty of teaching the prince. No amount of rewards or threats made the teachers reconsider their decision. The king had no option, but to oblige, but he wanted to teach his son a lesson and ensure that he mends his ways.

Hiranyakashyapa, tried to talk to the prince in a gentle manner on why he was chanting the name of Hari. When the young boy countered those attempts with logical arguments profound for his age, it unleashed the rage within him. He realized that he was being too soft on his son and decided to turn the heat up a notch. He ordered his guards to throw his son in a pit filled with hungry wolves who would devour any prisoner in an instant.

Instead of any signs of fear or worry, prince's face was beaming with a sense of calmness that only a confident person would have. The guards, despite being afraid, locked the prince inside the pit and left for the night. When they came back in the morning, they were surprised by the sight that greeted them. Prahalad was sitting calmly, petting the wild wolves that surrounded him and chanting the name of Hari.

The king was genuinely perplexed to hear that neither his son had given up his faith on Hari nor was he torn apart by the wolves. As a next step, he ordered his guards to throw the prince in a pit full of spears which would impale anyone who came in contact. Once again, the prince had shown no signs of fear while walking towards the pit. The guards flung the prince off into the pit, hoping to hear a shriek of pain. But they heard nothing of the sort. Their curiosity piqued and they bent over to see. Inside the pit, just hovering above the spears was the prince, calmly chanting the name of Hari.

Hiranyakashyapa wouldn't give up. Day after day he planned a new torture for the prince to give up the name of Hari. From being beaten with whips to being thrown off the cliff to being drowned in the river to being hanged as a common criminal to being trampled to death by an elephant, everything was tried, but it was the same story. Prahalad would show no sign of fear even if it meant a painful death and he was miraculously saved every time from each punishment. Nothing stopped the prince from chanting the name of Hari.

Hiranyakashyapa decided to burn his son in a pyre. To ensure that his son doesn't escape, he summoned his sister Holika who was granted the power of fire immunity. Once the guards arranged the requisite woods in a shape and lit it, the flames grew to dangerous heights Holding the young prince's hand, Holika led the way to the pyre. She felt a bit guilty when the prince showed no sign of fear. She didn't want to defy her brother openly. She sat in the pyre with Prahalad on her lap. The flames grew intense by every second, yet there were no shouts from either of them. By the time the flames died out, the guards rushed back to the king to apprise him of the situation. Hiranyakashyapa was dumbstruck to hear that his sister perished in the fire, while his son still continued to live and chant the name of Hari. It seemed like Holika sacrificed her life and powers to protect the young prince. It's a regional variant on how the festival is celebrated.

One fine evening, Hiranyakashyapa wanted to try talking to his son for one last time before he had to take drastic measures like removing him from the inheritance. What sort of message would it send to his subjects that he couldn't even control his own son?

But his son was unrelenting and stood his ground on why one should worship Lord Vishnu. This defiance by the prince awoke the beast inside the Asura king who had enough of this nonsense and asked, "You speak so much about your Hari. Where is he?"

"Hari is present everywhere. He is the one who graces the morning sky as the sun and the night sky as the moon and stars. He is the raging fire, the cold gale, the lush grass, the torrential rain including the very breath we are taking," said Prahalad.

Enraged at this answer, the king picked up his mace and asked, "Is Hari present in this pillar?" When he received no answer from his son, he smashed the pillar into smithereens in a single blow. He went on to the next pillar and repeated the same question. He smashed this pillar too when Prahalad was still silent.

When the king hit the third pillar with force, it didn't break at once. Instead, it showed visible cracks with hints of faint light emerging out of them. Something living inside it had broken the pillar like a new life emerging out from an egg. It was a being that no one has ever seen in all three worlds. With the body of a human and the head of a lion, he was a weird amalgamation of man and beast, a being that can be classified as neither.

With a ferocious roar, the being emerged out of the pillar and sought a fight with the king. The being was named Narasimha, as he is part man - *Nara,* part lion - *Simha.* A fierce fight ensued between them. Hiranyakashyapa was confident that nothing could kill him. Halfway into the fight, the king realized that the boon from Lord Brahma was not working any wonders as he felt the claw marks on his cheek. In a jiffy, the being slashed off Hiranyakashyapa's mace as if it was made of butter.

Then Narasimha lifted the king and carried him towards the entrance of the palace door. Suddenly everything began to fall into place for the demon king. In the heat of the battle, he failed to notice some crucial elements that would ultimately be a cause of his demise. The half creature was neither man nor beast, rather a mix of them. A hybrid creature that the world has not witnessed before or was not part of Lord Brahma's creation. Since it emerged from a pillar, it didn't come out from any living womb. As Narasimha sat on the bottom frame of the door (also known as *ghumam* in Telugu or *dehleez* in Hindi) and placed the demon king on his lap, he had a chilling realization. It was neither inside nor outside, it was neither in the air nor on land. The demon king looked outside quickly to see what time of the day it was. It wasn't even complete day or night. It was twilight, the intermediary time in between. Using his claws which aren't man-made weapons, Lord Narasimha began tearing up Hiranyakashyapa's entrails. The lord managed to find an avatar that circumnavigated the boon granted to the demon king and used it to vanquish him. The order was restored and the universe was alive to fight another day.

Yet, the story of Lord Narasimha's didn't end with Hiranyakashyapa's death even though that was the sole purpose of the avatar. Killing with his bare hands made Lord Narasimha go on blood lust. His anger was amplified and the avatar began to lose all sense of reason. Nothing in his path withstood his ferocity nor his power. He was the ultimate symbol of untamed nature.

He only wavered for a second when the little prince Prahalad stood in his path without any fear on his face. He began chanting the name of Lord Hari and requested the avatar to cool down. Somewhere at the back of his mind, Narasimha realized that Prahalad must not be harmed at all. Yet the lord ignored Prahalad and continued on his path.

In his wake, the lord left a trail of destruction. The Gods were worried alike for if Narasimha was not stopped, they would simply be accelerating the doomsday of all the creation. Upon Lord Brahma's suggestion, they collectively prayed to Lord Shiva for deliverance, who had the power to match up to Lord Narasimha.

Lord Shiva obliged and took on the form of *Sharabha,* a humongous beast made up of lion and bird. He flew down to the place where Narasimha was heading towards and intercepted him on the way. Sharabha threw a challenge at the lord, goading him into a fight. Natural instincts kicked in and Narasimha accepted the challenge. There was no clear victor in sight. Both of them were equally matched in power and prowess, yet Sharabha had a flight advantage due to its wings.

To gain an upper hand, Lord Narasimha turned into *Gandaberunda,* a two-headed bird that has no lack of courage. (Fun Fact, Gandaberunda is the state emblem of Karnataka in India.) Sharabha, the form of Lord Shiva and Gandaberunda, the form of Lord Vishnu fought for eighteen days. The destruction from their battle was unfathomable, with no deliverance in sight.

The Gods realized that they needed to do something and they needed to do it fast before everything was lost. Before they could decide on what to do, they were treated with an appearance of a lifetime. A woman with the head of a lion appeared on the battlefield out of the blue. She showered the battle arena in divine light through her very presence. Looking at her, both the fighting beasts were stopped in their tracks. The light had a calming effect and both of the beasts reverted to their original forms.

The lion-headed goddess who managed to do this impossible was none other than *Pratyingira Devi.* She saved the world from potential destruction that could have undone all the work done since the time of Matsya avatar. No one knows who the goddess was, except for the fact that she was a fragment of *Adi Parashakti,* the primal feminine energy.

After all this, Prahalad assumed his father's throne and ruled for a long time, all the while being a devotee of Lord Vishnu.

Losing the Plot, Into the Chasm

As demonstrated by the Narasimha avatar, out-of-the-box solutions are required to sustain the growth momentum during the transition phase. The singular focus on devotion of Lord Vishnu by prince Prahalad is commendable. For it was the shield that saved him all the time from his father's wrath. Lord Narasimha's rage provided a decisive victory against Hiranyakashyapa. Yet it was not controllable and that threatened the very existence of life.

A singular focus, multiple strategies sound good on paper. But there are enough red flags in the planning and execution exercise one needs to look out for if a brand intends to cross the chasm. Marketing helps in converting sales, which in turn takes care of the top line of the company. But the brand also needs to be prudent enough that all the marketing spend is not eating away the numbers. It should not be a case of spending Rs 1000 in marketing to earn Rs 10 in revenue. Airlines stand as the best example of this. Kingfisher or Jet Airways have witnessed where undue expenses have unraveled their business journey after a flash start. Blindly going ahead with promotions and discounts without any stop date or real tangible addition to the user base is simply tantamount to shooting in the dark. Within India, Uber Eats is guilty of this charge. Using discounts didn't help it exclusively when the fight in the food delivery business with Zomato and Swiggy came knocking on its doors back in 2019. Companies with limited resources need to be congruent with this fact, as the firms with deeper pockets would simply adapt to bleed out their competitors to be the last one standing.

Satya used to run a sandwich cart in a busy road filled with colleges. Since he was new, he thought of running 50% off to attract students. For a week, the offer worked like a charm. However, once the offer expired, his sales dropped drastically as at the same price point, students preferred to eat at the outlets. So, to attract the students once again, he offered a 50% discount on the new prices. It worked for a while. But since he was running on a loss, he stopped the discount after two weeks. While this was happening, the other outlets too began to run the 50% discount. Since their competition was running 50% off, Satya had no choice but to continue with the discount. The only difference was the established outlets had some resources to count on, plus they offered other dishes too. Satya had no such luck. He couldn't sustain the discounts and had to close his sandwich truck.

At the risk of sounding obvious, a repurchase mechanism is needed for any brand to survive this stage. Otherwise, the brands run the risk of falling deep in the chasm. Think about it – as a brand it had done everything to attract a customer for the first time. But if it doesn't think on how to make the customer purchase again for the second time, there won't be any business model to survive on. Maggi Hot Heads is an example of the same phenomenon. To capitalize on the brand equity of mother brand Maggi, Nestle launched a brand extension under the name Hot Heads which included flavours like peri-peri, green chili, chicken chili, and barbeque pepper. Its immense war chest and the goodwill of the brand helped it pass the introductory phase with flying colors. The trouble started with the growth stage. Maggi was able to attract initial numbers who were induced to try out Maggi Hot Heads for once. When it came to repurchasing the same, customers weren't so keen that they went back to the usual Maggi brand. The team couldn't sustain the momentum and Maggi Hot Heads had to be taken off the shelves in less than a year of the launch. It's hard to even think of the resources that went into the whole exercise. One hypothesis is that the product is not up to the mark in terms of taste, which led it to fade away as a one-time spark. A different perspective to the taste hypothesis is that customers were familiar with the flavour of original Maggi and weren't willing to replace it with anything, even when it was from the same brand. Another hypothesis is the team made a miscalculation in the demand and supply which made it flood the market with Hot Heads products. But no one was that keen on repurchasing the product. This led to Maggi Hot Heads falling into the chasm before it could complete the growth phase and reach into the 'Maturity Phase'.

'Growth Phase' is an opportunity for the brand to introduce new features to the product which was released earlier in order to be attractive to early adopters. Brands and companies need to be conscious of how they navigate these changes. The fall of a brand into the chasm is not a pleasant experience and Parle has experienced the same through its Hippo brand.

The Hippo Vanish

Parle is a major player in the snacking segment with a plethora of products under its umbrella. To break into the packaged snacks segment brimming with potato chips and namkeens, Parle came up with a new brand Hippo, which offers baked wheat munchies. Parle is a powerhouse with brands like Frooti, Fizz, Parle-G, Monaco, etc., which are pioneers in brand building. Parle wanted to do no less for Hippo.

In the early 2000s, it came up with Hippo as a brand mascot with the core philosophy that hunger is the root cause of all evil. Hence don't stay hungry and be a good person. It launched a TVC where Hippo traveled around the world solving issues by placating hunger and spreading love along the way. It plays on the powerful insight that food is an emotion and brings people together. This definitely helped Hippo to stay relevant in the consumer mind space. Its quirky packaging with bright colors helped in standing out on shelves and succeeded in cementing this position in consumer space. Not to mention, Hippo also offered unknown and exciting flavours which aren't usually found in the chips segment. Some of the popular flavours that are found across brands even today are onion and sour cream, Indian masala, tangy tomato, etc.

While Hippo was ticking off the checklist of everything to ride on the growth wave, it failed to anticipate the demand it could gather for its munchies. After all, they don't technically fall under the usual biscuits space or potato chips space, which was the implicit decision to create a whole new category altogether. It played safely by being conservative in its estimates. It had successfully attracted innovators and poised itself for early adopters with its brand mascot and related campaigns. But unfortunately, it bit off more than it could chew. With a nascent distribution system, it was not able to cope up with the unanticipated demand.

To tackle this crisis, Hippo turned towards social media, which was also on a growth journey of its own. It created a Twitter account where it asked its users to inform in case of any supply shortage with a promise that they would be replenished in record time. Users loved the product that they flooded the account to keep the team posted with real-time updates. Parle even allocated a dedicated team to source out the information by manually browsing the social media accounts. While that was an innovative way to crowdsource, real-time information gathering on stock levels in various key markets, it wasn't a very long-term solution that could be banked upon. It was more of a stop-gap solution. The puzzling question is why an established brand like Parle failed to utilize its existing models for Hippo?

An aggressive expansion without factoring in the demand and required systems in place to satiate the demand would eventually be the undoing of Hippo. Its paradox of brand positioning with the choice of its mascot didn't exactly gel well with the audience. This was because once the novelty of a Hippo started wearing off, people started questioning if it is a healthy snack or not due to the contradictions in the communication. The philosophy of eliminating hunger is not exactly a strong or memorable proposition in the long run, at least for the target audience back then.

When Hippo realized that things were going out of hand, it decided to do a revamp. It launched a campaign that represented the humanoid Hippo in the shoes of a mother taking care of her children's hunger in a cute manner. But it was too little, too late. From then, the downslide has been accelerating at a pace where no one could apply the brakes. And the brand had to bid goodbye to the customers in no time.

Parle to date has never come out with a solid reason on why it had to kill such a popular brand. The supply issues are the first reason provided for removing the brand, the question of brand positioning has cropped up at the altar of postmortem analysis by the industry experts. The truth may never see the light, but the lessons from Hippo are hard to ignore. Or the fact that Hippo was poised to be the fastest-growing brand of that decade and it could never achieve its potential. The irony is that it acutely managed all the challenges in the introductory phase, but succumbed to the ones in the growth phase.

Musings from the Mane

Amongst the avatars of Vishnu, Narasimha is a turning point because he is a transition from animal-based avatars to human-based avatars, signaling the philosophies required at the time of creation are completely different than the ones required at the time of its thriving. He also symbolizes the internal journey the God himself undertakes from the ferocious force of nature to the serene being of divinity. As evidenced by the minute factors that Narasimha avatar included to find a work around the boon given to Hiranyakashyapa by Lord Brahma represents the tweaking of 4Ps to suit the changing business needs of the growth phase. The half-lion, half-man represents the eternal struggle for control between nature and humanity, how skewed control can cause unimaginable destruction as demonstrated by the lord's uncontrollable rage after killing the Asura king Hiranyakashyapa and evident in the collapse of Hippo after it couldn't deal in appropriate fashion with the growing demand.

While the next chapters explore the growth phase of PLC in detail, below is a quick summary of the learnings from man-lion in the context of crossing the chasm and reaching the growth stage.

- Attracting customers to the business/brand and thus increasing the market share in a sustainable way is the only way to ride on the growth momentum.
- With increasing the marketing share by attracting the early adopters as the singular focus, it ought to be done by deploying various strategies ranging from product to price to place to promotions to supply chain.
- Discounting as a means to attract customers should be limited and in a controllable manner. Otherwise it would derail all the efforts done till date.
- Repurchase strategy should also be in focus to enable existing customers make multiple purchases, thus strength-ening the brand/business in the process.

5

Ignoring the Dwarf Umbrella

Yagnabhoomimpuragatvaa
Padatryamayaa chadaha
Trivikramovyaptaha
Namaste vatuveshine ||

Amidst the Growth

Growth by implicit definition is trying to better oneself from a previous state. However, in the growth stage of the PLC, that understanding is not adequate. A business and by extensions its brands need to have the forbearance to adapt to any sort of disruptions in the marketplace and mint a pristine way for growth. As they say, all the best laid out plans go awry to things beyond one's control.

Before the demonetization, Paytm was just another Indian fin-tech startup trying to make an average user pay through digital mediums. However, in the light of disruption, it managed to acclimatize its user base to transact digitally. One would be surprised to find even a small-time fruit vendor would hold the QR code of his Paytm to accept payments. Other digital wallets like Oxigen couldn't manage to pivot to the altered scenario and had to bite the dust in the end. In due course, the Government of India has bought a novel medium of payments in the form of UPI and it opened up opportunities for players like PhonePe, Google Pay, Amazon Pay, Bharat Pe, etc., to make use of. Seventy four billion transactions worth

INR 126 trillion in FY'22 stands as a testament to how long UPI journey has come up and how brands had to adjust to the changing scenario.

In juxtaposition with the introductory phase, growth offers a window of opportunity to strengthen one's brands. As the sales numbers keep on increasing, the cost required to initiate a sale decreases. This in turn frees up resources to allocate more spending towards building awareness or shoring up the value chain that helps in bringing the product to the consumer's doorstep. While it is vain to tame the beast of unpredictability, a brand can take measures that would help in making hay till the sun shines in the growth phase.

"It's a V.U.C.A world" is a popular phrase heard across B-schools and business circles alike, which stands for Volatility, Unpredictability, Complexity, and Ambiguity. It supposedly depicts the market landscape in flux. A brand needs to ride the growth wave and increase its market share in such an ever-changing environment.

Few familiar companies have learnt the lesson the hard way. Kodak had hopelessly failed to grasp the emerging digital trends and was crushed out of business in the end. Interesting to note that Kodak was not lacking in digital technology. In fact, it had built its first digital camera in 1975 itself. But held back for fear of losing its market share amongst the analog camera market or was skeptical about the acceptance levels of the digital camera. Due to this misjudgment, Kodak went to lose all it had built to date, where it is now regarded only as a case study. One could wonder how things had gone south for Kodak as they couldn't read on how the market was changing and take up necessary defense measures.

It is one thing for a new fledgling startup to commit

mistakes that threaten its very existence. And it is a different thing for established brands that know the way the market is evaluated to falter around. One could hypothesize the reasons to be manifold – could the numbers paint a rosy picture for the existing category to dismiss the emerging trends with confidence? Or did they assume that they have enough resources to fight out the change? Or the sad reality that they were completely blind to the revolution that bought their downfall? One may never know the actual reason but can learn from the missteps to avoid landing in a similar scenario.

Tiny Steps, Giant Leaps

On a rudimentary level, the 4Ps of marketing drive the perception of a brand. The converse is also true. In the growth stage, the next set of customers who contribute to the growing market share is known as the 'Early Majority'. Product extensions (also known as line extensions) are essentially introducing new variants or products within the same category to strengthen one's portfolio as per the customer preferences. Coke happens to be a quintessential example on this front. It managed to build Diet Coke as a separate brand altogether, while in reality starting as a product extension. Product extensions are a means to reaching the next set of customers to add to the top line. Out of ten customers, five customers prefer chocolate candies, while the others prefer vanilla candies. The brand was able to target the five customers using its base variant who love chocolate. To reach out to the incremental five customers, it bought out a product extension in the form of vanilla flavoured candy under the same.

However, resorting to extensive product extensions in excess would result in customer confusion, logistical nightmares, lack of shelf space, rising accounting costs. For instance, if an ice cream brand has fifty flavours that are available in around five different formats. This alone leads to 250 SKUs (Stock Keeping Unit) that need to be mapped according to the customer preference, geographical considerations, etc. It would be counterintuitive to the whole objective of attempting a product extension.

Extensive distribution capabilities need to be built to withstand any form of disruption. They also lend a hand in sowing seeds of awareness and induce interest in the mass market. BharatPe, an Indian fintech startup managed to combine distribution with technology to turn it into a competitive advantage. By the time BharatPe was in the fray, various companies had provided individual QR codes for the merchants to manage. It started causing hassles to customers and vendors alike. Imagine the vendor saying they only accept Paytm, while the customer only has a GPay app. When one multiplies this across a large number of customers and various brands into play, the problem suddenly increases by manifold. Taking this into consideration, BharatPe has come up with a single QR code that can be linked to multiple companies. Now the merchant only has to display one QR code and irrespective of the payment application used by the customer, the transaction gets completed. Most of the merchants who accept digital payments would sport the QR code poster with the BharatPe logo on it. Using this, the company was able to generate awareness and break into a market filled with competition. Irrespective of whether it makes money out of each transaction or not, the logo of BharatPe is there for all to see.

Lowering prices to break into a customer segment is one of the most tried and tested pricing strategies the world has witnessed. The decision between low margin - high volume and high margin - low volume game is dependent on how the brand perception is being built. Brands that aim to build a luxury aspiration cannot resort to penetration pricing to acquire a new set of customers. One cannot even conceive the idea of Lamborghini slashing its price just to increase its sales. It may reduce its production, but would never resort to such a move to keep the luxury perception alive in its customers. Brands that intend to play in the mass market may not foresee higher margins as it needs to deliver a value proposition. In a similar fashion, Parle G cannot hope to command a higher premium as that would affect its volumes due to a mismatch with customer expectations. Pricing strategies in the growth stage should be carefully evaluated with an eye on the long-term horizon. It's a classic Goldilocks case, where it can't be too cold, it can't be too hot. It just has to be perfectly right for the audience the brand wishes to cater to. The risks fraught with penetrative pricing and discounts, in general, have been detailed in the previous chapter.

In the growth phase, a brand is expected to offer product extensions or auxiliary offerings like additional services, warranty; build an extensive and exclusive distribution network; adapt healthier pricing strategies, and in general create awareness in the mass market. All these actions indirectly assist in building a brand that is crucial for the remainder of the PLC journey. A similar journey was faced by King Mahabali that is better explored in the Vamana avatar of Lord Vishnu.

Hiding in Plain Sight

From Ravana to Sisupala, from Duryodhana to Kansa, they have a common element in the form of underestimating enemies. One story that vividly stands out is that of Bali Chakravarthi. Bali, the grandson of Prahalad wasn't exactly the evil stock of Asuras shown in mythology till date. Prahalad inherited the empire his father built and managed to rule in a benevolent manner. It was prosperous enough for his grandson to inherit without any fuss. He managed to impart his learnings of dharma so that his grandson wouldn't go astray.

Bali intended to expand the contours of his empire, yet not against his grandfather's wishes. So, he turned to his guru Shukhracharya in whom the wise sage saw the return of Asuras to their glory. He advised that Devas are protected by the blessings of the supreme gods. And the only way to break those blessings in a quick fashion apart from meditation is performing a yagna with utmost dedication. Yagnas are divine rituals that contain power within them. Ancient texts describe how sages used to bring in rain clouds by performing yagnas. Considerable willpower, resources, and attitude are required to complete a yagna. As suggested by his guru, Bali performed the yagna *Viswajit,* which essentially means winning the whole world. Armed with the divine blessings, Bali marched his army to Amaravati, the city of Devas.

Indra was surprised to see that Bali was able to mount a strong challenge for control of all the three worlds. He wanted to find out the secret of Bali before fighting him, for Indra knew that Bali didn't do any penances nor received any boons from the gods. To save themselves, he and his army fled the city, effectively making Bali, the emperor of all the three worlds. This act of victory earned him the title of Chakravarti.

Since then, Bali began to perform yagnas, thus counting his divine blessings. He had performed numerous yagnas during his lifetime, so much so that he was just one yagna short of becoming the 'Indra' of that era. But any yuga in the time flow can only have a single Indra. It was impossible for someone to complete yagnas on such a level. So, no one could fathom the idea of a person becoming a second Indra, let alone a mortal of Asura birth. Having two Indras would cause imbalance in the power of gods leading to unforeseen dire consequences.

On the other hand, Aditi, mother of king Indra was heartbroken at the fact that her daughter-in-law was living in forests. She asked her husband, sage Kashyap to provide a solution for this unforeseen problem. The wise sage suggested praying to Lord Vishnu. Following the advice, Aditi began to perform a pooja that would invoke the blue lord.

Once the pooja was completed, Narayana appeared. Aditi was astonished to witness the lord with her own eyes. "O Lord! Protector of Dharma. My sons, Devas have lost their city, their wealth and status in the hands of their cousins - Asuras. Please save them from this ordeal," said Aditi.

On hearing this, the lord smiled and said, "They will be saved. But I want you to grant me a boon." Aditi was surprised to hear this. She was not sure what sort of boon could she provide to the lord of the universe. Upon asking the question, the lord replied that he wanted to experience the joy of having Aditi as his mother. Aditi couldn't refuse this request as it was not every day one could have this opportunity.

In the other part of the world, Bali started performing the last yagna needed to clinch the title of Indra under guru Shukracharya supervision. During the process, it was customary to donate to the needy and those who ask for help without fail. Since Bali was the emperor, it would turn into a matter of prestige if he could not donate anything.

A small brahmin boy entered the yagna site carrying an umbrella and a kamandal. The boy sought out the king on guest rights and the traditions of the yagna. The king was amused to find a little brahmin boy who managed to turn all the attention towards him. Upon asking him, the boy replied that his name was Vamana. However, guru Shukracharya was not fooled so easily. He suspected something was fishy, the way Vamana was walking with an air of invincibility around him. The wise sage guessed that the boy could be a ploy of Lord Vishnu to distract Bali from the yagna. It could be a ploy to somehow obstruct the yagna or worse, attack the yagna site using the little boy as a distraction. He wished that king Bali didn't patronize the dwarf or entertain his requests.

By this time, the king was about to get started with the rituals of welcoming a brahmin boy into the yagna site by washing his feet. The sage asked the king to stop immediately. Pulling the surprised king aside quickly, the wise sage aired his concerns. Yet, Bali chose to not heed to the sage's words.

Undeterred and sticking to his principle, Bali went on to entertain Vamana. The first step was to wash Vamana's feet. In a bid to discourage and insult Vamana, Shukracharya reduced his size and entered the pot using his powers. He stopped the flow of holy water in the pot by placing himself against the outflow hole. Not having water to wash the feet of an esteemed guest was a bad sign. Such signs were considered inauspicious and might prompt Vamana to leave the yagna site in humiliation.

Vamana simply took a grass blade and started poking the mouth of the pot to clear out any obstacles. Unfortunately, in one of the poking actions, the grass blade injured Sukhracharya in the process. Bloody eyed, the wise sage simply disappeared from the pot. With no obstacle, the water flowed smoothly and Bali completed the task of washing the boy's feet. King Bali had not noticed that his guru had turned up with an injury.

After washing the feet, Bali asked him what gifts he would take as part of the offerings. Vamana politely asked the king to reconsider his promise carefully. Bali grinned for he had all resources at his disposal. He was confident that he would be able to fulfill the worldly demands of the poor boy with a snap of his finger. Besides what more could a boy who can't even grow a mustache for years can ask for? Bali simply agreed to provide whatever the boy asks for without any hesitation. Shukracharya was livid when he heard the king's words. He requested the king to not act out so rashly, but it was of no use.

"Oh! Great king! I only request you to provide me with three feet of land measured by my foot size," asked the nimble Vamana. Bali was surprised at this request. Just three feet of land? That too measured by the boy's foot size? It was nothing. Here he was, the emperor of all the three worlds and only three feet of land?

"I promise to provide you with three feet of land of your choice from my vast dominions," declared the Asuran king.

No sooner than Bali uttered out his promise, Vamana started growing in height. He touched the sky, but continued to grow without any end in sight. He didn't stop until his foot was large enough to cover all of the earth, while the other foot was still in the air. With that he covered the whole of earth and the netherlands as a single tract of land measured by his foot. There are still two more to go. Vamana placed the other foot which was in the air on the heavens. With that the second tract of land from the agreement was fulfilled.

"Oh! Great king! The earth, including the netherlands and the heavens could only be counted as two feet of the land tracts as per the agreement. How do you plan to fulfill the third tract of land?" asked Vamana, looking down upon the tiny Bali who was still at the yagna site. If Bali was surprised by the turn of events, he didn't show it on his face.

Suddenly the king had an epiphany. How could he have missed this? The dwarf boy was no ordinary boy. He was none other than Lord Vishnu himself. His guru Shukracharya's warning made sense now. Lord Vishnu must have come to restore the Devas to their rightful place in the universe. Yet Bali decided that he would not go back on his word, no matter what.

"O great one! You have blessed me by granting a darshan. There's nothing left with me except my own self. Please place your foot on my head and help me honour my word," said the king, bowing down before the mighty *Trivikram* (the one who measured all the three worlds). Lord Vamana obliged by placing his leg on Bali's head, sending him to the Netherlands, and claiming his third tract of land.

Lord Vishnu, in the avatar of Vamana, faced a dilemma of his own. Bali had not done anything wrong or anything that can be constructed as considered Adharma. He won the throne fair and square according to the rules of conquest.

He performed the yagnas as per the scriptures without any deviation. He was the grandson of King Prahalad, one of the greatest devotees of Lord Vishnu. Probably his only mistake was his arrogance of claiming that he can do anything? This arrogance was signified by his rash promise to Vamana. Yet, Lord Vishnu had already given his word to Aditi that he would restore her children, the Devas to their rightful rule. Even in the face of defeat, Bali behaved in a dignified manner honouring his word.

Though Lord Vishnu had thwarted Bali from becoming the Indra, he was pleased with his devotion. He made Bali the ruler of Nether lands. He declared that Bali could return to his kingdom from the Netherlands to spend time with his beloved subjects who cherished their ruler, just for a single day every year. Since then few stories claim that Onam, a harvest festival of Kerala is celebrated to welcome their exiled king. Bali is celebrated as one of the immortal *Chiranjeevis* and the ruler of the Netherlands till the end of time. A simple, innocent request of three steps turned out to be a completely unimaginable gift for Bali.

The Extent of Myopia

From Prahalad to Bali, the growth story of their empire is evident for all to witness. Even though the empire helped in characterizing Bali as the benevolent ruler through his actions, an unforeseen event and underestimation led to his downfall. Similar tribunals await the brand as it moves ahead in the PLC. Apart from the unexpected disruptions in the marketplace, another subtle blindness a brand falls victim to is 'Marketing Myopia'.

Marketing Myopia is a popular concept developed by Theodore Levitt, a lecturer of Business Administration at Harvard Business School. The concept essentially means how far the brand or business goes into a narrow-minded space that it fails to see the obvious changes around it. It deals with a fundamental question - "Are businesses customer-centric or product-centric?" If a brand/business needs to avoid being labeled as myopic in nature, then it cannot prioritize being 'Product-centric' over being 'Customer-centric'.

The fine line between being product-centric and customer-centric is not minute enough to ignore. For instance, railways are not in the business of running trains, but to provide transportation. The moment railways failed to address this concern, that was when it allowed other modes of transportation to grow exponentially, while railways decreased. Railways are conceived with the notion that their job is to always lay down rails, build infrastructure, etc., and restrict themselves to product perspective. If these changes are made without taking into cognizance the customer impact, these changes are for naught. When the customer convenience is not met, users began to look for other means that served their purpose. Think of it, would it make sense for railways to lay down stations and tracks where there is no customer demand at all? Instead of improving experience on high demand routes?

A company needs to be consumer-centric, instead of solely focusing on being product-centric. Otherwise, it risks moving one step closer to oblivion. Not to say that a company should completely ignore product-centric measures. But it needs to strike a balance between them both. Back in the 2000s, Nokia was ousted from the smartphone wars that were completely dominated by Samsung and Apple. When the whole world was embracing Android, Nokia still stuck its gun on its in-house operating system - Symbian. It sought to challenge the might of Android when it was going from strength to strength. In comparison, Symbian resembled a pale shadow of Android and couldn't match the customer preference. Also, Symbian wanted to be exclusive, while Android had opened its doors for a collaborative building which accelerated its acceptance amongst developers and customers alike. Had Nokia concentrated on the customer perspective, it might have still been a player in the smartphone market.

For example, two e-commerce companies are offering the same product, at the same delivery time, at the same discounts. The only difference between them is that one has greater after service and the other not so much. It is a no-brainer that a customer would mostly go for the company with greater customer service. The companies, in this case, are Amazon and Flipkart respectively. No doubt e-commerce companies are not exactly money-making machines, nor can one deny the state at which they treat their delivery fleet to ensure the promised delivery times to customers. But one can't ignore that Amazon swears by its customer-centricity. There's a reason for that. If at all there was no proposition in customer centricity, Amazon wouldn't even bother putting up such a façade. After all, Amazon is a behemoth on its own, conquering market after market, acquiring probable rivals, and unleashing its potential. On the other hand, there's not even a whimper about customer-centricity from Flipkart in India. Only time would tell. Had Snapdeal (another Indian e-commerce company) survived the battle for market share in the e-commerce space, maybe it would have used customer service as a differentiator. Alas, it didn't even make it to the next round and the whole e-commerce space has witnessed a revolution with the entry of Ajio, Tata Neu, etc.

Raju owns a mobile repair shop. He is a stickler for processes to ensure that he delivers the highest quality service to his customers. However, there are days when he goes too much by the book that he doesn't actively try to help the customer, thus losing the customer in the process. Even in cases where there is a warranty issue and the company needs to pay for it, he doesn't actively provide information for it is not his purview.

Marketing Myopia is a warning that a brand can't sacrifice the long-term goals in favour of short-term objectives. With even offline businesses aiming to create digital fronts as additional touchpoints to interact with the customers, brands need to decide what is absolutely required for the customer instead of blindly following it just because it was trending. Zerodha provides an excellent example of how to navigate the growth phase and build for the long term.

Zerodha's Growth Engine

Only close to 3% of the total population of India invests in the equities markets, while it is 12.7% in China and around 55% in the USA directly or indirectly in 2021. Not long ago, the Indian trading scenario was dominated by large and small brokerages who thrived in a niche bubble that was only accessible to a limited set of audience. The whole process of entering a stock market was so cumbersome and riddled with paperwork that customers who wanted to participate also shied away from it. It was all set to change when Zerodha arrived on the scene. Zerodha found a gap it could play with as the whole market was concentrated with high commission charges and exorbitant rates. Its founder, Nithin Kamath, wanted trading to be simple and exciting enough to attract young customers. He found a pain point that would help in differentiation and at the same time bring in new customers to the table. The idea of buying stocks at a swipe of a finger seemed exciting to the young customers.

They leveraged digital technology, built a sleek UI, and kept the commission rates low. The product was simple to use. The name Zerodha is a mix of names – Zero and Rodha, which is a derivative of the Sanskrit word meaning no hassles at all. Zerodha provided an offering of flat Rs 20 per trade, instead of having commission-based trades. This strategy is a reminiscence of penetrative pricing that was adapted to suit the market needs. It worked wonders to attract younger customers. There are almost one million users daily, executing around 2.5 million trades per day on an average. Due to its technology-enabled platform which reduces its operating profits and minimized advertising spending, Zerodha can garner higher margins.

Zerodha doesn't spend much on marketing. It relied on its trusted customers and the power of word of mouth. One can interpret it as a pure genius move for trading. Zerodha is a business laced with trust and it needs to inspire that confidence in its customers. Otherwise, it would have to shell out a bomb in a bid to acquire customers without any base to fall back on. Instead, it let its early adopters spread a positive word, which attracted customers like moths to a flame. This helped Zerodha play on volumes while maintaining low trading charges, thus fueling the exponential growth.

Traditional companies missed the trend and could only witness the platform growing from strength to strength. It managed to capitalize on the young generation's desire to be a part of trading and investment, but have no clue on how the system works. To ensure that these needs are met, Zerodha began building appropriate products and partnering with firms as a part of its ecosystem like Varsity, Coin, Small Cases, Investing in Finshots (a simplified financial news delivery startup), etc. Even till date it never ran expensive customer acquisition campaigns nor any form of referral programs. One can ponder if Zerodha had been advertising itself from the start, would it have achieved the level of customer stickiness? Or would it have been brushed off as another startup doling out deep discounts?

Zerodha managed to make the best out of its growth phase and continues to build a financial ecosystem that intends to educate the customer and empower them to make responsible decisions through its plethora of applications. It managed to break into a category in the most unexpected way while the existing players could only play catch up to the changes in customer behaviour.

The Dwarf Speak

Vamanavatar is a watershed moment in the annals of Hindu mythology. He is the first avatar that dons the human form to save the universe from going through an apocalyptic war and restore semblance to all three worlds. He is the first avatar to be the progeny of a human couple, but not the last one evident by Krishna avatar. Lord Vamana's story is aplenty with nuances for the keen eye to witness, for it is easy to dismiss the dwarf boy carrying an umbrella.

Shukracharya who warned Bali represents the soothsayers in any firm that are ignored by the decision-makers due to certain calculations which could be biased, leading to another firm usurping the market pole position. Bali hasn't necessarily committed any major crimes except for the fact that he let his arrogance dictate a few major decisions that caused his eventual downfall. Even though Bali was exiled to the netherlands, his benevolence earned him a place amongst the immortals and rulership. It implies having a strong core for any brand to weather storms that threaten its very existence. Vamana is the epitome of potential as he was a puny dwarf who measured all the three worlds using his giant feet, earning him the name Trivikram.

Before moving ahead to the final phase of the growth stage in PLC, here is a summary of wisdom from the dwarf that is applicable for any brand traversing the growth trail.

- ✧ Profit is also a key metric to be measured in this stage to track the performance, as the increase in volumes reduce the per sale marketing expense. Unprofitable growth may not suit well for a company after a point in time.
- ✧ The growth phase lays down the foundation of a brand that serves as a cornerstone for the remainder of the PLC. Without this foundation, the business could be simply running from goal post A to goal post B without any tangible direction for its growth.
- ✧ Any modifications made to the 4Ps of marketing influence the contours of a brand going forward and cannot be taken from a short-term interest.
- ✧ Product extensions are a way to introduce variants in the same category to reach out to mass-market customers, build a robust product portfolio that caters to different customer segments and protect the brand from the competition.

- Pricing strategy ought to walk the fine line between high volumes/low margins and low volumes/high margins, without disturbing the brand perception.
- The development of intensive distribution is crucial to serve a wider audience and build awareness concurrently, without which higher demand will scuttle the overall growth of the brand/business.
- A brand needs to be customer-centric over product-centric to avoid the trappings of Marketing Myopia to strike a balance between short-term goals and long-term outlook.

6

Escaping the Angry Axe

Nihatyaguruhamtaram
Kartyaveeryamsabaomdhanam
Ramaha kshatriyahamtaasi
Vasudeva namostute | |

For a marketer, in the grandiose purpose to build a strong and memorable brand, the growth phase offers a sublime opportunity for a business that was still attempting to test the waters in the introductory phase. Attempting to build a growth strategy by playing around the 4Ps of marketing continues to serve as a form of competitive advantage, going forward. And it needs to be rooted in strong consumer insights and brand locus.

Earlier marketers operated with a liability of data darkness that is difficult to fathom without the aid of current technology. With the availability of too much data in today's age, it is easy to disbelieve that the world used to exist without any data in the first place. Questions like - 'What is the size of the potential target group?', 'How many customers are aware of the brand X?', etc., were answered with less precision in those days. Even to date, there are no accurate answers, but the margin of error is significantly lesser in comparison across time periods. In those days, when a company wanted to check whether its new launch was working or not, the only way to measure was to use product sales numbers as a yardstick.

Having access to appropriate data is crucial in this

heightened scenario where the stakes are equally high for the brand and all partners in the value chain. Data of only one kind may lead to a bias, without marrying the insights with data from other sources. Complimentary to the available tried and tested methods of market research, the advent of social media has ensured that marketers can arrive at an elementary customer sketch consisting of likes and dislikes, preferred mode and time of purchase, etc., with one click. Social listening as a tool to scrape social media to hear what the customers are trying to communicate is gaining traction with the growing digital marketplace.

Armed with the ability to extract the keywords the customers are able to associate with, marketers are crafting interesting variations of communications and efficient customer journeys. For example, Amazon has started displaying keywords of what its reviewers think of the product, thus giving the prospective buyers a summary of what the product is like in the customer's voice without actually going through thousands of reviews. Zomato arranges a list of key dishes in the 'Hot Zone' of the application that it thinks are best sellers or must be tried from a restaurant based on past sales behaviour. There are various tools such as Sprinklr, Hootsuite, etc., that help companies track their digital presence, its brand health, and other key metrics associated with digital space. One can send out personalization communications to nudge the customers towards a purchase. If sales number that present the reality of on-ground presence are correlated with numbers of digital space through analytics, one can derive a 360-degree view of the brand. This leads to a tantalizing possibility to measure the conversion of marketing campaigns to increase sales numbers, allocate spending efficiently, and make appropriate strategic decisions.

Ramesh has set up an online business of delivering sweets in the neighborhood. He decides to invest in online advertising. Once enough traffic started coming in, he wanted to monitor the comments section to ensure that he can tweak his sweets according to the feedback received, which if not corrected, leads to bad customer experience.

Matrix of Many

Either for a fledgling startup with a single brand or a company with multiple brands under its umbrella, the desire to evaluate their position to rethink their strategy is common, as they foray into the growth phase without any end. BCG (Boston Consulting Group) matrix is one simple tool that helps in providing cognizance of one's brands to help in decision making. It is a framework used to plot out the position of the brand and its potential against the axes of market growth and market share that represent the industry attractiveness and competition potential, respectively. It was first conceived by the Boston Consulting Group, thus leading to the name BCG matrix. Each of the four quadrants in the matrix represents multiple market scenarios to recognize and move forward appropriately.

Individual brands that are performing exceptionally and the whole market is also growing at a pace are known as 'Stars'. They are placed in the first quadrant which represents a high market growth rate and relative market share. One Plus, the smartphone brand is one such example that plays in a market with a high growth rate and has enough space for market share increase. Stars are supposed to represent the ones who made the optimum use of the growth phase in a PLC cycle.

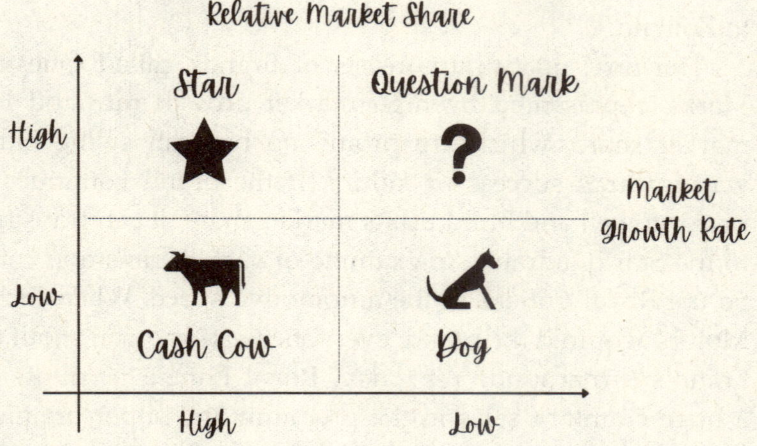

BCG Matrix

The second quadrant is defined by a relatively low market growth rate, but comprising top market share enough to sustain the brand's growth. Maggi is a classic example, where the noodles industry on a whole has poised a moderate market growth rate and it is in a pole position. It is a literal cash cow to the parent company Nestle, where Maggi contributes to a huge chunk of its bottom line. Brands placed in the second quadrant are known as 'Cash Cows'.

Brands with modest market share and meager market growth rate usually end up in the third quadrant and are known as 'Dogs'. If at all a brand ends up here, the company must do everything in its power to correct the situation, failing which leads the brand to oblivion, even before completing the remainder of the growth phase. Uber Eats, which was launched to capitalize on the growing food delivery industry is grappling with losses and stiff competition. It might not even find its place in this category as it had to eventually sell to Zomato.

The final quadrant consists of brands called Question Marks, represented by high market growth rate and low market share, which are promising but can swing either way towards success or failure. If the brand continues to perform well and build up its market share, it can transition to the Star quadrant. An example of such a transition could be the Royal Enfield in the automotive space. When Eicher Motors acquired the brand, everyone was skeptical about the brand's turnaround. Yet today, Royal Enfield accounts for a huge chunk of sales in the premium and super-premium motorcycle categories. What was supposed to be a Question mark, turned into a Star. New brands such as Dunzo, which is playing in the hyperlocal delivery segment is still a Question Mark, but promise potential growth.

Rounding the Noodle

The BCG matrix is a fairly self-contained concept that can be used as a reference to chalk out a future course of action. If a company finds few of its brands hovering in the Dogs quadrant of the matrix, it needs to take a tough call of diverting resources to performing brands or measures to revamp the brand premise with renewed focus.

If a brand is a Star, it is a testament to the fact of identifying the right opportunity to start a product from scratch and build a brand that solves consumer problems. However, since it still has the potential to reach, it may invite challenges from the external end. Any competition with deep pockets may force a showdown in the market, bleed out the Star brand and acquire it at a favourable price. This showdown impacts the Star brand all along the value chain without any respite in the short term as Nirma, the indigenous detergent brand witnessed in its fight for survival with Surf Excel.

In those days, detergent was considered a luxury product and priced accordingly. Nirma arrived at the scene with a price position that was irresistible to the housewives. Along with the product quality that was soft on the customer's hands and economic in value, Nirma managed to eat away Surf Excel's market share (owned by Hindustan Lever). For most of the time, Surf Excel ignored Nirma for the price point was not a sound business model. By the time Surf Excel recognized the threat, it was too late. To arrest the decline, Hindustan Lever introduced Wheel as a direct competition. Despite facing tough competition, Nirma managed to hold on to its position through its product and marketing actions. In the end, the detergent category was able to grow with brands like Surf Excel and Ariel serving the premium segment and brands like Ghadi, Nirma, Wheel, etc., continuing to cater to the mass segment.

If the brand happens to be a Cash Cow, it is an achievement to be celebrated for all the efforts that have resulted in increasing the bottom line of the company, which is the main objective of any business. However, a brand needs to ensure that it doesn't enter the zone of overconfidence and expose the chinks in its armour which another rival might take advantage of.

Maggi was ruling the instant noodle market with no competition in sight. It has a good tasting product, excellent communication that connects with its target base rooted in solid insights and its distribution network is extensive enough that one could get a plate of hot piping Maggi even amid snow-capped mountains. It is not even possible to fathom what could be wrong with the instant noodle brand? Turns out that was the same question rival firm ITC began to ask and their answers led to the creation of Yippee. Maggi consciously turned a blind eye to a couple of its faults which ensured that it would lose its market share from 73% to 60% back in 2016, even after a comeback from a debacle. Anyone who cooks Maggi and had a bad day while adding water than the optimum volume suggested, would know that the noodles turn sticky, thus robbing the texture and feel out of the dish. Or the noodles turn into a solid mess once it cools down, with Maggi in tiffin boxes being a case in point. Thirdly, one would have to break the square noodles to fit into any round utensils of the household, for none had bothered to invent a square-shaped utensil. It's safe to assume, the customer base strength didn't warrant Maggi to work on this feedback or it didn't have the bandwidth to address these concerns in a given timeframe. ITC, after three years of extensive research, precisely picking upon the points highlighted above, launched Yipee in 2010 which went on to become a one thousand crore brand in less than eight years. Since then, Maggi has tried to launch various variants to capitalize on the brand Maggi – Maggi Tomatina Noodles, Maggi Hot Heads, Maggi Fusion, Maggi Special Masala, etc. But it still needs to find its mantra to regain its pole position of 73% market share. A brand could be successful, but that doesn't mean that the issues with the core offerings should be ignored or get blindsided from a long-term perspective.

Wielder of the Axe

Long back after Vamana exiled Bali Chakravarti to the Netherlands, the known world was ruled by Kshatriyas. Being trained for the job, they managed to ensure that there was peace in the land. But after a point, the power started going over their heads and they managed to undo all the good work done by their ancestors almost single-handedly. Kartaveerajuna, son of King Kritavirya of Haihayas kingdom (the thousand handed one) received boons from the gods and started behaving obnoxiously.

On the other hand, sage Jamadagni was renowned for his prowess. Even Lord Surya was terrified of the sage's assault on him due to summer. The lord managed to pacify the sage by providing him with umbrella and footwear to survive the heat which later helped mankind. He even managed to gain the services of Kamadhenu, the divine cow goddess of bounty. He was survived by his wife Renuka and five sons, with the youngest being Bhargava Rama. She was considered the epitome of virtue and loyalty. So much so that mere sand turns into a solid pot to hold water for her husband's daily needs. Her devotion to her husband ensures that this miracle was sustained.

From a young age, Bhargava accompanied his mother on her journey to the river, partly to help her in her chores and also, to act as protection from the unruly king. One day, she failed to bring water to the ashram because she was lost in her thoughts due to the presence of a beautiful Gandharva couple on the river bank. This distraction caused a delay and in turn a crack in her devotion to her husband. Jamadagni's anger knew no bounds. He sought to punish her by asking his son to kill her for the transgression. His four sons refused to follow the father's orders for the love they bore for their mother. Jamadagni cursed all of them to be turned into ashes. When he commanded Bhargava to do the deed, he wielded an axe (his weapon of choice) to perfection and cut off the head of his mother without a second of hesitation.

Pleased with the display of loyalty towards him, Jamadagni granted a boon to his son. His son requested him to bring his mother back and restore the human form of his brothers. Delighted, Jamadagni obliged without much ado.

Life went on at the ashram without any hindrances. One day Ram was out in the forest to gather firewood. Kartaveerya Arjuna and his army were passing who decided to pay a visit to Jamadagni. Sage's family received them as per the protocol of a king and his entourage. He even used the sacred cow Kamadhenu to feed the entire army without breaking a sweat. The king demanded how much would Jamadagni be willing to accept as payment for the cow. The sage politely refused by saying that the cow was not for sale. Not a man to take no for an answer, Kartaveerya ordered his army to capture the cow. Jamadagni was helpless for he was not designed to be a warrior.

When Bhargava learned what had happened, his anger knew no bounds. He picked up his *parasu* (axe) and caught up with the king on the way to the capital and insisted on returning the cow without any violence. The king, drunk on his power, laughed off. Bhargava decided to answer through his axe. He single-handedly managed to vanquish the army. After a point, his axe was dripping red with the soldiers' blood, but he was not done yet. Kartaveerya was still standing and he was a formidable warrior in his own right, without even accounting for his strength granted by the divine boons.

A fierce fight ensued between the two warriors. For each blow Kartaveerya threw, Bhargava was able to match it with his axe. In the end, the latter prevailed. He chopped off a thousand hands of Kartaveerya and killed him in the end.

He returned to his ashram with the divine cow. Even though Jamadagni was happy, he wasn't too pleased to find the axe dripping blood. He shuddered at the actions of his son for he believed that a brahmin cannot kill a king. He ordered him to repent his sins by going on a pilgrimage and leaving behind the life of a warrior. Bhargava accepted his father's wishes without an argument.

However, his killing of Kartaveerya resulted in his sons taking the throne, but they are facing a tough time holding it. They were being reminded that their father's killers have not been brought to justice. Enraged, the prince and his brothers hatched a nefarious plan. Without any army, they sneaked into the ashram and found the sage deep in meditation. With no warning, the crown prince slashed off the head of the sage in a single stroke. The great sage Jamadagni, who caused the gods to tremble was put down by a cowardly Kshatriya.

Renuka returned from her daily work only to see her husband dead. Her grief was beyond measure. As fate happened to be, Bhargava came home from his pilgrimage. The sight that greeted him made him numb. On seeing him, Renuka beat her chest twenty-one times in her lament for the departed sage.

Bhargava's anger was boundless. He deduced that the crown prince would be the likely murderer of his father. Armed with his axe, he went to the capital with the aim to kill the crown prince and the associated bunch of Kshatriyas so that they couldn't harm another soul again. Bhargava was an unstoppable force who wielded his axe with precision. Armies trembled at his mere sight, warriors couldn't face his axe and kings conceded defeat in his mere presence. He purged the earth from the rule of Kshatriyas who were drunk in their power through his conquest. Since then, he was known as Parashuram.

After the conquest, Parashuram donated away all the lands he had won to sage Kashyapa and went into penance in the Mahendragiri hills. In due course of time, he came to know that prince Ram of Ayodhya had managed to break the great bow of Lord Shiva during a swayamvar in Mithila. He got enraged by this information on how a mere mortal could manage the feat. Prince Ram had married princess Sita with grandeur befitting the status of an Ayodhya royal. On their way back to Ayodhya, they were confronted by Parashuram. The air grew still, the sky rumbled with thunder and the army was motionless. Bhargava demanded that since Ram was so powerful, he should prove his strength by stringing the bow of Lord Vishnu and aiming an arrow with it. Bhargava assumed that Ram was a mortal who got lucky in the case of Lord Shiva's bow.

Prince Ram picked up the bow with ease and fixed the arrow for an aim. Bhargava was surprised. Then the realization dawned on him that Ram was also an avatar of Lord Vishnu like him. In his arrogance and anger, he missed out on this minute detail. Rama finally said that since Bhargava was related to his guru Vishwamitra, he wouldn't wish to aim an arrow at him. Since any arrow that was placed on Lord Vishnu's bow shouldn't be wasted, Rama gave Bhargava a choice between being rendered motionless for eternity or losing all access to higher worlds of reality that were gained through penance. Realizing his mistake and a lesson to reign in his anger, Bhargava chose to forgo his ticket to higher worlds and took penance in the mortal realm. He is counted as one of the seven Chiranjeevis, immortals who are roaming the earth in the aid of humanity should the need arise. In Dwapara Yuga, Parashurama served as the guru for Bhishma and Karna, respectively.

Coconut, Combat and Celebrant

As illustrated by Parashurama, uncalled acts of aggression must be dealt in the same coin to hold one's ground. It is equally important to not lose sight of oneself and miss out on finer points as evidenced by the incident between Rama and Parashurama. The tribunals Parashurama faced during his prime age evolved him into the wise sage immortalized over time, representing a brand journey.

Marico happens to be one of the prime examples that mirror Parashurama's journey towards defeating the anarchy he witnessed. An Indian-origin FMCG company, Marico has made its presence in a market dominated by towering foreign-based giants. Back in the early 90s, HUL was the largest company in the FMCG sector with its products spanning across various portfolios. In a bid to increase its market share, it sought to venture into new categories and expand its product portfolio.

Marico, which emerged from its family-operated business to concentrate on its core offering of coconut oil, happened to be an obstacle to Hindustan Lever's plans. It managed to acquire Tata Oil Mills Company (TOMCO) which had a coconut oil brand Tata Nihar Coconut oil. It was a popular brand in the eastern Indian markets and provided a leeway to play in the hair oil segment. Parachute, a brand owned by Marico commanded a market share of around 48% and was not allowing Nihar to grow in a double-digit market share figure.

Then HL (Hindustan Lever) chairman Keki Dadiseth with a penchant for making corporate acquisitions decided to acquire Marico, by all means, to possibly strengthen Hindustan Lever's dominance in the hair oil market. With that initiative, an assault on all fronts across the value chains broke out between Hindustan Lever and Marico. Starting from increasing advertising spending to discounting to retailers by giving higher margins to up to 35%, Lever was trying all tricks in the book to take advantage of its superior war chest.

Despite Marico having a strong brand presence with an excellent product, it didn't have enough resources to withstand a long-drawn assault by Hindustan Lever. Various analysts and the stock market seemed to agree with that assessment. It was reflected in the sharp fall in Marico's stock price. Naysayers believed that Harsh, chairman of Marico's best action, was to sell to Lever without a fight in a bid to arrest the stock price fall.

Amidst the market onslaught going on, Harsh received a call from Dadiseth asking for the price to acquire Marico. He promised that the price would be handsome enough to ensure Harsh and his future generations could live comfortably without any worry. Notwithstanding, Dadiseth upped the ante by stating the facts that Hindustan Lever was superior in terms of marketing and they boast of an extensive distribution network that couldn't be matched. He also added that it would be the best course for Harsh to sell the company before it's too late.

The reason these oil wars threaten Marico's survival was because Parachute contributes over 61% of its overall revenue. Since a hostile takeover was not possible as Harsh's family held over 65% shareholding in Marico, Lever resorted to an all-out war in the market. Harsh and his team decided to take advantage of their superior market understanding of branded coconut oil built over the years. Another advantage that Harsh enjoyed was that he was leading the battle from the front, while the person-in-charge at the end of Lever didn't enjoy similar decision-making power. While Parachute happened to be the bread and butter of Marico, Nihar happened to be just another brand in Lever's expansive portfolio.

To tackle the Hindustan Lever's assault, Parachute resorted to bringing up a packaging re-design and a revamped brand campaign that intended to position the brand to the masses. Parachute brought to the forefront the relevance of coconut as an auspicious offering in Hindu traditions and sought to drive home the connection to trust and purity. The brand campaign resulted in a reach of over eighteen million households.

It also identified that the chink in its armour happened to be a rural distribution that was nowhere as formidable as their urban counterpart. It built a blueprint of appointing close to 250+ super distributors in the rural heartland whose only task was to retail in these markets with an assurance from Marico in case of any expense excesses. The on-ground sales force was motivated to meet the battle-hardened Lever agents on the field.

In the end, Marico stood its ground and managed to hold on to its market leader position. After a war that spanned across six years, Nihar finally accepted defeat and was acquired by Marico itself. Today Marico has used Nihar to cater to a diverse segment apart from Parachute, combined through which it enjoys being in the market pole position.

The Swish of Growth

Born into a brahmin family, Parashuram was not hesitant to learn how to fight. Over the years he has learned to control his anger and morph into the Chiranjeevi revered. Today, he was able to pass on his teachings to various students who actively shaped the course of the sub-continent during the time of *Mahabharata* and beyond. He single-handedly fought multiple clans of Kshatriya who were troubling the denizens of earth. He stressed the importance of holding one's ground despite the mounting odds as long as the belief in one's cause is just as evidenced in the fight between Marico and HUL for market leader position in the hair-oil category.

Before moving into the territory of the maturity phase of PLC in the next chapter, below is a quick recap of the final stages of the growth phase.

- Collection of insights from all mediums, including digital, is important to build strategies affecting the 4Ps of marketing and is crucial for maintaining the momentum in the growth phase.
- BCG is a tool used to plot the contours of a brand potential using market growth and market share as its axes in four quadrants representing various scenarios. It is used as a barometer to take stock of the current brand situation and arrive at the next steps accordingly.
- In the case of a non-performing brand, tough decisions should be taken to kill the brand or set on a course for redemption from a long-term perspective.

- No brand should allow its success to blindside from its pitfalls that can be converted as a market opportunity by rivals.
- As a brand continues to grow, it needs to be prepared to take the challenger head-on using the market expertise gained over the years to build the brand.

THE PRIME

7

Strength of a Bow

Piturvakyamanukramya dharmam
Satyam cha palayas
Nihatyaravam yuddhe
Veerahakhalupuraahare ||

A ruler should never actively seek out war, but should be ready to don the conqueror persona if the need arises. The difference between a conqueror and a ruler is maintaining one's grip over the conquered domain, ensuring stability to avoid any potential rebellions, and ushering in peace. As brands enter the maturity stage, they need to walk the thin line between maintaining the momentum and consolidating the gains received from the growth stage.

The intent is to ensure that a brand builds enough backend infrastructure and front-end architecture to support its growth rate and attract new customers on the block. In this scenario, the term new customers is used to point out the untapped potential within the addressable target group decided in the previous stages of the life cycle. This distinction of new customers becomes evident as we deal with it in detail in the forthcoming chapters. The challenge in this stage is to maintain market share within this addressable TG itself, without succumbing to the threat from competitors. Rama's journey from a prince to an emperor who established the perfect rule that goes by the epithet *Rama Rajya* provides wisdom on how a brand should navigate its goals and challenges at the start of the Maturity stage.

Unsaid Truce

At this point in the life cycle, companies would have achieved or would be in the way to achieve economies of scale, thus resulting in low production costs. It would have cultivated a strong network of stakeholders – Suppliers, Distributors, Logistics, Media Agencies, etc., to ensure its products reach the consumer doorstep without any hassle. Apart from the marketing actions, these additional aspects provide the brand with a recipe to mount a solid defense for market share. The defense of a market position can be charted to diverse scenarios. Earlier the brand was a challenger in the growth stage, but now is in the role of a defender, an irony that isn't lost on anyone.

In the start, any new entrant would find the barriers of entry too strong to overcome in an established market and the existing supply chain being dominated by the market leader with no room for others. Hence, the new entrant's lookout for ways to disrupt the existing status quo to be taken seriously by everyone. Punching the market leader head-on is a symbolic gesture from any new entrant in that perspective. If the gambit is successful, it implies that the new entrant or rather known as the challenger is to stay in the market henceforth. They would have carved out space in the market pie and would try to hold on to it. Jio disrupting the telecommunication game for Airtel in India or Patanjali, and other indigenous brands taking the fight to Colgate are a few examples in recent times where the challenger has turned into the incumbent after tasting success.

In the second scenario, two incumbents each in their respective maturity stages of the product life cycle would battle it out for market supremacy, unlike the fight between an incumbent and a challenger. Interestingly, this fight not only involves customers, but also the external stakeholders in a prominent manner. Tales of such coups would be told by grass-root personnel who bear witness to the events and the corporate meeting rooms where strategies are hatched to gain market share. A major distributor or retailer using the tacks of under-cutting (effectively reducing their margins to off-load more inventory in the market in comparison to others) to increase their sales; a competent advertising agency moving their existing account to a key competitor; not being able to match the price drop executed by the competition are a few of the tactics used by the incumbents as there is no dearth of resources. Despite scoring few victories in the short term or making strategic retreats, the result of the battle is a stalemate in most cases. In due course, the incumbents would come to terms with the changed scenario and form an informal, non-verbal truce respecting each other's dominions. One look at the Indian newspaper market and it can be observed that *The Hindu* dominates the southern markets, while *The Indian Express* takes pole position in the northern markets.

This is reflected in the battle between Vali and Sugreeva, the *Vanara* princes of the Kishkinda kingdom. Vanaras are the divine incarnations of various Devatas who are to assist Lord Rama during his time on earth. Once Sugreeva and Vali went on a hunt for a demon who was troubling their subjects. In the course of tracking, they found the trail marks in a deep cave at the end of the forest. Vali went ahead in search of the tracks, while he asked Sugreeva to guard the cave entrance in case anyone was foolish enough to ambush the brothers. The battle between Vali and the demon went on for days with enormous shrieks and grunts emanating from the cave. Sugreeva stood silently at guard with worry written all over his face. One fine day, the cave got silent and Sugreeva observed blood flowing out from the entrance. Sugreeva assumed that his brother was slain in the fight. He closed the entrance of the cave to ensure that the demon didn't cause any more trouble by pursuing him. He had already lost a brother. He didn't want any more harm to his citizens. Despite being devastated, with a heavy heart, he assumed the kingship as a part of his responsibility upon the suggestion of the couriers. An empty throne or no leadership at the top is an invitation for the vultures to pick everything apart.

However, one fine day, Vali returned only to find Sugreeva on the throne. His fury knew no bounds. Sugreeva's pleas that it was a misunderstanding made no difference to him. Vali challenged Sugreeva to a duel, to which the latter agreed only in self-defense. There was no warrior who could match Vali in a duel. Even Ravana, the demon king of Lanka had to taste defeat in Vali's hands. The brothers fought valiantly, but only Vali prevailed, as expected. He had a boon from Lord Brahma that if he stood before anyone, half of the opponent's power would be transferred back to him, thus making Vali powerful as the fight went on. No matter who the opponent was, Vali was always invincible. In order to save his life, Sugreeva ran to take shelter in Rishyamukha hills where Vali was cursed that he couldn't step his foot. He was cursed by a rishi that if at all Vali dared to set his foot in the hills, his head would burst into a thousand pieces. No matter how angry he was, Vali still had some wits left with him. Since then, even though the siblings wanted to kill each other, they have been living in an informal truce, wary of each other. Even though they had information of each other's whereabouts and resources within their grasp, they couldn't do anything about the situation after a point. They were minding their own business, in their respective dominions.

Divine Core

Such truces in the world of business are not uncommon, yet brands do not have access to multiple aces in their sleeves that would drastically alter the status quo. Instead of completely limiting one's growth, these unsaid truces have consequences that strengthen a brand. It leads to the development of core competencies that a brand/business would be famous for, and which in turn helps in maintaining its market share despite stifling competition from all corners. In the Indian FMCG sector, nobody can beat the ITC stronghold of distribution which has a widespread clout. It's hard not to find a small shop in the midst of a deserted highway which doesn't have an ITC branded cigarette. On the other hand, HUL is known for its marketing actions that pave an advantage. It boasts of a large product portfolio in India, so much that every six out of ten advertisements run during an hour of television belongs to the stable of HUL. Such core competencies are built and add further credence to the stalemate. In a few cases, it takes a new challenger as discussed in the first scenario to change the equation. Such battles between the challenger and incumbent are inevitable as the market is always in flux.

Building on the work done in a growth phase, a brand is almost able to leverage its brand value as a source of competitive advantage along with its core competencies.

The consumer goodwill earned by the brand over a while is termed as 'Brand Equity'. A source of competitive advantage, it is the bedrock upon which brand extensions are built, which are required at the later phase of the maturity stage (more details in next chapter).

The goodwill a brand earns through its lifetime would allow it to weather any storm and live to fight another day. Coke nearly witnessed its downfall when it tried to dabble with its original recipe by introducing a drink concocted using a different formula. The customers were not amused at the loss of their favorite drink and took to the streets in protest against the company. Their loyalty made the company bring back the original recipe in a matter of weeks. Otherwise it would have been a disaster for the company. The original recipe was rebranded as 'Classic Coke' and continues to be a star of Coke's portfolio. On the other hand, when Maggi was taken off the shelves in India due to a government ban, many wrote off the brand. Competitors wasted no time in bringing out alternatives for the consumers. In due course, when the ban was eventually lifted, Maggi came back triumphant like the proverbial phoenix rising from its ashes.

The epitome of the Brand Equity analogy in the mythological annals is defined by Lord Ram, the eldest son of King Dasharatha and Queen Kaushalya from the kingdom of Ayodhya, who also happened to be the seventh avatar of Vishnu. Due to queen Kaikeyi's handmaiden Manthara's machinations, Rama was deposed as the crown prince and was exiled for fourteen years. Utilizing the boons given to her by the king, Kaikeyi made moves to glimpse her son Bharata ascending the throne instead. Dasharatha was honour-bound by his illustrative legacy to fulfill the boons he had promised to his queen. A person's integrity is measured by their ability to make good on their promises, no matter what. Rama also followed suit by declaring that he had no intention of going against his father's wishes and was happy to give up the crown for Bharata. He never resented or chided his father for commanding him about the exile. Rama willingly followed the order to not go against his father. Lady Sita and her younger brother-in-law Lakshmana also insisted on accompanying Rama to the forest. However, the people of Ayodhya were grief-stricken on hearing the news of their prince's punishment. Questions were asked ranging from 'What wrong did Rama do?' to 'Did Dasharatha lose his mind?' Bharata was on a diplomatic visit to his maternal grandfather Ashwapati's kingdom in the north. In due course, King Dasharatha went into a state of depression and a longing for Rama that was fatal to recover from.

When Bharata returned to Ayodhya, he was shocked to hear about his father's death. He was furious at his mother for hatching such a nefarious scheme for a throne that was not his by rights.

Wasting no time, he followed the trail of Rama to Chitrakoot, only to find that the crown prince attuned to the life of an ascetic with ease. He apologized profusely on his mother's behalf and requested Rama to return. Rama was happy to see his brother, yet he politely refused Bharata's offer saying that he cannot go against his father's wishes.

A kingdom cannot be leaderless. Bharata categorically declared that he too has no wish to take the throne for himself. It was a stalemate between both the princes. Understanding his brother's position, Bharata requested Rama to give him his footwear to place them on the throne and rule in Rama's name till the end of the exile period. He also declared that he would not return to Ayodhya till Rama himself came back. From a nearby village, Bharata managed to give peace and stability to the kingdom that was going through a difficult time. When Rama returned triumphantly to Ayodhya, he witnessed the similar devotion from his people last seen fourteen years ago. It's a testament to Rama's characterization as *Maryada Purshottam* that enabled him to tide over the hurdles he faced. It was his values, his steadfast devotion to his word that created an aura around him. This aura enabled him to survive the fourteen years of exile and return triumphant to the kingdom of Ayodhya.

Co-branding to the Rescue

The most visible sign of the maturity phase is the stagnancy witnessed in the sales department. By now the company would be engaged in setting up processes, quality systems in place for smooth functioning of the well-oiled value chain built in the previous stages of PLC. As mentioned earlier, an ace that any brand has to arrest the reversing growth trends and also possibly break out of the informal truce is to employ actions that increase brand awareness to generate new sources and reinforce old sources of brand equity.

For a firm in the onset of the maturity phase, short-term measures are employed to maintain the market hold achieved as the decay in the sales growth is yet to be realized completely. As a brand continues in the maturity phase, long-term measures are needed as the customer churn would be high and it is imperative to add in new customers at an equal rate or higher (more details in chapter 8).

'Brand Partnerships' form an avenue to attract new customers, apart from any brand's usual target group. In the specific circumstance of a brand partnership that doesn't involve acquisition in any format or the prospect of buying out or the chance of investing for a stake, is termed as 'Co-branding', where two brands come together for synergy from the marketing prism. An alliance of sorts where both the partners contribute to the objectives either of them deem important, respectively. Co-branding is one of the options any brand can use to maintain its market hold, while attracting new consumers, differentiating itself from its competitors, and ensuring that the brand equity remains intact. While Co-branding fosters the source of brand equity, the intention behind such marriage of convenience should be decided upfront. It can be between in-house brands or with external brands, as long as there is visible synergy amongst the brands and the respective categories. Before crafting a co-branding strategy, various factors like the expenditure involved to communicate the alliance and packaging-related changes, the customer reach that can be achieved, a clear demarcation of liabilities in case of any mishap, and no deviation from either brand's essence ought to be evaluated with gingerly consideration.

Raju had recently opened a small fruit and vegetable showroom to cater to local neighborhood needs. To get new customers, he requested the popular juice vendor to open a small front in his showroom. This ensured that loyal customers of the juice vendor started visiting the vegetable showroom and in turn increased the customer footfall.

Co-branding could be broadly defined in four formats, each with a definitive characterization as per the good folks at Henry Stewart publications. 'Reaching In' is a strategy employed when a brand wants to have a higher penetration in its intended target segment, while the partner brand strengthens its core offerings. 'Reaching Out' is employed when the brand is looking to reach out to newer consumer bases and complement the core offerings. On the other hand, 'Reaching Up' is a strategy defined when the partner brand enhances the brand image, without adding anything significant to the core offerings. Lastly, when a partner brand offers both newer market reach and enhances the brand image, it is known as 'Reaching Beyond'.

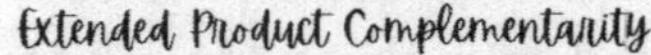

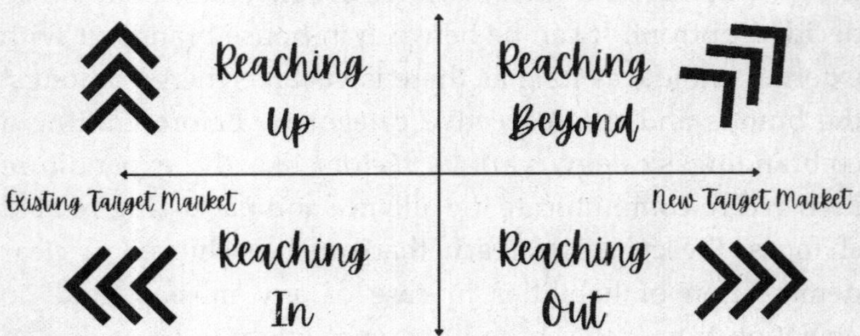

Oreo from the house of Mondelez has managed to use co-branding to its advantage. The tasty chocolate cookies filled with vanilla filling are popular with youngsters and adults alike. Apart from having a product that most of its customers adore, their marketing team managed to create an iconic eating ritual for Oreo – 'Twist, Dunk, Eat'. They wanted to break new grounds to reach out to potential customers apart from the usual retail, grocery stores, or online mediums. In foreign markets, Oreo is available in various flavours imaginable.

Within India, Oreo flavoured drinks at McDonald's, Kwality Walls ice cream mixed with Oreo cookies, etc., were visible efforts of the company's new strategic thinking. Such alliances provided Oreo a break into untried segments or capitalized on novel touchpoints with consumers and introduced the flavour profile to them in a new manner. Without the alliances in place, Mondelez would have paid an exorbitant price to reach out on its own capacity, the cost of customer acquisition is still high. From the perspective of an alliance partner, it is more prudent to offer an ice-cream flavour of a favorite taste than to expend resources in materializing the original flavour profile to the customer palate. It's a win-win situation where Kwality Walls gets to sell its ice creams and Oreo earns some fee for loaning its flavour.

Another classic example of co-branding is evident in the computer peripherals industry. AMD, a semiconductor company specializing in making chips has been Intel's competitor for a while. It can offer its product at lower prices, yet AMD has not been able to make a dent in Intel's market hegemony. Intel's positive brand image is so ingrained into the consumer mind space that grants them an unfair advantage. Customers have a proclivity to purchase a laptop only with an intel processor. Despite AMD having better processing capacities in a few instances, customers still view Intel from a positive prism. Since it doesn't leave the laptop manufacturers with many choices in terms of selecting the processor, they would have to make the best of co-branding with Intel to further their sales numbers. The power of alliances is illustrated vividly in the tale described in the Kishkinda Kanda - a subsection of the *Ramayana*.

Monkey Alliance

After being sent into exile on Queen Kaikeyi's orders, the trio of Rama, Sita and Lakshmana have been living happily in Panchavati, a part of the Dandakaranya forest system. One fine day, Surpanakha, the sister of Ravana, made her way towards Panchavati. Upon seeing Rama, she was immediately attracted to him and requested him to marry her. However, Rama refused citing that he followed monogamy and was already devoted to his wife Sita. Enraged, Surpanakha attempted to kill Sita in a fit of jealousy. In a bid to safeguard his sister-in-law, Lakshmana accidentally cut off Surpanakha's nose. Due to this unfortunate incident, Ravana was forced to avenge his sister's insult. At a time when the brothers were out of the ashram, Ravana came up in a disguise and kidnapped Sita. Jatayu, the mighty vulture died trying to stop the Lankan king from taking away Sita. When the brothers returned, they were greeted by the sight of an injured Jatayu, who informed them of what had transpired with his dying breath. Heartbroken, Rama decided to search for Sita wherever Ravana might have hidden her. They tried to search for any lead that might help them.

During their quest, they ended up in the land of Rishyamukha hills. It happened to be the same place where the vanara prince Sugreeva was seeking refuge from his brother Vali. Sugreeva from his hiding place in the hills assumed that these warriors were sent by his brother to kill him. So, he sent his trusted minister Hanuman, who using his shapeshifting powers fished out the information about the brothers and presented them before Sugreeva. After hearing their story, Sugreeva promised to help in the search for Sita. He also bought out a bundle of jewellery that Sita had thrown out while Ravana was carrying her in the *pushpak viman* (the mythical aircraft). As a mark of alliance between Ayodhya and Vanaras, Rama promised to secure Sugreeva's throne from Vali. They sealed their coalition with fire as the holy witness.

Upon Rama's suggestion, Sugreeva challenged Vali for a duel that Vali won without breaking a sweat. Vali sent a missionary to Rama seeking his collaboration and suggested that he could use his good terms with Ravana to broker peace between Lanka and Ayodhya. Rama politely refused saying that he couldn't support a person who has forcibly taken someone else's wife, a similar mistake that Ravana had committed. When Sugreeva challenged Vali for a second duel, this time Rama was able to kill Vali without any hesitation as he was able to differentiate between the brothers using a garland. He crowned Sugreeva as the king of Kishkindha.

By the time this happened it was already monsoon time. They waited for two months before any search operation could begin. As per their original promise, Sugreeva summoned all of the vanaras who formed the army and was sent to all corners of the world in search of the Ayodhya queen. Vanaras who went east, west, and north returned empty-handed without any trace of Sita. The team that headed towards the south found a lead in the form of Sampati, the brother of slain vulture Jatayu, who confirmed that it was Ravana who had taken Sita to Lanka. Hanuman even crossed the mighty ocean to obtain proof that Sita was indeed in Lanka before an assault could be launched. The leaders of Vanara were crucial in finding the whereabouts of Sita. The Vanara army also built a monumental bridge spanning from the tip of the subcontinent to Lanka in no time. Their battle prowess turned the tide of the war against the Lankan empire and their mighty army. Even though Lord Ram was a powerful warrior in his own right who vanquished countless demons during the exile, he still had to seek the help of Vanaras, who possessed a natural advantage in their home ground of forests for the effective success of the search operation. Additionally, he needed an army to fight the powerful captors of Sita. Had he not taken the alliance, the contours of *Ramayana*, the first epic in Sanskrit literature would have been completely different. In the end, alliances are supposed to bring mutual benefits to the table. Airtel happens to be an example in recent times of how to form co-branding partnerships.

Airtel, Pepsi and Happiness

The Indian telecom industry has been transformed beyond recognition in the last three years. From its inception, Jio has been on a marathon sprint with no breaks to market leader Airtel's juggernaut. To match the aggression displayed by Jio, Airtel slashed its prices following Jio's pricing strategies, while Idea entered into a marriage alliance with Vodafone to consolidate synergies. The above steps proved to be prudent for survival, but it was short-lived as the Supreme Court of India had a surprise waiting for the telecom players. In 2020, the Supreme Court ordered the telecom players to pay the AGR (Adjusted Gross Revenue) dues amounting to almost INR. 1.47 lakh crores. Airtel and Idea-Vodafone combined suffered a loss of 73K crores due to the price war in 2019. Amidst this, the Supreme Court order was no less than a death knell for Airtel. Naysayers and well-wishers began to doubt the tenacity of the telecom industry. Parallelly the loss of subscriber base for Airtel, Idea-Vodafone didn't contribute to the financial health of either of the firms.

Under the shadow of impediments, the telecom players reached out for an uneasy truce whose first proclamation was to allow market forces to bring back the product prices to normalcy. Jio used penetrative pricing to capture the market share in the early days of its launch and the impossibility of the product experience to disrupt the status quo. Forced by Jio, the other players also had to play the price game to ensure their market share remained intact and avoid a massive consumer drain. With price taken off the table, the discussion of future strategy shifted back to offerings, services, product quality, ethos, etc.

At this opportune moment, Airtel decided that it needed to pivot away from being recognized as just a data service provider to improve its market share. It started venturing out into alternate offerings that could be bundled with its core telecom service. It inked deals with Google, Lionsgate, Nokia, Juggernaut, Apollo Hospitals, Zee 5, strengthening partnerships to provide an enhanced user experience. Airtel wanted to break into newer consumer segments and strengthen its existing base to regain its lost market share to Jio. The above-mentioned partnerships are primarily digital and cater to target groups that are subsets of Airtel accustomed customers. Airtel wanted to attempt something radical to truly break into newer segments. From that perspective emerged the co-branding partnership with PepsiCo.

A telecom giant and a snack and beverage giant are as disparate as they could be, but the synergy recognized between the parties is undeniable. As per the deal, PepsiCo's snacks and beverage packages in India would carry codes, through which users could redeem free data via the 'Airtel Thanks' app, and the logo of Airtel would be used in every packaging. PepsiCo would get to be a part of Airtel's marketing campaign, where its brand could be displayed across 344 million phones. This alliance paved a way for Airtel to break into non-traditional segments, while PepsiCo looked to benefit from repeat purchases, thus creating a win-win situation for both parties. The cost of acquiring a new customer might have been steep if either had followed the old-fashioned methods.

Challenges of Nexus

A person's integrity is measured by their ability to make good on their promises despite being in demanding situations. Myths are peppered with figures ranging from Dasharatha to Karna to Sibi Chakravarti who have been shaping the adage into our collective consciousness. The same principle holds for brands to a degree higher than humans. Throughout their lifetime, brands would be responsible for a significant number of humans in their value chain. As the brand continues on its trajectory, it is bound to clash with ideas of time against the brand foundations established a while back. Despite making the right noises and moves against perennial challenges, a divergent problem arises in an unexpected manner, throwing all the brand's existence into question.

A vocal minority of customers take up the call against the brand in a bid to stay true to their ideals. Such a move has been termed as 'Brand Activism' by modern lexicons. For instance, in a country obsessed with fair skin and a brand dutifully pandering to those sentiments instead of taking a moral stance was pulled up by the vocal minority. With the 'Black Lives Matter' protests picking up steam, the debate on racism was waged in the subcontinent too. An insight that emerged was that the customer was no more interested in fairness or anything remotely related to the promotion of racism. A by-product of customer awakening that the brand ought to have foreseen for a while. With a growing chorus each day, HUL, the parent company of the brand 'Fair and Lovely' finally bit the bullet. It opted to go for a rebranding exercise and distance itself from any sort of communication that promotes racism explicitly or implicitly. Even though it is a bold move from the brand, one can't help wondering with regards to the timing of the move. The brand rechristened itself into 'Glow and Lovely'. The jury is still out there if the rebranding exercise addressed the issue of not perversely promoting racism.

Myntra, an Indian fashion e-commerce company had to face a crisis due to brand activism. An activist pointed out on the internet that Myntra's colorful logo 'M' was offensive to women from a perspective. They even went ahead to register a complaint on the same. By the time netizens noticed it, Myntra made up its mind to redesign the logo and it came out with an improved version a day later. It was a massive expenditure to revamp any logo and the company had to go through this tribunal because a person had a different perspective and the internet amplified it.

In the light of brand activism, the question that needs to be answered is would there be a possible outage against any brand en masse? Would a brand activist be a user of the brand in question at least once in a lifetime? It's a given that brands are humanized in consumer mind space to some extent (more details in chapter 9). This leads to an interesting phenomenon where customers expect the brand to champion the causes of righteousness, along with expectations of ethics and moral values within the confines of their brand core. Any breakaway from these ideals is not a pleasant experience for the brand. However, the fine line of fulfilling the wishes of the silent majority and the vocal minority must be walked upon the basis of understanding the customer's pulse. From time to time, companies have faced public ire, and how they dealt with it made them the iconic brands today.

Lord Rama faced a similar ethical dilemma that nearly broke him and his family, as described in the Uttara Kanda of the *Ramayana*. Ayodhya was jubilant for the return of their beloved royal couple. One fine day a washer man was furious that his wife was late to return from her maternal house. When she finally turned up, he accused her of infidelity. When the people around suggested he seek king Rama for justice, he discarded it immediately. He declared loudly that he couldn't seek judgment from a person who allowed his wife to return after staying in another man's house for more than a year. People were shocked at how someone could utter such a malicious string of words. They pointed out that Sita's *agnipariksha* was done which proved her chastity. The washer man simply brushed it off as propaganda and added that no one in Ayodhya had witnessed the event.

Soon the washer man's comments reached the king's ear. It directly challenged the integrity of the king and questioned his right to rule. If a king isn't respected by his people, he couldn't have the moral authority to be a sovereign. With the institutions of order called into question, the only thing left for the kingdom was to fall into chaos. Rama wanted to avoid chaos before the voice of one could turn into an avalanche.

He couldn't bear to ask Sita to go through the trauma of questioning her integrity once again. He wasn't willing to take any coercive actions on his citizens. He wanted to be a king who leads by example and doesn't want to be the one who besmirches the good name of his ancestors. Rama sought to do what he thought was necessary to preserve the integrity of Suryavanshis and made the hard choice. He banished his queen who was pregnant during that time to forests. In the end, the story of Rama and Sita does finally have a bitter-sweet ending (explored further in the chapter), but it was not without its tribulations.

As elucidated by Rama's confrontation of public opinion, there is no way to determine the right course of action. A brand can only ensure that when faced with a crisis of sorts, it can opt for solutions that are in line with its fundamentals.

Satya worked in the operations of a potato chips manufacturing plant. During a quality check, they found few bad samples. Instead of taking the risk or writing it down to the marketing team, he took the decision to recall the entire batch produced for the day and destroyed it. Even if one customer makes allegations of receiving bad product – real or imaginary – it hurts the brand.

The Conquest of Conquests

'Emergence of New Competitive Forces' is a substantial threat as the brand continues in the maturity phase of PLC. Brand Alliances/Co-branding are short-term measures to be resorted to defending the market share at the incipient of the maturity phase. It is difficult to fathom how a competitor would challenge the incumbent. To counter the ambiguity and stay relevant in changing scenarios, it is prudent to neutralize the threat through acquisition. The decision is adequate if the cost of building in-house capabilities or the expense of fighting out the challenger in the open market or both is higher than the actual acquisition price.

While it is reasonable to shell out a premium for the acquisition rather than the efforts to develop it in-house and bring it to similar market quality any day, the hidden cost of integration with the parent company shouldn't be ignored. Another reason why the acquisition of a brand is attractive is because it paves the way to build a myriad portfolio that addresses the spectrum of top-end to low-end segments. As a brand, an acquisition increases its stature with the potential to turn into a market leader which facilitates in negotiating favorable terms with stakeholders in the value chain. It also signifies strength and the capacity to grow, as others might have to think twice before throwing a challenge.

Facebook was the lead in big-ticket tech acquisitions in recent years. It willingly opened its purses to acquire WhatsApp and Instagram. Facebook knew that nowhere it had the ability and bandwidth to build WhatsApp and scale its current level of operations. Hypothetically, WhatsApp uses the valuable time to bring new offerings to the table, while Facebook was still stuck with creating a basic product to challenge WhatsApp that was no longer of market interest. A similar story slammed out for Instagram acquisition too. It realized that Instagram has built capabilities to disrupt the social media space and Facebook was nowhere near to it. Plus having a sizable chunk of the user base interacting with the application daily is a positive sign. Additionally, the acquired brands/companies wouldn't pose any threat to the pole position the acquirers occupy in the market. Before the acquisition, Instagram must have brainstormed ways to beat Facebook and the irony is that it now has to develop strategies to integrate its platform with Facebook and popularize the social media giant.

Further, acquisition assists in monitoring the future trends and ensuring product readiness when the time is ripe for action. Flipkart, has acquired the AI-based LIV–AI which has built the capability to convert speech to text in various Indian languages. Flipkart believes that the future would be dominated by regional languages, thus making the experience more democratized.

Amazon acquired 'Lovefilm.com' back in 2011. It integrated seamlessly into its infrastructure and was able to roll out the offering of 'Prime Video' to all key marketplaces in 2016. Using Prime Video, Amazon was able to make significant strides in the OTT space. Any acquisition at the conclusion should fulfill the objectives for the acquirer and create a positive delta for them. Otherwise, it is flushing good money down the drain.

Ashwamedha yagna is elucidated in the ancient myths as a ritual to be performed by kings and emperors alike to establish their puissant presence and expand the confines of the empire. The yagna bears resemblance to the strategy adopted by market leaders in the face of competition.

The Saga of Twins and Sacrificial Horse

Kingdoms being forged and decimated at the command of swords for conquest was not an unknown word during Treta yuga. It was a time when Lord Rama was ruling Bharatavarsha at the helm of the Ayodhya Empire. Owing to terrible circumstances, he was forced to exile queen Sita in order to uphold his Suryavanshi oath. At that time, Lady Sita was not by herself. She was carrying Ayodhya's descendants. But after Sita's banishment, the empire lost its sheen. Rama sunk deep into the sorrow forsaking his primary responsibilities. In a bid to bring back the lost glory of the empire, his advisors suggested that he perform Ashwamedha yagna to extend the empire's boundaries. They pointed out that even though he had banished Sita to govern the realm to avoid any black mark on the ruler's reputation, he was not honoring the sacrifice made by refusing to govern. Finally, Rama relented and agreed to perform the yagna. *Ashwa* essentially means a horse. In this yagna, a ceremonial horse is let loose on the land with an army following it from a distance. Wherever the horse steps its hooves, that land belongs to the empire. If anyone thinks otherwise can battle it out with the accompanying army. If the challenger wins, the army would leave the land alone and recognize their independence. If not, they will have to bow down to the new emperor.

The beast faced no challenge in the start as none wanted to test out the might of the Ayodhya army. But when it entered the ashram of Valmiki, it was captured by twins - Luva and Kusha. Earlier, the twins toured the kingdom singing the paragons of Ramayana written by sage Valmiki. The twins were not aware that Rama was their father nor that the horse belonged to Ayodhya. When Bharata, the commander of the army, tracked down the horse to Valmiki's ashram, he asked the boys to return the beast without any violence. The boys refused to give away the horse for they didn't fancy the way Bharata spoke. It came down to a fight where the boys managed to defeat Bharata and the army almost single-handedly. They held Bharata captive in the ashram.

Rumours began to fly thick and thin about the missing horse. It was not a great story that a mighty empire has been humbled by two little boys. Rama was forced to confront the boys as it was a matter of prestige. An all-out archery fight broke out with neither side gaining an upper hand. Before any permanent damage could happen, Sita reached the battlefield and brokered peace between Rama and the princelings. At this juncture, Sita was glad that she was able to fulfill her obligation by entrusting the future of the *Ikshvaku* clan to Rama. She then went to call the earth mother, to take her away. Despite the turn of events, Lord Rama began to groom the princes for responsibility and entrusted them with a larger empire before departing to the heavens.

Even Yudhishtir performed the Ashwamedha yagna in Dwapara yuga to expand his empires by adding kingdoms to boost influence, ensure longevity and remove rivals. Airbnb happens to be the best example to elucidate this perspective in a modern setup.

Airbnb - Tech, Travel and Trivia

Airbnb started as a platform to match property owners with short-term tenants, and has revolutionized the travel industry in a way. Despite the proposition of being lighter on the pockets, Airbnb can connect on a deeper level and capture the essence of travel for its customers.

When Airbnb was doing a rebranding exercise, it effectively zeroed that it represents 'Belongingness' at its core, along with the affinity it brings to customers during their travel through hospitality. The new logo of Airbnb depicts a heart, a location pin, and a person, a reflection of the brand core it mostly cherishes.

In the customer journey, Airbnb comes into the picture once the customer decides to travel to a place and decides to look for a stay. Earlier Airbnb was in no position to influence the customer's deliberation to travel or their judgment on a place to visit. But it wanted to change this equation and be involved in the end-to-end customer journey.

From this perspective, Local Mind fits into the customer journey puzzle that Airbnb is trying hard to crack. It was only a two-year-old startup when Airbnb concluded the acquisition process. Local Mind's cynosure is to draw out local nuances to the forefront, helping customers form improved opinions. It believes that the best way to experience a place is through the lens of a localite.

It allows users to connect with locals to answer questions with regards to the place. This serves as Local Mind's USP, which elevates the experience more than having a robotic voice answer queries or checking out articles with clickbait links that may not provide complete and unbiased information. For Airbnb, Local Mind helps in solving the major bottleneck of building customer trust. If a customer is interested in checking out the local cuisines of Venice in an authentic manner, all he needs to do is hit up the Local Mind site and ask questions that would help in forming an opinion. Engineers at Local Mind have created a sleek Q&A platform that could be organically scaled up by both parties – who post questions and answer them, respectively. Using this, they have managed to build quite an invaluable catalog of local neighborhoods. Anyone could proclaim that the Eiffel tower is the must place to visit in Paris, but a localite would accurately point out where to get heavenly macaroons from boutique bakeries or to grab a hot cup of chocolate to beat the weather. With such information in one's grasp, Airbnb would be in a pivotal position to nurture enriching customer experiences. Airbnb has acquired Local Mind for an undisclosed amount, including the team and intellectual property.

Pillar of Strength

The crux of Lord Vishnu's seventh avatar is to showcase the potential of a mere mortal in a world filled with gods, demons, and otherworldly beings. Despite his birthright being taken away at the nick of the moment, he never flinched and still honoured his father's wishes. He never entertained Supranakha's advances citing his vow to remain faithful to one woman. Even when Sita was carried away by Ravana, he didn't despair and allied with the Vanaras to rescue her. His alliance with Vanaras represents the partnerships the brands need to form to sustain the growth in the maturity phase. Even with the tough choices, he attempted to do his duty in line with his ancestors' illustrious achievements. He never went back on his word. This unflinching stance is required by a brand as it cannot afford go away from its marketing promise and is a redemption factor in the maturity phase.

The reason Rama is celebrated as *maryada purushottam* is due to his ability to stand tall and strong, reacting to situations in line with his code, notwithstanding the cost attached. More than that, his rule is fondly remembered as *Rama rajya*, the ideal functioning of the state. He expanded his empire and took it to glorious heights through the Ashwamedha yagna; where a brand might also have to look for acquisitions and mergers for the next phase of incremental growth. He managed to transform the empire he inherited from his father, governed it through his life experiences, and passed on a successful entity for his children.

His philosophy provides a perfect antidote to Lord Krishna's imparts that are relevant in the next leg of the maturity phase. Before moving on to witness the world from the peacock feather's eye, below is a brief summary of the lessons from the Rama avatar.

- ✧ Consolidation of gains achieved in the growth phase and combating the slowing growth rate are the main objectives at the start of the 'Maturity Phase'.
- ✧ In various markets, competitors (mostly incumbents) playing in a specific segment hold on to their market base and have no means of threatening others' boundaries in a serious fashion, leading to an informal truce between players.
- ✧ 'Brand Equity' can be cultivated and maintained, that comes to a brand's rescue in time of dire need. It also serves as a source of competitive advantage.
- ✧ To combat slow growth rates and enter into newer customer segments, 'Co-branding' or 'Brand Alliances' can be formed with partner brands to fulfill one's objectives on a short-term basis.
- ✧ Acquisitions can be explored as a long-term measure to combat the emergence of competitive forces, a major peril of the maturity phase. They help in consolidating the existing base, creating diverse portfolios for a diverse audience, and turn future-ready to stay relevant in the consumer mind space.
- ✧ 'Brand activism' is one challenge a brand needs to face in contemporary times by sticking true to its core, irrespective of the price involved.

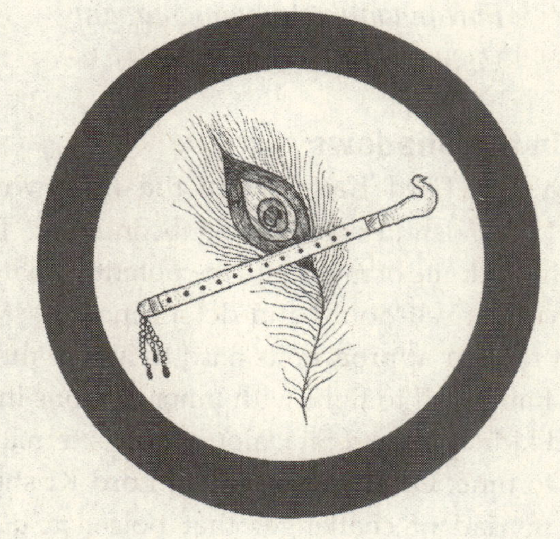

8

Peacock Feather Musings

Krishnosi dwaparekaale
Dharmam bhoomau pravartayan
Paramaadbhuta bhavastavam
Vasudeva namostute | |

Defense in the Shadows

Lord Rama and Lord Krishna are the most worshipped avatars of Lord Vishnu across the subcontinent. They both represent the epitome of mankind, the potential that is hidden beneath layers of self-doubt and determination. While they are distinct in their approach, its hard to ignore their similar core. Lord Rama had to fight with inner demons in the form of exile and kidnapping of Sita, along with external obstacles from time to time. On the other hand, Lord Krishna had to deal with myriad of challenges that poised a question to his mental balance and focus. The dichotomy of Rama and Krishna avatars is visible in the maturity phase. While the first half of the maturity phase is focused on inward outlook, the reminder part champions outward outlook to keep the growth cycle running. A brand tries to defend the existing market position and aims to bring in new customers to keep the market share intact.

Everything is fair in love, war, and marketing (except for slandering or calling names). Numerous marketing gospels dictate road maps, commandments for the brand to navigate the choppy waters of the market environment. While there are many to choose from, as a brand goes deeper into the maturity phase, it needs to find its voice to stand out. After decades or months of mimicking, improvising, going about its marketing strategizing, the brand needs to do something out of the box to help it cement its status in the eyes of the customer. History has been a kind reminder, for a brand needs to go way beyond conventional marketing strategies for relevance in the competitive landscape. If Lord Rama is known for his steadfastness in the light of challenges, which is analogous for Brand Equity, Lord Krishna represents the epitome of making unconventional moves to reach one's objectives.

Losing market share leads to the decline stage at an accelerated speed, so brands try every trick to ensure that brakes are applied at the appropriate time. In this pursuit, one erroneous metric that is warranted undue preference is the count of repeat buyers. Market share is made up of a) Repeat buyers and b) One-time buyers. It's easy to assume that any brand needs to have a significant portion of repeat buyers. In reality, one-time purchasers or non-frequent purchasers make up a large chunk of any brand's revenues due to their numerical superiority within the buyer's segment. For instance, if the average usage of toothpaste is one month, a marketer cannot envisage its most loyal customer purchasing the product more than twelve times in a given year of measure. Similar scenario with high ticket purchases like mobile phones, automobiles, electric appliances, etc., where it would be a utopia if the customer turns to be a frequent buyer in a specific time frame. This phenomenon has been explored deeply by Bryan Sharp in his book – *How brands grow?* Regrettably, marketers ignore this segment that brings in revenues and go after loyal customers, which would not be appropriate resource utilization.

The intent of market share defense is already flawed due to considering wrong inputs. Additionally, one cannot overlook 'Customer Churn' which is a natural phenomenon amongst all brands and segments, for no customer base is monolithic in nature. The trouble starts when the inflow of customers is less than that of the outflow. It is a sign of losing market share. Retention of customers is of note, but a marketer should never lose focus on bringing in new customers as they have numerical superiority, unlike loyal customers. Loyal customers would stay true to their name, but no amount of marketing actions would influence the loyal customer to purchase higher than the average purchase quantity or would dissuade them from making a purchase at all in the first place. Such marketing actions are akin to a rainfall in the midst of an ocean. If a customer is already purchasing Coke thrice a week, higher than the average, it would be tough to convince that customer to consume it daily. However, the probability of convincing a new customer to try Coke once a month is fairly possible.

Attracting new customers is characterized by the term 'Market Penetration' and ignoring this metric is a sure shot ticket into the decline stage. Any brand or business has to eventually move into the decline phase. The only thing that varies is the time taken by the business to reach the decline stage. It is a prophecy that can't be thwarted. The more a person tries to run away from a prophecy, the more they aid in its fulfillment. During Dwapara Yuga, King Kansa, the king of Mathura had given away his sister's hand in marriage to Vasudeva. While driving a chariot back to the in-law's palace with newlyweds in it, Kansa heard a prophecy given out by a voice in the sky. It declared that his sister Devaki's eighth son would be his bane. He immediately tried to kill her as the survival instinct kicked in, but was talked out of it by Vasudeva who promised to handover the child. He knew that Vasudeva always kept his word. Kansa sealed his fate by imprisoning Devaki and her husband in the dungeons. He probably could have avoided his eventual downfall had he not imprisoned his sister. That eighth child turned out to be Lord Krishna, the eighth avatar of Vishnu, who survived into adulthood and vanquished Kansa.

The key difference between different stages of maturity phase is that earlier the brand plans for short-term measures to acquire new customers. In the later stage, the brand prefers to tap into new, unexplored markets where it has a slight luxury of making changes to the product to create a robust portfolio from a long-term lens. Within the 4Ps of marketing, the last P - Promotions, is used during the initial phase of the maturity stage. The remainder of the maturity phase witnesses subtle manipulations of the three Ps (Product, Place, Price) extensively to bring in new customers.

One way for a brand to go about is to engage in brand extensions to offer new customer offerings and capitalize on its existing goodwill. The success of brand extensions is not guaranteed, for the extension needs to stand on its own without harming the mother brand. Maggi had learned this lesson when it tried to foray with Maggi Hot Heads and Maggie Fusian, both offering spicy and Asian flavours, respectively (as illustrated in chapter 6). While Hot Heads failed to take off after a fiery launch, the jury is still out on Fusian. Dairy Milk has successfully carved out Dairy Milk

Silk as a separate brand and identity of its own. Virgin airlines have performed brand extensions without a proper analysis of core brand fit and suffered for its actions. No matter the choice of extension taken, it should not deviate from the brand core and brand promise. The moment it does, the brand is destined for failure.

The other route is to explore new markets and customer segments that have been earlier untapped. This could involve introducing new SKUs or being available in different mediums or experimenting with optimum pricing points. Amul (a pioneer in the dairy segment) still rakes in sales due to its comprehensive product portfolio and competitive pricing which is relevant to all customer segments (ranging from mass to premium).

Any brand can employ to tap into newer markets by inward-looking: trying to crack the puzzle of the rural heartland (India or any country for that matter), or by outward-looking: to move beyond the international borders where exports are the game. It is not a compulsion that an inward-looking approach is important before moving on to an outward-looking approach or vice versa. The underlying point being – both are equally important for a brand to sustain its growth in the later stages of the maturity phase. This expansion is imperative as a company could have maxed out all the growth opportunities available and needs newer avenues. Certain categories like luxury items, heavy machinery, etc., may completely skip the first step (rural targets) to directly advance into an export setup which is quite understandable. However, in the case of categories like FMCG, FMCD, Automobile, etc., it would be prudent to win back at home than directly going international.

From Gokul to Vrindavan to Dwaraka, Lord Krishna has always been exploring opportunities, adapting accordingly to the situation to create a better lifestyle for his people. In Gokul, he was a mere cowherd, but the journey from Gokul to Vrindavan was necessary for Lord Krishna to grow as an individual. The warrior king witnessed in Dwaraka, the man who went on to change the fortunes of the subcontinent was only possible through the experiences of Gokul and Vrindavan, making his initial journey profound.

Operation Shakti

The majority of the brands start their journey in the dazzling cities before they spread out. Brand leaders like Kellogg's even while having around 70% market share, are not even present in 20% of total households in the country. On the other hand, HUL has finally managed to put together a solution that helped them win rural markets, adding a significant delta to its bottom line. HUL is the largest FMCG company in the subcontinent, a subsidiary of Unilever, and boasts of a plethora of brands like Lifebuoy, Lux, Pepsodent, Dove, etc., under its umbrella. The basics of microeconomics dictate that demand and supply forces need to be in perfect equilibrium for any business to thrive. In FMCG industry, demand is always skewed across categories, despite catering to basic needs of day-to-day life. For example, the buying patterns for toothpastes would be different in urban areas in comparison to those rural sectors. HUL understood this better than anyone else. Statistics prove the rural demand is significantly higher compared to urban as ~70% of the population lives there.

The rural market is not as straightforward as the urban market due to reasons ranging from an effective distribution network to the spread of information to the disposable income available. It's not possible to imagine a day in the metro cities without any of the applications making life easier on a single click. On the rural side, such basic amenities are still considered a luxury. In retrospection, cracking the rural piece was a labyrinthine exercise. HUL has decided to take this problem head-on to ensure that the company's bottom line is positive. Their conventional techniques have failed consistently over the years against the rural paradox. What worked in urban markets need not be replicated in the rural market, because the variables are different. To win this market, HUL had to brainstorm something new, something that was quite unconventional. It had to be a one size fits all solution for the villages in the subcontinent. That's how Project Shakti came into the picture.

In Project Shakti, HUL partnered with various women who had the entrepreneurial zeal and passion to be financially independent. They were trained to be ambassadors who would sell smaller SKUs of HUL products in their respective villages, HUL executives carefully curated villages of more than 2000 population and employed women who would be called as *Shakti Ammas*, earning around 3-10% margin on the goods sold, along with an exclusive HUL discount of 3%. This project worked wonders for the company. It has rapidly expanded all across India after it was first tested in the villages of erstwhile united Andhra Pradesh. Instead of going for a full-fledged sales hierarchy, HUL went ahead on incorporating existing customers as their own ambassadors to crack the rural market.

Today HUL has around one lakh microentrepreneurs across eighteen states who help in last-mile distribution.

Men too have been roped into this scheme, by giving them titles as *Shaktimaans*. The advantages for HUL by this Shakti scheme are limitless. Not only has it gained the crucial last-mile distribution into the rural heartland, but also has ambassadors who would propagate the goodness of HUL and its various products. Its product portfolio ranges from home care to personal care, which makes the job of Shakti Ammas easier, by convincing their customers to take the bulk of products from a single place in a single time, instead of purchasing multiple times across a month. Every fortnight, an HUL supervisor visits his area to deliver the orders placed by Shakti Ammas, to take account of the issues they are facing, and keep a track of the sales being done.

Only HUL has the manpower and resources to undertake such a massive project to crack the rural puzzle. One interesting thing to note is that this is not a part of any traditional marketing principles that are taught as a part of any basic marketing curriculum. Restricting this move to one form of marketing would be an injustice, as Project Shakti is as unconventional as it sounds. Maybe the sheer brilliance of it hides behind the simplicity and the democratization it truly achieves at the grassroots.

Rural Blueprint

When the objective is to gain numbers from a rural market, the 4Ps of marketing get rechristened as 4As of Rural Marketing, as unconventional moves are at the very heart of the strategy. 'Acceptability' is at the top of the four As list. One common characteristic of the rural market is that it tries to derive value for money. So, any product needs to be acceptable to the consumer perception that it adds value to them. For instance, the product basket of HUL fits right into this mould. Adding to that, Shakti Ammas and Shaktimaans are from the same closely-knit community that the villagers are familiar with. The factor of acceptability increases, as the consumers would have higher trust in their words, compared to advertisements or influencers.

'Availability' of the products in the vicinity of consumers is an unsaid rule, otherwise one runs the risk of consumers moving to other brands. At a closer inspection, for lower price points, the tradeoff between a brand and a value, increases as one goes below a price point. In few cases, the customers would switch to another brand without hesitation if the said brand is not available at all or has increased its prices. With distribution issues rampant in rural areas, the unavailability of products ensures that consumers are forced to develop loyalty to the available products. This adds an extra disadvantage to any product trying to break the rural stranglehold. Project Shakti solves this issue by ensuring that stocks are replenished once in fifteen days accordingly, as they have micro-level data of which household purchases what kind of HUL product at what frequency. Using this, they can persuade other non-committed consumers to join the HUL bandwagon.

'Affordability' is next on the list. Any marketer worth his grain of salt would understand that the rural market is extremely price-sensitive and only smaller SKUs would be the right strategy to penetrate. Smaller SKU enables a lower pricing strategy, which helps the rural consumer with low disposable income to sustain, along with giving them the luxury to try out new brands without any kind of hesitation.

'Awareness' is a must for any brand success and traditional marketing techniques may not work due to different landscapes. Radios and newspapers are the best mediums to deliver your message effectively in a shorter period. Now with the growing speed of the internet and its usage, this might change soon. Project Shakti scores a brownie point here, as the Shakti Ammas and Shaktimaans turn into brand ambassadors themselves who go door to door to create awareness for a plethora of HUL brands without much effort. This is much more effective compared to other BTL activities, as it is the cost-effective and optimum usage of existing resources.

Various brands have tried to align their product portfolio on the lines of four As of rural marketing to have a shot at the potential rural India provides. As unconventional as it sounds, it still stays true to the spirit of 4Ps of marketing. Kellogg's is the latest in the bandwagon, which has introduced SKUs ranging from Rs 5 to Rs 99 and has initiated sampling trials in schools of tier 2 and tier 3 cities.

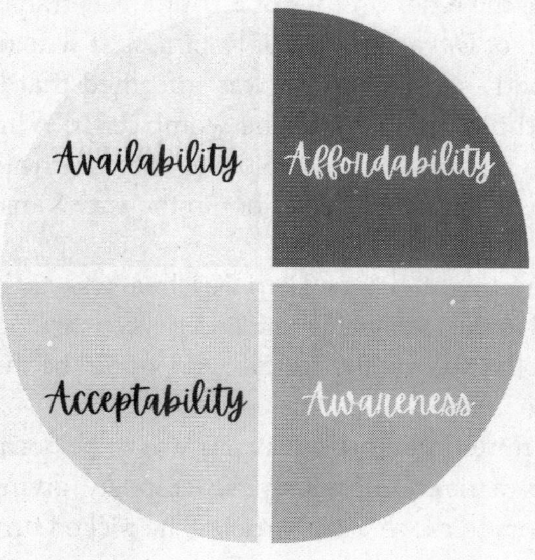

Pallav used to work as a software engineer in a metro. Thanks to the lockdown, he had to return to his village during the peak era of remote work. He expected the village to have the same facilities that are available in the city. He understood that there is an opportunity and tried to replicate in the same manner, but couldn't get the requisite results as the customer's psyche is different in both places.

From Gokul to Vrindavan

Lord Krishna's story of enlightening the villagers of Vrindavan stands true to the objective of rural marketing. Before reaching Vrindavan, Lord Krishna's origin story was completely different. Despite promising to not harm any children, Kansa smashed the heads of Devaki and Vasudev's six children against the jail walls. It was near the seventh child pregnancy that something happened.

Lord Krishna suggested Adi Sesha, to take birth as his elder brother. Using his magical powers, the fetus of Balarama, the elder brother of Krishna was transferred from the womb of Devaki to that of Rohini, first wife of Vasudeva and Yashoda's sister. Kansa was informed that the seventh child died naturally within the womb itself. What he didn't know was that the original child was very much alive and was still a son of Vasudeva, albeit not in the way Kansa imagined it to be.

The midnight before Lord Krishna was to be born, he appeared in the form of Vishnu and gave instructions on what needed to be done to the couple who would be the parents to the divine force.

Mere minutes before the avatar was to be born, the chains to the legs of the couple fell off miraculously, giving Vasudeva the freedom to move. As instructed, he picked up the baby in a basket and placed him over his head. He proceeded to move out of the jail expecting resistance. Yet everyone was asleep as if in intoxication. Despite raining heavily, Vasudeva was not drenched for even a bit for behind him was Adi Sesha, who protected the lord like always. His destination was the village of Gokul, which could be accessed by crossing the river Yamuna. He needed to replace the baby with that of the daughter born to Yashoda at the same time as the lord. The river parted midway to allow Vasudeva and the baby to walk without any hassles. In no time, Vasudeva reached the home of Nanda where everyone was asleep. He quickly swapped the babies, took a long look at his son Krishna and headed back.

The moment he entered the jail cell, the swapped baby started crying, the guards woke up suddenly as if nothing had happened and Kansa was alerted about the arrival of the eighth child. He was surprised that it was a female. He tried to smash the baby against the wall without any remorse. Instead of blood and pulp, something unexpected happened. The baby flew off and turned into a bright light. Out of that light emerged a divine goddess, the Yoga Mata – mistress of all illusions. She simply laughed and claimed that all of Kansa's power couldn't stop the eighth child's birth. She also declared that his doom was now certain. Kansa panicked and returned to his advisors for the next course of action.

In the meantime, the whole of Gokul was overjoyed due to the birth of their chief Nanda's son Krishna. If Lord Krishna had an unusual birth story, then his childhood was as unconventional as it goes. He vanquished Putana, a demon henchwoman sent by Kansa to kill all newborn children during that time. He began to defeat all sorts of obstacles sent by Kansa; yet his existence was unknown. After such daring feats, little Krishna used to be known for his playful nature, mischievous pranks he pulled off on people, the charades done to steal butter from everyone's house, etc. When Yashoda caught him eating mud, he simply opened his mouth to show that the whole universe was inside him. He once managed to run a stone mill, ten times his size in the midst of two trees and uprooted them. As time went by, Krishna too grew up, much to the adoration of villagers.

After a while, his family decided to move to Vrindavan. Vrinadavan was a beautiful village under the backdrop of luscious Govardhanagiri mountain standing tall near the river Yamuna. Every year the residents of Vrindavan used to worship Indra - King of gods and lord of rains, for bountiful harvests.

During the ceremony of that year, Krishna questioned the wisdom of dedicating the yagna for Indra. He argued that while Indra was still the ruler of heavens, people in Vrindavan were living in harmony thanks to the eco-system created by Govardhana giri mountain. Instead, he suggested the mountain Govardhana deserved the admiration of the villagers, for the mountain protected them, provided them with food, and ensured a steady supply of fresh water. If the rain was plentiful, it was due to the presence of the mountain, he argued.

Convinced by his logic, villagers began to worship the mountain and everything was going well. Yet Lord Indra was not happy and wanted to make sure that no one would ever dare to question his powers or insult him again in the future. Indra unleashed an army of clouds on an unwitting Vrindavan.

Within seconds, the downpour turned into an intense rainfall. Villagers ran amok with their possessions and livestock to take shelter, but the deluge proved too much for them. After witnessing the disaster unfolding before his eyes, Krishna decided to take things in his own hands. Without flinching for a second, he simply lifted the Govardhan mountain with just the tip of his left-hand little finger to use as an umbrella. He asked the villagers to gather below the shade, while he effortlessly carried the load of the mountain on his little finger.

It rained continuously for seven days, yet Krishna carried the weight with a smile on his face. Indra realised his mistake as he forgot that Krishna was none other than Lord Vishnu himself. He came down from the heavens and the rain immediately stopped. The king fell down on Krishna's feet for forgiveness. Since then, Vrindavan has never had issues with rainfall.

The one takeaway from this mythological tale is that even though one region had a common worshipping pattern, it was tweaked to suit the local needs as the exact procedure of worship didn't work out appropriately. Additionally, Krishna's story is a reminder that certain problems need unusual perspectives to reach the desired intent as long as the spirit of the conventional practices is held. It shouldn't be the case where anything and everything is done in the name of unconventional without a care for consequences.

The Ambit of Societal Marketing

Plans of giving back to a society run in the minds of most firms when they are in the maturity phase. The usual route of CSR (Corporate Social Responsibility) is taken, as the firms would be in an influential position to champion any cause, add in their voice to any social issue, and bring in a real difference on the ground. Any brand which contributes its part to society or drives a social message that impacts society as a whole through its marketing actions comes under the ambit of societal marketing. A brand's primary objective could be the bottom line and a consequence of it is a social impact or vice versa. Nonetheless, there is nothing wrong with brands contributing to a positive impact and generating sales at the same time.

One such example could be, during the 2018 Kerala floods, Ola sent out motorboats with its logo painted over them as a part of rescue efforts. Ola didn't advertise openly, but the logo and message were for all to see. It gained precious mind-space which wouldn't be possible using traditional methods in an envisaged timeline. Another instance is Vicks ran an ad campaign about the discrimination faced by transgenders in the country. It showcases the beautiful story of a little girl who narrates her love for her mother, all the things she does to keep the girl happy, and what the girl hopes to do in the future set in the backdrop of adoption. The twist in the tale is that her mother was a transgender. In both cases, brands have directly and indirectly driven a message to society, all the while promoting their brand. During the recent Covid pandemic, various companies have stepped up their contribution by donating funds to multiple PM and CM funds, vaccines, masks, etc.

Societal marketing actions need not be restricted to simple advertisements or logo placements for that matter. Nor should they be force-fit events where the product or the brands are present for the sake of being present. Unless and until the marketer finds an organic way to integrate a brand onto the CSR activity without being too obvious, it is imperative to avoid such mishaps. In such a scenario, a simple display of a corporate logo would do the trick rather than leaving a bad taste for the customer.

No doubt, Project Shakti was an attempt to make HUL's product portfolio appeal to rural customers as per the rulebook of four As of marketing. Even so, it is also a classic example of societal marketing done right. The whole crux of Project Shakti is to empower women into the corridors of financial independence. Its impact on the Shakti Ammas and their families cannot be fathomed. They are grateful for the chance to stand on their own feet. In Gita Devi, one of diamond Shakti Amma's own words - "I was able to pay for my daughter's sewing classes who was bedridden due to typhoid." The consumer's impact, as they witness the change in the lives of Shakti Ammas due to closely-knit communities in villages, is unparalleled. No celebrity ambassador could hope to deliver similar trust for a brand.

Societal marketing actions may probably have a higher impact than the usual activities in terms of brand recall. It could also be the forerunner in bringing taboo topics to the table in a subtle manner that is impressionable. The red label by HUL is another example of a brand that has always tried to bring in a social theme in its advertisements in a skillful manner that is not often touched upon. The story of Lord Krishna and his childhood friend is a testament to the fact how subtle CSR actions create an influence that can't be matched by charity alone. Not all CSR activities should be forced product fits.

The Secret of Puff Grains

Lord Krishna's story first began with his purpose of rescuing his parents from his evil uncle – Kansa's clutches. Kansa happened to be the king of Mathura by imprisoning his father. Eventually, Krishna vanquished Kansa and returned the throne of Mathura to his grandfather. Yet Kansa's brother-in-law Jarasandha was unhappy with the status quo for his sisters were married to the ex-king. He attacked Mathura seventeen times while Krishna was the defender. After a point, Lord Krishna realized that this defense strategy was detrimental to his people. He decided to find his fortunes in some other place, far away from Jarasandha and Mathura, so that he could never be bothered again. He wanted to build a peaceful life for his people.

In a quest for such a peaceful land, he finally chanced upon the place in the middle of the sea, near the western coast. Using the engineering prowess available, he built a city in the middle of the sea, surrounded by water on all sides. A perfect impregnable fortress where only an enemy with a powerful navy could attack. Rest all conquering attempts could be foiled before they could even begin in the first place. In a single stroke, Krishna brought a fresh leash of opportunity for him and his people. He ensured that Jarasandha's threat was neutralized, even at the risk of him being called *Ranchod* - one who ran away from the battlefield.

The kingdom of Dwaraka was prospering at unprecedented levels. While Krishna was at Dwaraka, his childhood friend Sudama decided to pay him a visit after ages. They studied in the same gurukul of sage Sandeepan, where they were versed with various subjects, arts, and scriptures. Back in their childhood days, Krishna promised to help Sudama in whatever capacity he could, should the need arise. Down to the last penny, his wife suggested he make Krishna come true on his promise to help them come out of their poverty. Sudama initially was not in favour of asking for anything. However, one look at his hungry children's face changed his mind to an extent. Convinced by his wife, Sudama agreed to go to Dwaraka.

The grandeur of Dwaraka mesmerized him so much. It could rival Amaravati, the capital of the gods. He was apprehensive that Krishna would not aid him to come out of the financial trouble, or worse, not recognize him at all.

However, Krishna did nothing of that sort. As soon as he saw Sudama, he stopped all his royal activities and went on to greet him as they used to back in their childhood without any difference. The warmth between the friends was for all there to notice. On witnessing Krishna's gesture, Sudama was so ashamed of doubting Krishna's intentions that he decided not to ask for help. Krishna, an omnipotent being, understood his friend's problem and decided to not hurt his friend's pride. He vowed to help his friend in a subtle manner.

He asked Sudama to feed him the delicious mix of beaten rice and jaggery, just like old times. He was surprised at how Krishna knew that he was carrying the mixture. Yet he fed the same for he knew it was Krishna's favourite. Krishna had taken exactly three handfuls of the mixture, before giving Sudama a tour of Dwaraka. After a complete day of catching up, they both finally bid goodbye. Sudama journeyed back to his home, only to find a palace waiting for him. He was confused on how his shabby hut could change into a royal mansion in its place. The palace was filled with treasures that could last for a lifetime. His wife exclaimed that it appeared out of nowhere. When asked about the time at which the riches started appearing, she said it was near mid-noon and on three occasions, where it seemed to multiply. Putting one and one together, Sudama understood that for every bite Krishna took from the mixture, wealth started appearing at his house. He was thankful for his friend honoring the childhood promise. Krishna didn't directly provide any money to Sudama, even though he could have. He helped out Sudama without harming his self-respect. Thus, we have a tale at hand of Krishna's *leelas* where it is demonstrated that subtle actions have better influence than what charity alone could have achieved, which is exactly how CSR activities are supposed to be designed.

Into the International Waters

From humble roots in Vrindavan to setting up a powerhouse in Dwaraka, Lord Krishna had come a long way. Yet his journey was not over as he had to play an indispensable role in the *Mahabharata* war, in shaping up the course of the subcontinent and humanity alike. On a similar note, a company that has been looking inward to increase its growth rate needs to look at an outward perspective also, to ensure similar growth levels even after saturation kicks in the domestic market. Many companies in the maturity phase do look out for exports or at least set up an international business operation to sustain their top line. Scouting for newer markets to access helps in increasing the customer base as they are a delta to the growth equation. For instance, Airtel has operations in the African countries that contribute to its operations or Godrej Consumer Products is present across three continents playing in various categories that have a synergy with its domestic portfolio.

alive as he promised to not harm the other four brothers. He was already cursed that he would forget the incantations of divine weapons at the most appropriate moment. Arjuna and Karna danced a deathly dance with no winner in sight. Arrow for arrow, missile for missile clashed on the battlefield of Kurukshetra. In an attack aimed at Karna's chariot, it got stuck in the mud. Karna left his weapons to remove the wheel. However, upon Krishna's command, Arjuna attacked Karna who didn't have any means to defend himself. With this move, the war was more or less decided as the last warrior of Kauravas was vanquished. Had Krishna not taken this gamble, the fight between Karna and Arjuna would have gone on forever, resulting in a stalemate.

On the last day, Duryodhana challenged Bhima for a duel with maces as their weapons. Duryodhana issued this challenge as a last resort to win the war, as his army was totally annihilated. They fought fiercely with no result in sight. Duryodhana was well versed with mace warfare. Krishna signaled Bhima to hit Duryodhana below the waist to win the war. It was against the rules to hit any man below the waist in any form of a duel. With the death of Duryodhana, the Mahabharata war was over.

From the peace talk negotiations to navigating the war strategies, Lord Krishna made many unconventional moves to win the day. Some might even claim those moves are immoral to the point of rule-breaking. Irrespective of the ethical debate, one thing those moves have in common is they upend the existing playing field and ensure that victory is the outcome. The greater good is the main objective that unites all the unusual moves made by Lord Krishna.

Similar is the approach needed to tackle international marketing to expand any brand's presence and bring in new customers. International marketing is a complex labyrinth, like a Chakravyuh ever-changing, unlike the domestic aspect of marketing that is fairly simple to navigate in comparison. As established earlier, marketing need not be restricted to only communication, but it ranges from product to manufacturing to supply chain. All moves within each perspective need to be viewed from a silo prism and the big canvas. Every country, every market needs a differentiated approach, starting from overhauling the supply chains to crafting the 4Ps to bring out a relevant product to the customer. That itself is unconventional, yet tweaking the strategy to go against unsaid norms may be the need of the hour as long as it is within the legal framework of any sovereign and meets the brand's objective. Even with unprecedented moves, a marketer should ensure that the core of the brand is not diluted in the process as Lord Krishna showcased in this unwavering support of Dharma. On a similar note, Bajaj showcases the blueprint on how to utilize the principles of international marketing to expand into exports business and be a market leader in various geographies.

World's Favourite Indian

Bajaj Chetak brings back fond memories of childhood, where standing in the scooter while the father skillfully navigated the roads was a thrilling experience for any kid. From Chetak to date, Bajaj has come a long way. It started its roots as a distributor in 1948 for importing 2-wheeler and 3-wheelers vehicles from Piaggio, like every other current Indian automaker. It was during the time where the winds of liberalization were yet to blow and the manufacturing sector was suffering in the myriad of license regimes. By that time, Bajaj had gained the lead in the market. When the government of India opened the licenses to manufacture automobiles in the country, Bajaj obtained a license from Piaggio to manufacture and market Vespa scooters in 1959.

It introduced the scooter Chetak in 1972 and started exporting scooters and 3-wheelers to countries like Yemen, Nigeria, Bangladesh, Australia, Hong Kong, etc. Chetak turned out to be a hit and the iconic tagline 'Humara Bajaj' proved to resonate with the audience. However, turn to the mid-'90s, where various automakers have turned to India succeeding the liberation movement. Honda launched its scooter line that gave stiff competition to Bajaj. Eventually, Bajaj decided to discontinue its scooter segment and focus only on its motorcycle line. It introduced the premium line through its 'Pulsar' range and since then there was no looking back. It is a strategic decision, an unconventional move to back out of a segment where Bajaj had a popular brand. But it decided to focus on its two strong segments – 2-wheeler motorcycles and 3-wheelers, which it is leading in for almost fifteen years. It is similar to how Lord Krishna sacrificed Ghatotkach to ensure that Arjuna survives to win the war in the end.

After gaining a foothold in motorcycles in the domestic market, Bajaj decided to increase the share of exports in its revenue. It has launched various brands and products (Discover, Pulsar, Rouser, Boxer, Avenger, Dominar, Master, Maxima, Qute, etc.), clocking over half a million motorcycles exported in 2008. It has expanded its presence to more than seventy countries spanning across Africa, Latin America, Europe, and southeast Asian regions. Tne challenge is multifold as the brand needs to be communicated in a localized way without changing the essence of the core.

While the main utility of any motorcycle is to serve as a means of transport, it is also a ticket to economic freedom and a license of expression. Especially in markets of Africa, a two-wheeler is used as a ride-hailing service, providing livelihood to millions. Bajaj positioned 'BM 100' as a durable vehicle to suit the necessary usage conditions of African customers who clock more than a hundred km run on a daily basis. In no time, Bajaj turned up as the market leader in various African markets as its product was durable in comparison with cheap, Chinese models. BM 100 is essentially used as a taxi motorcycle where almost three to four passengers travel in a single ride. Such a vehicle may not suit Indian palates or legal requirements. However, to win the African markets, Bajaj had to go back to the drawing board and create a new vehicle from scratch that would be appropriate to the customer segment.

North American and European customers view motorcycling as a passion in comparison to utility and thus crave higher cc engines that are rated on performance and vehicle form. It got a foothold in the European markets due to its acquisition of KTM and Husqvarna which make the super-premium motorcycle range with engines more than 250cc. If it was serving up lower engine capacity vehicles in the African market, it ensured that it was making higher engine capacity vehicles for the western markets, using the know-how from the acquisition of KTM and Husqvarna. In order to reduce the time to do in a market, it went through the acquisition route. This also helped to extend the brands KTM and Husqvarna to other markets, without compromising on time or quality.

Gaining market share in Latin American markets was a tough task where there's a mixed crowd of utility users and luxury users. It didn't help matters as the terrain of most Latin American countries is mountainous. Bajaj tied up with prominent distributors to help in gaining a foothold and introduced the Pulsar range of motorcycles that do not compromise on the style factor and at the same time are suited for the typical terrain. As of date, Bajaj stands fourth in number across the continent and has dethroned the Japanese brands (Yamaha, Honda) in markets like Guatemala, Dominican, etc. It was the brand value of these distributors that Bajaj was able to piggy ride to some extent before customers could recognize Bajaj as an independent, quality motorcycle manufacturer.

On the other hand, Southeast Asian markets contribute to more than 30% of the global 2-wheeler industry behind India and China. To date, Bajaj has a significant presence in the Philippines market only, with its KTM range being introduced in other markets. It intends to change that, but there was a slight delay due to the pandemic situation. The company also declared that there would be a dedicated sales and marketing office which would cater to the needs of the region based out of the Philippines.

One can observe that Bajaj has moved ahead with a differentiated approach, ensuring that each regional product fit is formed based on a solid understanding of the market. This differentiated approach is similar to how Lord Krishna dealt with a myriad of situations in an unconventional manner. This includes meeting the government regulations in terms of emission norms (Euro 3, Euro 4, GSO, BS 4, BS6, PROMO, etc.) which involves making technical changes to the product, all the while having the features customized and maintaining SKUs of various colours. Amid the product customization conundrum, it didn't fail to customize the brand communication too. Cultural aspects have been woven into how it wanted to communicate to its audience. For instance, the creatives of Discover 125, a commuter motorcycle brand are not just lifted and shifted from India, they have been customized from the visual aspect to the copy lines to features, ensuring the brand positioning is not too far off the mark.

Indian brands do enjoy the same perception of quality and make on the lines of Japanese brands so much so that one can observe the lines 'Made in India', 'Built-in India', etc., on the packaging to convey the message. While ensuring that it is creating strong brands on the go, Bajaj realized that it needs to leverage its strong connection with its audience and create Bajaj like a house of brands that is a global powerhouse. Taking a leaf out of 'Humara Bajaj' of the 80s, Bajaj has come up with a line 'World's Favourite Indian'. On a very granular level, the campaign is quite simple and effective. It reinforces the presence of Bajaj across the world, portrays the popularity it enjoys, and showcases the technical prowess of India. Bajaj still goes into localized marketing customs to different countries, but this unifies all its efforts reflecting on its global attitude. A motorcycle is more than a vehicle to most consumers. This simple catchphrase would mean many things to various stakeholders, but in the end, it shows Bajaj in a subtle, positive way by reinforcing emotional connections like Humara Bajaj.

The usual template indicates that the parent company brand and messaging is consistent, while its brand portfolio is customized to the country. This is evident in FMCG giants like

Unilever, P&G, where its portfolios are quite different in India and that of the USA, yet what Unilever stands for is the same across both markets. Bajaj has upended the usual playbook and went for something different so far as to bring in a layer of sentimentality to its corporate communication strategy. Its other Indian competitors who play in the international market can't even claim that space anymore, even if they turn to be the market leader shortly. Another aspect why this move by Bajaj is unconventional even to the standards of international marketing as it has not been attempted by other market leaders. There haven't been examples where Dominos claims to deliver the 'World's Favourite Pizza' or Apple claims to be the 'World's Best American' or Samsung claiming to be 'World's best South Korean'.

From the incipience of its journey to foray beyond the proverbial subcontinent waters, Bajaj has been taking a leaf out of Krishna's playbook by embracing the unconventionality of international marketing, ranging from all aspects to achieve its larger objective of increasing its customer base in the maturity stage.

Endings of the Flute

Lord Krishna has always been an enigma since Dwapara Yuga and beyond. Some legends claim that Dwapara Yuga was counted as the entire life of Lord Krishna. His actions are celebrated as leelas by his devotees, which would take an entire book to sum up. He essentially lived two lives, one as a cowherd in the pastures of Gokul and the other as the kingmaker in the kingdom of Dwaraka. One thing that unites his dual life is his knack for challenging the status quo and ushering in thinking that was considered unconventional in those times. It would be technically erroneous to classify the blue lord sporting a peacock feather as a mere rule breaker.

His stance of rewarding Govardhan mountain for bountiful harvest and succeeding lifting of the mountain through his little finger is a feat in itself and also a template for brands to venture into rural markets for the next engine of growth. His role as an advisor, strategist in the war of Kurukshetra provided tactics for a brand to establish itself firmly in the international market arena (as demonstrated by Bajaj). Lord Krishna recited Gita to Arjuna on the battlefield of Kurukshetra. Bhagawad Gita is considered a guide for humanity to follow as they move into Kali Yuga. Any brand or business that has survived till the maturity phase to tell its story turns out as a muse for nascent brands that are yet to embark on their PLC journey to learn from.

Out of all the ten avatars of Lord Vishnu, Lord Rama and Lord Krishna's time on earth spans over two yugas - Treta and Dwapara. Both of them intended for humanity to forge a better path through their actions. On the surface, they may seem opposites, but at the core are very much united in the goal of the betterment of others. Similarly, the maturity phase of the PLC cycle for any brand is lengthy, depending on the brand's intent to pursue the objective of bringing in new customers to its fold. Both the avatars of Lord Vishnu together represent the maturity phase where Rama's relentless attitude is required in the initial stage while Krishna's temperament is vital to maintain the growth rates in the reminder part.

While we head to the next chapter that deals with the preachings of Lord Buddha and its relevance as we embark on the last stage of PLC, below is a quick summary of musings from the blue lord adorned with a peacock feather.

- Any brand in its maturity phase that plans to add new customers to sustain its growth rate needs to ensure that its prospects are not harmed due to the worn-out beliefs accumulated in the previous stages of the PLC cycle.
- Prioritization of adding new customers over retention as per business categories is fruitful to the business objectives.
- Venturing into the hinterlands of the rural market or moving beyond the international boundaries are two ways for a brand to add new customers.
- 4Ps of marketing need to be tweaked into four As of marketing (Acceptability, Availability, Affordability, Awareness) to ensure the product portfolio fits rural consumers.
- Societal marketing is an avenue to explore and win consumers and, make a difference in their lives in a subtle manner. CSR activities should be organic in nature with regards to specific brands and products.
- Trade indicators along with consumer insights provide crucial inputs to decide on which country to export to and its subsequent GTM (Go-to-Market strategy).
- International marketing forms the crux of unconventional strategy to cater to different geographies, all the while maintaining a uniform brand status quo.
- Different forms of entry modes: Direct operations or Alliances (Acquisitions, Shareholding, etc.) or Franchise model or Export/Import model dictate the level of control over the whole marketing value chain.

THE EBB

9

Peepal Tree Worth

Tripuramjayaadhatum
Mahesasya purakhalu
Khyatosi bhudharoopena
Danvimaanaharak | |

For more than half a century, marketers have tried to humanize brands. In layman's terms, a brand is nothing but a sign of any form – graphical, words, colors, etc., that represents a value and evokes a trust factor to the consumer. There's a subtle, but major difference between any shoe and a shoe with 'Swoosh Mark' on it. One can recognizes it and purchase the product because of the inherent trust value developed by Nike. While this mark is inherent, it would be easier for the customer to connect with the brand if it was made relatable. Any mark of multiple designs would do the job, yet it's the swoosh mark that invokes an involuntary emotion in the customer which the other designs fail to replicate. And in that process, the formation of a brand persona, a humanized representation with values and attributes, is witnessed. Nike as a brand is humanized in customer's mind space allowing it for a better connection and recall. The moment someone asks for shoes, the answer immediately comes out to be Nike for those who are familiar with it.

A brand persona is not something that could be willed out of thin air. It is an amalgamation of the traits, emotions, attitudes and values that have been shown consistently across all communications of the brand over the years. A brand persona could be anything – a person or a mascot, a character, or even an idea. For instance, the brand Dove from the house of Unilever is on a quest to bring natural beauty to the discussion. That is its way of being sympathetic to customer's issues while promoting itself as the potential solution. Nowhere it goes too technical on the lines of speaking the intricate chemical formulas and their uses. Our favorite Amul girl keeps winning hearts with her relatable and quirky take on daily events. All such moves aid in humanizing the brand on a subconscious level.

Shivansh and Shubham run a kirana shops near multiple apartment complexes. Shubham carries on his services in a business-like manner. Shivansh on the other hand is care-free and jovial in nature. He also allows items to be taken on credit. So, for the residents, Shubham's brand persona is 'no-nonsense guy'. On the other hand, Shivansh's brand persona is 'friendly and helpful man'. These subtle markers play a role in what sort of customers Shivansh and Shubham attract.

Myths and Symbols

Back in the age when kingdoms were still popular, different kings used to have varied symbols like lions or tigers in their insignia as a mark of courage and easy identification. That imagery is used everywhere from pillars to sculptures to shields to weapons, thus strengthening the perception of the royal dynasty.

Similarly, brand personas are a mosaic of ideas that have been compounded over time. The thing about ideas is that they are quite powerful and once formed, it would be difficult to erase them (for they are bulletproof). If a marketer's job is not challenging already as witnessed across the initial stages of PLC, keeping a track of brand persona from the start so that it bears fruits at a later point in time is a task in itself. A brand can lose track of the larger picture of building a brand persona as it gets entwined on firefighting day-to-day issues. Should such a scenario arise, the difference between the customer perception and the marketer's expectations would be a tough hand to deal with. If one happens to ask any customer which characters their brand represents, half the battle is already won as it indicates the delivery of the intended message. The commonality between books, movies, songs and brands, is archetypes and likable personas. People would love to witness characters that are multi-dimensional with strong likable factors and teeny tiny flaws that represent human nature. A similar phenomenon is attempted across brands too as imitation is the greatest form of flattery. Hindu mythology encompasses the stories of deities with flaws to signify the essence of divinity being human and the potential they have.

Having a brand persona helps to form the connection and aids in easy recall amongst customers. Cadbury's 5 Star advertisements in recent times have a common theme of a laid-back attitude represented by twins who take no worries in the world by eating the chocolate This laid-back attitude is the brand persona that the team has strived hard to communicate.

Not every communication has to be verbal in nature. Subtle visual cues make a significant difference too and the better part of them are represented by symbols. Symbols have been a part of humanity's collective consciousness since times immemorial. These symbols could be anything – archetypes, visual imagery, motto, motifs, metaphors, etc. One of the noteworthy archetypes belongs to the story of David vs Goliath. The question that needs to be asked is what makes it more memorable? Is it because it pits an underdog against a powerful person who could crush without even lifting a finger? Trained warriors were afraid to take on Goliath and laughed at David when he expressed his wish to fight the giant. Turns out, we, humans love to root for a powerless person who goes on a quest to learn and take control of their destiny. Archetypes of such manners are ubiquitous. The Greek pantheon reeks of archetypes and symbols that it is hard to ignore when companies are named after the deities and heroes (Nike, Trojan, Amazon, Ajax). Nike is the Greek goddess of victory and by taking inspiration from the goddess, Phil Knight (Founder of Nike) subtly implies that their products signify the path to victory. Choosing the apt name for the brand is also one step forward in creating a brand persona.

The name, logo, principles, communication, all together in a melting pot give rise to a brand persona with whom the customer relates. And having this brand persona as a barometer can make the job of communicating to an existing/potential customer much easier.

Santhosh wanted to sell samosas that are easily identifiable. So he simply began to stamp the samosas with the letter 'S' before frying them. Once fried, the samosa shell has an attractive 'S' etched on them, thus differentiating him from the competition. It also turned into a visual piece for conversations on social media, thus making Santhosh popular.

Even after a brand persona is forged with the utmost deliberation, as the brand moves ahead in time, it needs to

There is no specific rule on whether a company should focus solely on rural consumers or international markets to gain new users. If the firm has the bandwidth and the capability, it can put a strategy to operate in both perspectives. After all, increasing the customer base helps in negating the impact of customer churn that is a natural phenomenon to all brands. The question of interest is how can a business go ahead in its international strategy.

The setting up of an international business arm need not be restricted to exports only. It could be fashioned in different ways, provided it is in line with the business objectives. A brand could launch full-scale operations in a foreign country – ranging from manufacturing to distribution, the complete value chain - or it can enter into a franchise agreement allowing the partner to use the brand name and is responsible for the operations (while the brand can reap benefits in the form of royalties). A joint venture could be an option with a local partner for the collective responsibility of operations and lastly where the brand can export the products with a local partner solely appointed for distribution. Any of the above options could be chosen based on the cost-benefit analysis performed and the long-term vision of the firm. *Mahabharata* war beholds similar tactics employed by either side of Kauravas and Pandavas to boost their army numbers through marriage alliances, treaties, feudalism and conquest.

Once the business objective is set, choosing which country to zero in for international expansion is a tricky task. There are more than hundred countries that could serve as potential destinations for any brand to aim for. Secondly, one cannot overlook various aspects of the political environment and government policies that form the support pillars for the operations. Apart from the external factors, certain technical considerations have to be deliberated before a decision to export is arrived upon. These considerations are based upon the 'Trade' rule book which caused the rise of ancient empires and would certainly pave the way for modern countries into financial powerhouses. Globalization has opened up the markets for exploration, which in turn allowed global MNCs like Unilever, P&G, Nestle, to enter new markets.

While the term trade doesn't sound fancy enough to be related to marketing, it does open up new prospects. Marketers have found a way to make use of trade regulations and indices to explore countries for export purposes. Imagine a country having a restriction that no mobile phone can be sold without meeting a minimum requirement of 8GB RAM. As a brand manager, the product exported into that particular country needs to be modified accordingly which inherently leads to a new SKU to the portfolio. It's a win-win situation if the said company is the only one with technical know-how to supply the requirement. The new product may seem like a one-off case, but it can be extended to another country with similar requirements. Conventionally, such moves are made on a case-to-case basis. If the country doesn't allow the use of particular imagery that is associated with the brand, the team has to come up with an alternative messaging that suits the palates of its new customers and does not harm the brand's global positioning. Price is a tough rope walk in managing increasing costs (including duty and taxes) and new customer's purchase propensity. Turns out, the outward perspective into international also alters the norms of 4Ps of marketing as we know it and is equally challenging in comparison to selling in the rural markets.

Following the Map

A framework with trade indicators has been designed to assist a company to decide which country to extend its business to. Apart from the usual sales numbers, trade indicators try to provide a different perspective on this matter. Trade indicators are wide enough a subject with humongous data collection that is of interest for various stakeholders. Nonetheless, around four to five indicators are required for any marketing professional to make required calls on the overall business strategy. Even if the top management decides that a certain objective needs to be fulfilled, the onus of finer details, due diligence, and execution is on the marketing team, starting from market research. Despite the trade indicators, customer insights still stand tall on the priority list of any marketer.

As a first, Regional Competitive Advantage (RCA) is a measure that tracks the products or the particular HS codes that provide the country an advantage when it comes to exports. It would be a logistical nightmare if every product is entered into the database as is without any commonality that helps different countries understand the nuances. HS codes are the international classification of products for easy recognition amongst countries for efficient logistics. In Bangladesh's perspective, textiles provide them leverage through which they contribute to their country's export volume. This translates to textiles being Bangladesh's regional competitive advantage which it has utilized to the fullest. For a business, it could play out in two ways – either its supply chain could be shifted to Bangladesh to make use of the ecosystem that propelled the country as an export powerhouse or the business may need to relook at its brand strategy where textiles are in surplus. It's a modern outlook of ancient popular geo-associations: *Kanjeevaram* for Silk, *Lakkapalli* for wooden dolls (on a more granular level), China for tea, India for textiles and spices, etc. While having a regional competitive advantage doesn't necessarily mean that it is implicitly prohibitive. Rather a brand needs to be smart about playing in a field that is advantageous against competition.

The second metric, Trade Intensity Index (TII), is a ratio of the share of the partner's exports to the country to the partners' exports to the world. This ratio provides a measure of which partner contributes most significantly to a particular HS code. For instance, Europe imports a lot of mangoes, Alphonso mangoes to be precise. Out of the total share of the mangoes exported to the world by India, it contributes a larger share to Europe. In such a scenario, the brands would be able to command a premium, obtain deals across the value chain which helps in generating gains for all stakeholders. Even in the *Mahabharata* war, a significant chunk of the Pandavas' army was made of the Panchala kingdom, which meant that they were able to call the shots. The kingdom housed their children, during the exile of the five brothers. The unsaid deal was Yudhishtir's eldest son with Draupadi, the grandson of Dhrupad would be the heir apparent to the throne of Hastinapur. Marketing is as much about finding the right match to the demand as much as it is about introducing a product utility to a customer. TII helps in mapping innate demand to supply to generate value for any brand.

In a few cases, certain products are imported to meet the domestic demand that isn't met by domestic supply. In recent times due to scanty rainfall, onion was imported from Turkey to ease the short-term demand that arose. The third metric,

Import Penetration Index (IPI) is a ratio of import's share of a particular product to that of the domestic demand, thus throwing some light on the paramount need to import. For example, in case of India, crude oil has a high IPI, as it forms a huge chunk of India's domestic consumption due to the paucity of local oil resources. It aids the marketing team to explore the possibility of an alternate product as a substitute for the imported product. India has been exploring the use of ethanol-based fuel for mobility to remove the dependency on fossil fuels. Plus, the surplus in sugarcane produce is being directed to manufacture ethanol, making it a win-win situation. Ethanol-based vehicles are still in a nascent phase, nonetheless, IPI provides a good start to explore the possibilities of alternative product fits.

Another key non-quantitative parameter that needs to be tracked is the FTAs (Free Trade Agreements) inked between various countries. FTAs provide a comprehensive view of different products/HS codes slotted into tax slabs starting from 0% duty. It endows a perspective to finalizing the product and pricing strategy to play in that market. Smartphone manufacturers attract less duty as they assemble the units in India in comparison to importing the complete handset, thus offering them at a competitive price. While FTAs are a good schema to provide a direction to overall strategy, scrutiny to the fine print is required as not all HS codes fall under the purview of 0% rate or the FTA. Bhishma Pitamah, the grand old man of the Kuru clan, may have been a champion of justice and would have supported the Pandavas in a heartbeat. Yet, the fine print of the promise he made dictates that he would always remain loyal to the throne of Hastinapur. Hence, he fought on the side of Kauravas in the *Mahabharata* war.

	Old Product	New Product
New Destination	Extending the product	New Product Development
Old Destination	High Marketing Efforts	Minor Product Changes

Based on the above discussions, a rudimentary matrix is derived basis which a brand can decide on the product strategy to be employed while scouting for a market to play in. In the first scenario, if one continues with the old product in the old destination, more efforts are required on the marketing spending (since no major changes are done to Product or Place in the 4Ps). Secondly, a completely new product can be introduced to suit the palates of any existing destination or to the new policy defined by the ruling dispensation. On the other hand, if any similar destination is found to an existing one the same product (that is going to different geography) could be extended, thus leveraging on the existing supply chain in place. Lastly, if it is a completely new destination with no similarities, a new product may have to be designed from scratch. The major question a brand needs to ask is how it can leverage its resources and the insights derived from trade parameters to craft a winning strategy to raise the brand flag in unexplored territories.

Beyond the Maritime Trade

While trade indicators are crucial pieces of the puzzle, it would still be an incomplete decision without having a clue about the customers. Trade indicators provide an indirect view of the customers, not a direct front row seat for his/her purchase decision process. The data may confirm that Sri Lanka has been importing several scooters, but it won't throw light on why they have been purchasing scooters. Marketing takes a pole position in securing this missing puzzle piece to ensure that the overall strategy is not compromised. Imagine a scenario where a brand manager ends up with non-moving inventory in a foreign location (due to favourable signs from trade indicators) as the consumers are not aware of the brand? Or worse, set up a manufacturing unit by reading the trade tea leaves in an erroneous manner. Any company would avoid such nightmares from emerging in the first place. Krishna and his leelas are made popular through art, stories, songs, dance and drama, but the innate meaning behind them and what it means for humanity could only be deciphered by learned men of caliber. That won't diminish the value of stories alone, as the stories still push the users in the right direction.

In the quest of understanding various geographies, numerous marketing gospels agree upon the fact that it is tough to change a user's behaviour that is set in stone. It is always easier to set one's sails to the wind rather than going against it. Gillette provides a perfect use-case of a product extension that didn't derive the expected results for the team missed out on gaining crucial insights about the market. Counting on the market potential of India, Gillette decided to launch its iconic razor portfolio in the subcontinent. It tried the product on a few test Indians living in the United States. Based on the positive response, it sought to marry the findings of US-based Indians to launch a razor for Indian men. Unfortunately, when the launch didn't get the intended response, they were forced to find out the actual conditions of an Indian user. As the team finally arrived in the country to understand how a common man used to shave, they observed that Indian men did not have the luxury of a razor or perfect setup to shave (proper washbasin, running water, large mirror, etc.). A typical man used to shave with a mug of water and a small mirror to aid him in the task. All he cared about was a quick shave without any cuts. Armed with this realization, the team revamped the product to suit the Indian terrain. If it had not been done, maybe Gillette would not have been an iconic brand in the subcontinent. When McD entered India, it had to curate to the vegetarian taste buds of the country to attract all sorts of customers. Harley Davidson learnt the hard way that no proper research while entering into a new market would amount to burning cash, as it had to exit its operations in India in the end.

The takeaway is that a brand cannot rely on trade parameters alone to devise its strategy without understanding the customer. At the same time, when a brand is aiming to expand into multiple geographies, it cannot take shortcuts in the due diligence of market research. A brand might have a complete experience of Country A, but it shouldn't make the mistake of assuming that the insights of Country A would work for Country B. As the saying goes, there is no single cloth that fits all. This applies to all aspects of marketing, ranging from the market research process to 4Ps to the positioning the brand has to take. One can comprehend the level of magnanimity the marketing division plays, just by extrapolating the efforts required to build a brand in dozens of geographies.

Lord Krishna is the epitome of the phrase 'No single cloth fits all'. He is a formidable warrior in his own right, with equal or more strength in comparison with the combined strength of the Pandavas. When Lord Krishna faced Jarasandha, he chose to run away and build prosperity in Dwaraka city on his terms. On the other hand, he advocated war to Pandavas when Duryodhana refused to give up the throne after the period of exile and talks of peace had failed. The scenarios may seem similar, but the subtle differences warranted separate strategies. Krishna didn't pose an existential threat to Jarasandha's throne, whereas Yudhisthir was a rival claimant to the throne of Hastinapur. As long as Yudhisthir was alive, Duryodhana would not rest until the threat was neutralized. Thus, war turned inevitable as Lord Krishna followed a different tactic, unlike the one he used in a similar situation. For a company in the maturity phase, it cannot hanker around a single approach. It needs to be flexible to have multiple approaches governed by a single principle.

International marketing is quite complex and fun at the same time due to the quantum of variables involved with countless scenarios. How should a marketing division function in the first place? What should be its protocols to operate in different geographies? Should it be anchored in geography-wise portfolios, for instance, complete product portfolio of South Asia would be handled by one single team) or should it be bifurcated on a brand level, for instance, A brand across more than thirty countries, is one team's responsibility)? What is the counter-strategy that needs to be employed where a domestic competitor turns up in the export country after witnessing the success of the incumbent? What is the ideal way to challenge a strong local player in an export country? Should the brand aim for a uniform way of branding across all countries or should it adopt a decentralized approach where each country would be treated differently? What should be the extent of control a central team can have on local marketing action, if one is talking about sixty to seventy countries? How should the teams react when one country's strategy is threatening to upend the carefully built cart in another country? The purview of international business is complex and exponential.

Irrespective of the entry mode chosen to start a business in a new country, maintaining a uniform essence of the brand, as well as customizing product offerings to increase sales in that particular market is not a piece of cake. While proceeding ahead with a uniform branding approach, the basic error possible is a mistranslation of tagline that could snowball into a PR disaster and move towards the grave one of reading the consumer insights wrong, which would upend the country-specific strategy. As established earlier, the insights that worked in Colombia may not work in Bangladesh. In such a scenario, would the brand prefer to make cosmetic changes to its product while keeping prime parts intact, or would it bite the bullet in creating a completely new brand from scratch to enter that specific market. In case of a mismatch in insights, it wouldn't be a wise move to extend the product portfolio as it is. Wheel from the house of HUL is one of the brands that was created specifically for the Indian audience who preferred effective detergent that wasn't harsh on hands (unlike their western counterparts who could afford washing machines and the detergent being harsh on hands was never a factor to start with. They only had to concentrate if the detergent was potent enough to remove stains, no matter what). Such moves aid in ensuring that the brand experience is similar across various geographies. In the case of Royal Enfield, any user visiting the showroom in Denmark or Hyderabad would have the same experience. In the case where the incumbent is in charge of the value chain, it is easier to maintain uniformity in brand positioning. Following a uniform brand approach would lead to consistency, significant efforts are required to overcome any deviations from the expected fit between the brand and its target consumer group.

On the other hand, having a decentralized brand approach has its advantages. It would provide more breathing room to incorporate local factors in a nuanced fashion to communicate and connect with the customer on a remarkable plane. Netflix in India seems to be following this approach where it captures the microcosm of the sub-continent to make its tailored offerings tempting to Indians. It even went ahead to create a separate social media handle 'Netflix India South' to talk about the new content released in the regional languages of southern India (Telugu, Kannada, Tamil and Malayalam). One unsaid line that never should be violated is that the core of the brand, the essence of what it stands for, shouldn't be diametrically opposite in two different countries. For instance, a luxury brand in Country A shouldn't alter the price offerings that it is no longer perceived as a luxury brand in Country B. Earlier it would have been possible to get away due to the paucity of information, but now with internet breaking digital barriers, users have all the information at their fingertips. For example, someone sitting in Bangladesh could google for Apache reviews (a popular motorcycle brand from the house of TVS) and the four out of the top ten results are that of bike content generated by Indian influencers. Anyone could access any sort of content from anywhere in the world as long as they are not banned by the government. This is not just restricted to marketing content. It can be applicable in case of product decisions also. In case Country A has additional product features, customers in Country B don't hesitate to demand the same.

There is no right answer to what sort of branding approach needs to be followed – uniform or decentralized – after deciding to enter a country using insights derived from trade parameters and customer understanding. The overarching marketing processes and strategies that govern a brand's foray into foreign lands is known as 'International Marketing'. An unusual beast from normal marketing one usually encounters due to the challenges that go beyond the contours of 4Ps. As a brand approaches the mid of the maturity stage, it needs to look forward to expanding into unexplored territories to maintain the growth rate, and International Marketing is integral to it which runs by the playbook of moving out of the conventional tactics. Lord Krishna demonstrates how to play in an unconventional manner, starting from tackling the disagreement between the cousins of the Kuru clan to defeating Kauravas in an eighteen-days war that involved most of the country.

Outside the Status Quo

Long before Kauravas and Pandavas fought in the field, seeds of destruction were planted in the 'Game of Dice' played between Duryodhana and Yudhisthir. Yudhisthir lost his city, his wealth, sold himself, his brothers, and his wife into slavery. What followed was the darkest episode when Draupadi, queen of Pandavas, was disrobed in the court of Hastinapur. Not even her five husbands raised their voice, despite Draupadi thundering vengeance on all who sat silent against a woman's pleas. It was Lord Krishna who saved her from humiliation by ensuring that the saree she wore never ends in length as Dushasana attempted to disrobe her.

Before it was too late, king Dhritarashtra, father of Duryodhana, intervened. He finally found a voice and spoke out to broker a compromise between his sons and the Pandavas. As part of the deal, the latter was supposed to spend twelve years of exile in forests and one year in complete incognito mode. In case anyone recognized Pandavas, they would have to repeat the exile cycle of thirteen years. This notion was brought forth with the thought that Duryodhana and his heirs would bring the throne under their grasp, thus solidifying their position. Lord Krishna did support Pandavas and Draupadi on occasions during their stay in the forest.

A few years down the line, Pandavas completed their exile and incognito sentence of a total of thirteen years, turned up at Hastinapura for their fair share of the kingdom that was promised long ago. Earlier Arjuna revealed himself in a war between the Virata kingdom and Hastinapur during exile. Even though he won the day for the Virata kingdom, Duryodhana was delighted that he broke the incognito period before the completion of one year. Krishna had been making a case for Pandavas to not go into the second exile. He argued that Kuru's clan traced their lineage back to Chandra, the moon god, and are honour-bound to follow the lunar calendar. While Arjuna might have broken rules as per the solar calendar, by terms of lunar calendar they were well within the limit of the exile period. The Kuru elders couldn't argue against the logic and accepted the terms. The terms included providing five villages to Pandavas after the completion of the exile period. However, it's a different tale that Duryodhana rejected the terms proposed by Krishna and concurred by elders of the court. This led to the war of Kurukshetra. In a distinct scenario, any reasonable man would have accepted the terms and avoided the war, in the light of out-of-the-box tactics displayed by Lord Krishna. Unfortunately, it was Duryodhana who refused to see the rationale.

By now, the war was inevitable. Both sides started making alliances, calling in favours, increasing their army count, and shoring up their defenses. Kauravas had an army of eleven akshauhinis (2,405,700 warriors), while Pandavas could muster only seven akshauhinis. At the request of Arjun, Krishna himself sided with Pandavas as Arjuna's charioteer, while he loaned his famed Narayani sena to fight alongside Kauravas. The *Mahabharata* war went on for eighteen full days. In those days war was governed by a set of rules and regulations that strictly adhere to the warrior dharma. No warrior generally tended to break the code to ensure that battle was fought fairly.

With the greater good in mind, Lord Krishna changed tactics, employed strategies for Pandavas to win. He actively encouraged the hesitant Pandavas to do what was required to win the war and save themselves by breaking rules from an enemy who has sought to kill them. He gave the recitation of Bhagavad Gita, a holy text for a way of life to soothe the frayed nerves of Arjuna who was reluctant to fight his teacher and grandfather Bhishma who sided with the Kauravas. Even though Krishna's actions could be dismissed as usual war campaigns to win, they are too unconventional or unheard of on a battlefield.

The first warrior to fall down was Bhishma Pitamah. He had taken a vow to not raise arms against women or children. He also had a boon that he could only be defeated when he willingly gave up his weapons. Krishna decided to bring Shikhandi to the battlefield. On seeing Shikhandi, Bhishma threw away his weapons as he took a vow to not raise his weapons against women. Arjuna shot a volley of arrows utilizing this window of opportunity. Those arrows pierced the old man, who resembled a person resting on a bed of arrows, thus closing a warrior chapter in the most unexpected manner.

After the death of Bhishma, Dronacharya commanded the Kaurava forces under whom, both armies broke the rule of fighting after sunset. To gain advantage, Krishna advised deploying Ghatotkach and his band of rakshasas who were adept with magic and equipped to fight in the night. Krishna forced Karna to give up his Pashupatastra, a divine weapon that never misses its mark to vanquish Ghatotkach. Karna had intended to use it against Arjuna, but was forced to save his army from annihilation in the hands of Ghatotkach and his minions, by Lord Krishna. Hence saving Arjuna's life and also securing the throne for Yudhishtir's eldest child with Draupadi, for at that time Ghatotkach was the eldest of the Pandavas children and could technically be the king.

The next day, Dronacharya planned a new strategy to capture Yudhishtir and end the war. It was *Chakravyuh,* a literal war maze that moves on constantly that only three people knew how to break – Krishna, Arjuna and Dronacharya. Abhimanyu only knew how to enter the maze, but not how to exit. With the promise of help, Abhimanyu entered the maze. Yet he was trapped, cut off from his army in the maze and brutally killed by all the Kaurava warriors. Arjuna vowed that he would kill Jayadrath, the main perpetrator, and avenge his son's death. If he was not able to do so by sunset, he declared that he would kill himself by submitting to fire. Kauravas devised their strategy and hid Jayadrath well. Hardly a few minutes were left before the sun moved below the horizon. Kauravas were already celebrating for Arjuna would kill himself and Pandavas' side would lose an efficient warrior. Lord Krishna used his divine discus to cover the sun, thus causing an illusion of a solar eclipse as a sunset. Jayadrath fell for the trick and came out of the protected army ranks. Arjuna in no time used his arrows to eliminate him, thus fulfilling his vow.

Ashwatthama was the only person guru Drona cared about the most and sided with Kauravas because of his son's loyalty. Krishna decided to use this to make the guru vulnerable. He made Bheema kill an elephant named Ashwatthama. Yudhisthir who was known for not speaking a single lie ever was asked to convey the news to Dronacharya. He loudly proclaimed that Ashwatthama was dead, and added the words 'an elephant' in a feeble manner. On hearing the first few words, guru Drona collapsed in grief. Dhristudyunma swiped the head of Drona, thus killing the great teacher.

After the death of Drona, Karna was made the commander-in-chief of the Kaurava army. On the seventeenth day, he went into the battle with the notion that only Karna or Arjuna would survive. Either way, his mother would have five sons

keep adding personality traits to remain relevant. Advertising over the ages is the best available proof of these changes made to the brand persona. One can find a stark difference between the Thums Up advertisements of then and now. The methodology may have changed, but the brand essence – 'Taste the thunder' and the brand persona as 'one who seeks adventures' remains the same which is the primary trait. How the main character seeks the adventure are the secondary traits that kept changing over time. Popular bathing soap Santoor attests to this notion. It represents a forever young character despite life happening. Its ads mainly feature a young woman doing impossible stuff and in the end a kid runs up to her and calls her "mommy". The audience are shocked on how such a young woman can be a mother of a 6-year-old. The secret of the young woman is that she uses Santoor soap. While this has not changed, how the main character is portrayed in response to modern times has been tweaked.

As the saying goes, no brand is too old to learn a trick or two. To date we have discussed how a brand should be cognizant of its product relevance, ensuring that it keeps a track of the customer pulse, and expands its horizons to shore up its market share. Nevertheless, it also needs to overhaul how the brand is perceived by both internal and external stakeholders. *People change with time* is an adage that is accepted around the globe. But that line of thinking may be a bit erroneous. What essentially changes is how they respond to the situation, not who they are at their core. If that core changes, then essentially a person has truly changed for good or for worse. Analogously, a brand may not radically change who they are at the core, but pick up certain extra traits that are best suited for the circumstances. There is no hard and fast rule that the brand needs to keep on adding new traits as it moves forward. A brand or rather a brand manager should keep an open eye when the opportunity for change presents itself to stay relevant.

Sapna has started an organic hair oil business and began to communicate about the benefits of using organic oil on human hair. While she managed to get early buyers, she was struggling to scale up her customer base. She decided to tweak the communication a bit. She started showing a mother applying an organic, herbal hair oil on her daughters. Through this strategic move, Sapna managed to add a motherly trait to her brand persona of "Healthy & Natural" in the consumer mind space.

First Cut

Industry in which the brand is playing and the creative freedom a brand manager enjoys determines the brand persona that is to be created. Not to mention customer understanding would always be an inherent part of any decision-related process. Sprite, a beverage giant from the house of Coca-Cola, is always associated with a 'cool-guy, no worries, laid back' person who is the main character in any advertising material. Zomato, a food tech startup gives out quirky vibes through its witty advertisements. A brand catering in a B2B setup would not require an extensive setup that a B2C environment would demand. Having said that, any brand's ability to add personality traits is truly a test of time.

Airtel, a telecom giant in India had declared in its recent campaign that it intends to improve its customer experience. For the same, it has vowed to answer all customer questions such that the number of unaddressed queries is zero. An impressive and impossible target, given the circumstances of the industry. It has claimed on national television that it would do all in its capacity to set the counter of customer complaints to zero. It implies that Airtel wants to showcase its capability in ensuring the readiness of all its systems and processes ranging from sales to service to provide an exemplary customer experience. Imagine a brand that has been in the market for more than a decade, trying a different tack to win the confidence of the customer who is extremely tech-savvy in the ever-connected world. Every brand dreams of providing a top-notch customer experience, yet only a few would agree that they have flaws and only a handful are willing to work on them. Or probably for some brands, customer service is just an afterthought, a cost gobbling scheme with no tangible returns. Claiming that you are the best in the market is one thing and being willing to admit that there are some issues and showcase willingness to course correct is another thing. In a single move, Airtel has once again reminded us that customers perceive brands through a humanized lens. Irrespective of the success or failure of the campaign, Airtel has added another trait to its brand persona – being transparent. The brand personas built over time are the lifelines that are required by any brand to ensure that they are in the customer's mind space.

The question is... why?

Final Transition

The transition from 'Maturity' to 'Decline' phase is the last change over between phases in the PLC cycle. While the challenges of the Introductory and Growth Stage were a mixed bag with a skew towards external in nature, the brand battles now are waged on an internal turf. From a fledgling startup to a giant spread across international borders, there is a high chance that its growth has made economies of scale viable. Nonetheless, even with all the advantages considered, no company can escape the complexities it represents. To put into perspective, 'The company has turned into an elephant that is slow to move, but it surely does move'. As the brand/business grows, its internal challenges play a crucial role in how it staves off external threats.

After a journey full of experiences, it is quite natural for a brand to follow its established norms and procedures to take future decisions. One could say it's a rather cautious attitude, but the marketer is aware of the fact that one misstep and redemption would be hard to come by for the brand. It is also practical. Think of it, brands have existed for a long time than the human force managing them. To ensure the brand continuity is in place, they have these guidelines and processes so that any manager picking up the brand mantle wouldn't disturb the status quo too much. Just because there is a change in the person leading Thums Up, doesn't mean that it should abandon its brand positioning.

One curious asset at this stage, in comparison to any other stage, that a brand can use to its advantage is Brand Loyalty. It exists in diverse forms, but even so, it turns out to be a lifeline for a brand that is soon looking at the horizon. Brand Loyalty to such an extent that customers fondly keep the brand alive just based on the experiences they share with the brand. A yesteryear motorcycle brand, Jawa was able to survive the wilderness, thanks to its fans running clubs and meets, even though the brand was virtually nonexistent for ages. There was no production of vehicles or any requisite parts for almost a couple of decades. Yet that didn't dither the fans from being loyal to the brand. In fact, it was one of the factors for Mahindra to bring back Jawa motorcycles on Indian roads. If we extend this phenomenon to an international audience, it won't be a tough ask to find a Harley Davidson fan to have the logo tattooed across their arm! That is simply a measure of the brand loyalty Harley Davidson commands. Even if it were to go off the roads, its customers would find a way to keep it alive.

Divyanshu has recently moved to the city of Bengaluru as his company moved to a hybrid model setup. After an extensive search for his momo cravings, he managed to find a small shop run by an Assamese fan. Before he knew it, Divyanshu became a regular customer. Suddenly the shop closed. He almost went on a weekly basis to see if the shop was open or not. But the shop didn't open for three months. During this time, he didn't order from other restaurants or venture out to explore new momos' places. Even in his absence, Divyanshu never explored other options, as he liked the product and was loyal to it even if the shop was not present.

Another question that comes up is – How to build brand loyalty?

Brand loyalty is intrinsically derived from the carefully established brand persona. As one gets the persona right, loyalty is bound to follow on. Loyalty can be inspired for sundry reasons, but the communication and the persona are the key foundations that are built over the years.

The luxury of time is not something fledgling brands can afford. They could find themselves directly into the decline phase, even without navigating all other stages, and before they can utter the name brand loyalty. A brand or a business cannot simply exist because it has to exist. It came into being for it had a problem to solve. After all this time, despite having all resources at hand, it's a slippery slope for the brand if it fails to ask itself – 'What is the problem the brand is trying to solve'? This is much required for the brand before it loses the last vestige of connection with the ground reality.

The Existential Crisis

It's a profound question – 'What is the problem that the brand is trying to solve?' It is not a herculean effort to forget why one is driving along a road after driving for over twenty years. One can get so entangled in the nitty gritty of the journey that it is easier to forget the destination itself. After all this time in the journey of a brand, the undecorated questions are tough to answer. It doesn't help one's case if the marketers are revisiting the question after a while.

In this stage, there is no shortage of resources nor expertise, but is the brand trying to solve any problem? Is it trying to stay ahead in the curve of trying to anticipate the next customer need? Or is it simply running around from one goal post to another? This epiphany is one of the reasons why brands are observed to re-invent their purpose in changing times. Today Mondelez's purpose (Company that makes popular brands like Oreo, Cadbury, Bournvita, etc.) is to make snacking healthy and all its efforts from product to advertising are focused on that. Think of it, Mondelez is in the business of selling snacks and confectionery which are far from healthy. In a time where health consciousness is a trend, a move to reinvent the wheel and make snacking healthy and guilt free for the customer is no hare-brainer. While Mondelez is the parent company, a definition of its purpose definitely percolates to the brands it operates.

Having multiple brands doesn't dampen the impact of an existential crisis. If handling a single brand is a multifaceted job, imagine a scenario where the organization is dealing with a legion of brands spread across manifold segments and categories. The legion of brands could be operated in two ways – a) House of Brands and b) Branded House. As the name suggests, House of Brands is essentially having multiple diverse brands under a single roof. For example, Unilever is the best example of the House of Brands approach. It has brands like Kwality Walls, Dove, Knor, Ponds, Olay, Rin, Surf Excel, etc., under one single roof. On the other hand, Branded House refers to a strategy where every brand is named after one thing. For example, Google Maps, Google Pay, Google Ads is an example of this.

In both the scenarios, the question of what is the problem that the brands are trying to solve gets complicated. Navigating the labyrinth of the hierarchies, functions, divisions, and departments where everyone might have their own objectives and agendas is a tough task. It is not surprising for the brand to lose out on focus. In such a melting pot scenario, the twist in the tale comes when a team is trying to build a brand from scratch. Utmost care is taken to ensure that it doesn't injure an in-house brand consciously. For example, a company has brand A with 100kmph performance priced at INR 10,000. The team comes up with a new brand B which has a performance of 200kmph and is priced at INR 8,000. This pricing strategy eventually hurts brand B. In terms of resources like media slots, marketing budgets, signing up of ambassadors, it is always going to gladiator matches. Or in the case of Amazon, the home page landing banner has the highest conversion rate. Different categories and brands would be making their case to have a presence on the banner to catch the eye of the customer. While a little intra competition is healthy, it can get ugly real quick and affect the overall health of the company. To ensure that this doesn't happen, few companies do have employees in place who look at the big picture. If such checks are not placed, one might end up witnessing a new brand, cannibalizing existing brand's sale due to a mismatch in strategy. In the end, a brand losing its focus has adverse effects on other aspects of business apart from the bottom line for either a startup or an established company. Investors would lose confidence to keep the cash flowing in, employees would lose motivation to work for the objectives, new talent might not even consider the company a great place to work, suppliers would have no incentive to collaborate and the gravy train that keeps the show running may stop in the end.

Poison of Attachment

Placing processes and checks in place is a sign of maturity that ensures minimum error within an organization. One of such processes is the formation of a "Brand Key" containing crucial information about the brand, so that no brand manager would go on a wild adventure when showcasing the brand to the customers. Think of it as the recipe of Coke that is only known to a few. It is almost the equivalent of a trade secret. Such documentations help in maintaining a continuity while adapting to the fluid situations.

Even though marketing has a tinge of creativity associated with it, it is a science that governs all the decisions taken, starting from gathering relevant consumer insights to taking the brand to the masses. Lines are blurred between following the letter of the processes and ensuring that the spirit of the process is sustained as the organization grows. If one part of the problem is forgetting what is the problem the brand is trying to solve, the other problem is getting too attached to the processes that one loses sight of innovation.

Without one's realization, every person involved in the decision-making process gets so attached to the processes that they lose track of what is needed. This attachment may turn unhealthy after a while and it begins to adversely affect the brand in ways that are not fathomable. The scenarios are countless to illustrate. The competitor could launch a product and gain a first-mover advantage while the incumbent brand that had similar plans is still stuck in paperwork, without realizing the urgency of the market. Brand managers could be looking at the wrong metrics to arrive at insight to make a decision, leading the brand away from the intended objective. They could wait for the perfect data and the perfect analysis that insight itself becomes stale to act upon. They could also give in to internal pressures and prioritize short-term measures over the long-term goals of the brand. One brand playing in the same category could be developing a new product that would harm another in-house brand.

These sticky wickets are not restricted to small, marquee brands, but also giant behemoths in respective categories. If startups are applauded for their quick decision making, then the converse is also true. In major established companies, the decision making is slow, taking into account all the processes in place. Losing focus and accelerating towards the decline stage is a sure shot consequence of ignoring the primal question – 'What is the problem the brand is trying to solve'? Another derivative of it is to ask – 'What is the objective we intend to achieve with the resources at hand? It is no brainer that solutions vary from the question one is trying to answer at hand. No amount of careful brand personas or the brand loyalty garnered would help the brand in case it loses focus. In simple terms, brand loyalty exists only if the problem the brand is trying to solve resonates with the customer and he/she connects with the brand persona. One cannot technically exist without another. Eons ago, a certain prince named Siddhartha went on a quest to answer a similar question for humanity and his learnings may have a bearing on the brand dilemma.

The Tusk of a White Elephant

Long ago, somewhere in present-day Nepal, there lived a childless royal couple longing for a bundle of joy. They had visited every temple they could, praying to every deity who would help. But it was to no avail. Despite all the setbacks, they still held onto hope.

One particular night, the queen had a dream about a white, winged elephant with four tusks charging into her womb. If anything, the elephant resembled divinity, resembling an answer to the years-long prayers of the royal couple. The next day, the queen felt different from normal. She was immediately taken to the royal physician who broke the good news that the queen was pregnant. After nine months, the kingdom rejoiced at the arrival of a prince. The royal couple's happiness knew no bounds, for at last their prayers had been answered.

As per the custom, the king summoned the royal astrologer to write down the horoscope of the prince. Usually horoscopes (*Kundli* in Hindi) are written down at the time of birth, based on the planetary position in that exact time.

It's a tradition that is still followed in majority households. The astrologer was bemused when he saw the astronomical calculations as per the prince's birth timings. He proclaimed that the prince would go down in the annals of history as the greatest emperor the world has ever witnessed, who would rule swathes of land or the greatest hermit who dedicated his entire life to eradicating the suffering of everyone. Either way, he was destined for greatness, declared the astrologer.

The king was alarmed at this news. He wanted to do everything in his capacity that stopped his son from turning into a hermit and be an emperor of the emperors. He named his son Siddhartha. For a major part of his childhood, Siddhartha grew up in a closed environment where there was no place for pain or the aged or the diseased, or the suffering. Siddhartha was given utmost care by the royal physicians that he never fell sick at all. Any servant or courtier, who possessed the slightest of the signs of aging or sickness was banished from their positions. No one in the prince's household served for long. Sometimes the prince used to wonder why his royal entourage was being changed often at regular intervals, yet he never bothered voicing out his doubts to his father. He was brainwashed into living in a utopian world where he never knew what was outside the little safe bubble built by his father. Yet, destiny had something else in its sleeve for the carefully laid out plans by men who think they can control everything.

As the heir apparent, the prince used to accompany his father to all the council hearings to understand governance. Yet, he failed to understand the nitty gritty of the problems, for he never had to face them. Using this as an opportunity, Siddhartha requested his father to allow him to tour the capital to gain insights, thus being able to contribute to the council hearings in a better fashion. His father reluctantly agreed. He assumed that by now, he had put his son on the path to the throne and couldn't deviate from it.

He asked his trusted charioteer to give the prince a tour of the capital. He strictly instructed the charioteer to take the prince only on the prescribed routes and not to deviate at any cost. The father (the king) hoped that he could try to shield his son as long as possible. The prince was elated on the king's decision. It has been his cherished dream to visit the outside world. The charioteer as instructed took out the prince to see parks and other tourist spots within the city. The prince was surprised to find not a soul on the route. As a safety measure, the king had already cleared up the roads and filled them with the palace servants. The prince wasn't content with going out as it didn't feel a difference at all. He wanted to be free.

Just when he was about to return to the palace, he saw a person with brown skin tone moving towards a narrow road. He had white hair instead of black. Siddhartha couldn't recall seeing a person of such complexion. He asked the charioteer to follow that person. The charioteer hesitated, but when the prince insisted, he obliged. Siddhartha saw the old man enter into a colony. In there he saw a variety of people whom he had never encountered before. It was at this exact moment the prince got an opportunity to witness real life without any smokescreen or whitewashing. Few of them had a darker complexion, while some of them sported a wheat complexion, a couple of them were healthy to the core and clean to the slate, while loads could not help being dirty. One person was picking up rice grains fallen on the ground to his plate. On the opposite side of the road, he saw a mother tending to her daughter who was ill with chickenpox with red boils all over the skin. He never knew the concept of falling sick or going hungry or not having enough money. He thought everyone would be well fed and well dressed like him. It was nothing he had ever witnessed before at the palace. He was deeply disturbed by this experience.

He wanted to understand how all the humans born on the same earth have such drastic differences? He wanted to seek the answers behind the just and equally cruel diversity of all forms in humanity. When posed by the questions, neither his parents nor mentors could provide a satisfactory answer. In fact, his parents discouraged him from pursuing such questions for his own well-being. Yet, he began to search extensively for answers within the confines of the palace for those questions that haunted him day and night.

Alarmed by his son's proclivity towards becoming a hermit, the king decided to marry off the prince in the hope to keep him occupied in domestic affairs till he ascended the throne.

Things were quite normal for a while. The king believed that the danger had passed as Siddhartha was married to a beautiful princess Yashodhara and they had been blessed with a son named Rahula, thus securing the future of the throne. The king was overjoyed at the prospect of a grandson. Even in the most joyous occasion in the life of any man, something was gnawing at Siddhartha's heart. He did the duty that was expected of him as the crown prince. Yet, he was still disturbed by the question of 'why' for all the experiences he witnessed. It was eating him up from inside. He could not take it anymore. He had to find out the reason for everything.

Finally, one midnight, he made up his mind to leave his wife and newborn child in the quest of finding the truth. The quest for finding answers to all the unanswered questions. It was not an easy decision. Yet he did it for his own sanity.

He soon found out the stark difference between a prince and a wanderer. He was living off solely on berries and alms. He traveled a lot, mostly on foot, and talked to many people about their problems, their experiences and their perspective of life. But he could not arrive at peace with his queries. Finally, he reached a place in present-day Bihar which eventually would be known as Bodh Gaya. He found a Peepal tree in the way and sat down to take rest for a while. As if on an involuntary action, he started meditating under it. He concentrated on all the experiences he had to date, all the observations he made to zero down and find out the root cause of suffering. Why does a human being suffer?

He continued his penance without any food or water. Siddharth's focus was only on the why and nothing else. After forty-nine days of penance, he finally found the answer he was looking for. He attained *nirvana* or spiritual enlightenment. Since then the Peepal tree obtained the name *Bodhi* tree for that was where Siddhartha attained enlightenment and turned into Gautam Buddha. The tree is still rumoured to be present in Bodh Gaya.

The answer Buddha zeroed on was that the attachment was the root cause of all suffering. And the attachment could be anything – identity, material, abstract ideas, etc. Getting attached to one is where the seed of suffering germinates. Even after getting the answers, Buddha continued to meditate in the same spot. One day two merchants Tapussa and Bhallika were passing by and stopped to see the radiant Buddha with a calm demeanour on his face. Upon listening to the prince's story, they fell on his feet to accept them as his students. He elaborated that people did not see the big picture for they were drawn into labyrinthine webs caused by attachments and hence suffer in the process. These two were one of the first disciples of Buddhism and in due course the number of disciples grew.

Buddha's philosophy began to resonate with the masses and began to adapt his way of life. People began to find solace in his teachings. He began to be associated with peace and non-violence. His legendary disarming of the notorious Angulimala, the bandit who wore a necklace of human thumbs using non-violence was propagated as a myth. Several kings began to adopt Buddhism as a religion even after the end of Buddha's mortal life.

Buddha's father might have gone narrow-minded due to his singular focus on averting his son's future that he ended up causing the same future. Siddhartha's relentless quest on finding answers to the purpose of life may have saved humanity from a collapse. He attempted to bring the learnings from the golden age of Satya Yuga to help humanity navigate the nascent stages of Kali Yuga where man is destined to lose out on all values. It is for the same reason Buddha is revered as the ninth avatar of Vishnu, for trying to untangle the dilemma of one's suffering.

Back to the Podium

Buddha's life teaches the brand about two pitfalls it needs to avoid in order to survive the decline phase. The first is finding out the problem it is attempting to solve in relation to the current environment. And the second pitfall is to avoid getting attached too much to processes and hierarchies that it hurts the brand in the long run. Microsoft is one of the companies to face this twin trouble in recent times and managed to come back from the brink in an unexpected manner.

It's hard to imagine a desktop or a computer without any Microsoft product installed in it. Yet there was a time where Microsoft was making mistake after mistake. And the stock markets reacted sharply by driving down the share price. Despite having Windows as a household name, Microsoft didn't do well till the time it was under the stewardship of CEO Steve Balmer. It's a known fact that the tech behemoth built its core business through operating systems. But it managed to miss out on most of the new-age digital trends. The search engine space was completely dominated by Google, with Bing being a poor lookalike. It re-invented Internet explorer, then introduced Bing and shut down Internet explorer altogether. Yet it couldn't challenge Google for the market leadership position. The next trend that came with the advent of smartphones was mobile computing and operating systems. Before Microsoft could make concrete plans on how to be the dominant force for mobile operating systems, Android won the race by becoming an open-source platform for various companies and collaborates to build an ecosystem on it. Around 7 in 10 smartphones are powered by Android operating systems. For a company that still is known for its computer operating systems couldn't crack the code on how to be a leader in the mobile operating system space. It still sought to salvage the situation by acquiring Nokia for 47 billion USD to build smartphones with Nokia hardware and Windows OS (Operating System). But that gamble didn't deliver the desired results. Another digital trend that was a consequence of smartphones was cloud computing. With too much data and applications in the market, it became a necessity to have a backend infrastructure in the form of servers, storage equipment, etc. It's hard to imagine today's world without any digital infrastructure empowering us. Even if Instagram, Microsoft Teams don't function for a minute, the whole world goes bonkers (which was witnessed in 2022). In such a $200 billion critical market, Amazon steamed ahead with its AWS (Amazon Web Services) product with no resistance from Microsoft.

It's hard to peg the logic behind Microsoft's business moves in the early 2000s without addressing Bill Gates in the room. The charismatic founder who started Microsoft from scratch. He was the CEO of the company for almost two decades. Bill famously said that he wanted to see a computer on every desk and in every home. Twenty years later, when Bill's successor Steve Balmer took up the CEO mantle, he was still motivated by this vision.

Being from a sales background, his approach to leading a tech-company was drastically different from how a tech person would lead it. In his tenure, Microsoft was fighting battles on multiple turfs without too much focus on the end goal. It was fighting with Samsung and Apple for a pie in the Smartphone market, it was challenging Google on search engine and mobile operating system front and with Amazon on the cloud computing market share. Somewhere amidst all this chaos, Microsoft lost its purpose on what customer problem it was solving. This percolated to different functions in the company. The internal windows teams amassed too much power to shut down any movement of resources to new projects that they felt could challenge its hegemony within the company. The performance measurement turned into a combative framework that no one in the company bothered to utter the word innovation. Internal politics with regards to resources and performance appraisals dented the employee morale. This resulted in the perception that Microsoft was no longer an aspirational company to work for, which ultimately led to attrition of talented employees.

Ultimately when Steve Balmer announced his resignation as Microsoft's CEO, the markets reacted positively by the stock increase of 7%. The entire world held their breath on who would be anointed as the CEO of the largest tech company. Despite not being in a good shape, Microsoft still commanded a 76% market share in the desktop market. Everyone was of the opinion that an outsider would be brought in as the CEO to turn the fortunes of the company. They were surprised when Hyderabad born Satya Nadella, the head of enterprise and cloud business (Microsoft) for over ten years was promoted as the CEO.

When Satya took over the reins, he started hitting the ground from Day 1 onwards to reinvent Microsoft. He came to the profound conclusion that Microsoft had lost its focus and forgotten its true purpose. And in order to change the organization, he undertook a spiritual journey of sorts to find the soul of Microsoft. He approached an independent consultant to conduct a survey to evaluate the current working environment within Microsoft. He realized that the root-cause of Microsoft's suffering was its unhealthy attachment to the Windows operating system, which was not letting the company grow or move forward. He understood that Microsoft could not bet on a single horse and should create multiple streams of revenue. For one of the revenue streams, he realized that cloud-computing was the future and Amazon shouldn't be allowed a free run. So, the first move he made was to shift the focus to cloud computing. They have created a cloud computing solution called 'Azure'. Conscious of his decision, Satya never even once mentioned Windows in his interviews when he was talking about Azure. And by 2014, they dropped the name 'Windows' from 'Azure' to ensure that it stands as an independent brand in its own right. As the third CEO of the company, Satya dared to imagine a future for Microsoft away from the shadow of Windows

The second move in the focus of cloud computing to pivot 'Office' products from a Windows licensing model to a 'Office 365' subscription model. In such a scenario, theoretically a user can still use Office products like MS Word, Excel, PPT, etc., without even having a Windows operating system. To ensure that such a thing happens, he managed to do the unthinkable. He inked a pact with Apple to release Office products for iOS users also. Microsoft of the old strongly believed in the playbook of not letting the competition grow or to keep picking up fights with them to wear them down. Because of this, Apple users couldn't use office products on their devices for a long time. It is also a known fact that Google pays a hefty fee to keep 'Google Chrome' as the default browser on iOS devices over Apple's own browser - 'Safari'. Satya managed to shock the tech-world by taking this bold move to allow Office products in Apple devices. By the start of Q1 2022, Microsoft has reported that there are more than 56.1 million Office 365 subscribers.

The third move to affirm Microsoft's renewed focus on cloud computing was to write off Nokia's acquisition as a sunk cost. Satya believed that it was not possible to fight battles on all fronts and he took a bold decision to not enter the smartphone warzone anymore. He didn't sanction any further investments into Nokia and deprioritized the agenda of smartphone manufacturing.

Satya managed to identify the main attachment that was the problem of Microsoft and managed to bring the focus to a revenue generating business model that is suited to modern times. But he had another problem to solve. The independent survey revealed that innovation became secondary, turf wars between departments and teams have ceased growth of any form. Satya wanted to tackle this *us vs them* attitude that was the heart of all process related tangles. He identified and appointed seventeen change leaders who would try to inculcate an *us with them* attitude. He went a step ahead and managed to change the company's mission statement to suit the current environment. It stands as to "Help empower people wherever they are, whatever device they are using". A statement that seeks to remove Windows from the center of focus and put back innovation in the game. He also advocated a customer centric attitude that can be reflected in everything, ranging from making technological changes to communicating with the users.

Cut down to today, Satya's renewed attempt to bring back focus and ushering a new line of culture by cutting off unhealthy attachments has paid off rich dividends. Microsoft has already crossed the one trillion USD mark, earning overall $184.9 million revenue in 2021. Once again, Microsoft is back as an aspirational brand to work amongst the human talent, which also has a ripple effect on how the products are designed and marketed. He literally hit the refresh button for himself and for Microsoft as it isn't an easy task to bring back a mammoth company from the brink to the spotlight.

From the Peepal Tree

Lord Buddha's life journey is rooted in empathy and compassion, as much as it is in understanding the cause of suffering. His non-violent ways and ability to connect with the other person has made him reform many, including the notorious Angulimala, which effectively led to the creation of several stories and thus cemented his brand persona. His teachings have given birth to a religion that has a significant presence in the Asia-Pacific regions, which attests to his brand loyalty amongst his followers. Despite being born with a silver spoon and being shielded amidst palace walls for most of his life, he started asking the right questions and found his answers through introspection. He became the greatest hermit the world has ever seen just as the royal astrologer has proclaimed.

Lord Buddha's story is important because it highlights the internal struggle with self to withstand the external forces. The story also evidences the fact on how easy it is to lose one's way when one is hell-bent on the destination without looking on the path they are walking as showcased by Gautama's father and by a tech-giant like Microsoft. As per the timelines available, the Buddha avatar takes place during the nascent stages of Kali Yuga before the prophesied end for Adharma happens. His teachings were of importance to survive the age of Kali and live a content life till the emergence of the Kalki avatar. Before moving on to the next chapter that deals with the lessons from the Kalki avatar on the last stage of the PLC cycle, below are the key takeaways from the teachings of Buddha.

- Brand personas are integral for a brand and should be crafted carefully over the duration of time as it leads to brand loyalty. This helps the brand survive the last stages of the maturity phase.
- The thumb rule for brand personas is that they should be fashioned in a relatable way to customers with an inspiration from archetypes (Hero, Rebel, Joker, etc.) that appeal to the customers. They should be consistent over time, but also should be flexible to add a trait or two in line with changing times.
- Periodically, the brand/business should evaluate the answer to the question – 'What is the problem it is trying to solve?' and should chalk out future strategies accordingly.
- A brand should never lose focus or grow an unhealthy attachment to narrow-minded objectives based on existing processes, policies and politics and lose out on the big picture.

10

New Age Destruction

Nighrahaya chadushtanam
Shistanam palanaayacha
Ashwanrudobhavankhadgii
Kalkireva prakirtasyase | |

Mortals are engaged in a perpetual dance between life and death. It would be futile to fight the inevitable as the cycle of life could never be upended. The *Bhagavad Gita,* one of the holy books that guide the followers of the Hindu religion, captures a similar sentiment within its pages. While the essence of this life principle is true for living beings, it holds importance for brands and businesses alike. Brands try to mimic human behaviour in a curious fashion - full of energy but with limited resources in their young age, pursuing a goal with a singular focus in their adulthood, and coming to terms with mortality and life truths in old age.

After having a glorious run from the introductory stage to the maturity stage, any brand has to prepare itself for the final stage in the product life cycle – 'Decline Stage'. Not all brands would have crossed all stages in the product life cycle to reach the Decline Stage. They could have come in a shorter time frame also. The only thing that is certain is that every brand/business has to reach the Decline Stage. The inevitability can only be delayed, but not destroyed.

In their final moments, people react in different ways. Similar story plays out in the world of brands. Some marketers would attempt to milk out the brand till the last drop without a care in the world. If there is an impending government ban coming up or there are some quality issues with the existing product, they may be tempted to run massive discounts to liquidate the existing stock. Others may have a twisted sense of pragmatism where the golden goose at hand is killed to garner all treasure at once, instead of speaking the language of patience. In the name of making sales, they promise the moon and stars. After the sale is done, they don't care for anything, which hurts the brand, robbing it of its future. A brand's time could be done for a variety of reasons – not a new trend in the market or doesn't resonate with the customer anymore; changes to the political and regulatory norms; internal management decision to shift focus of the company, etc. In such a scenario, the writing on the wall is ignored with a healthy dose of optimism, which may not bode well for a brand grasping for survival.

Amidst the grey area of the Decline Stage scenarios, there lies a crossroads for the marketer to choose. One such scenario is the decision of how to launch new products. The launch of a new product always leads to the decline of an existing brand/ product. When a business decides to move ahead with new product launches, the question arises – under which brand it needs to be put on? If it's a new startup, the answer is pretty straight forward. However, the company is mature enough to already have a robust product portfolio, the alternative in front of them is to choose between crafting a completely new brand from scratch or opting for the brand extension route to capitalize on the existing brand equity. Neither of the choices are easy, but a pragmatic brand manager ensures that the decision won't hurt the product portfolio in the long run. This scenario is slightly different from the intra-brand fights and cannibalization as highlighted in the previous chapter. It shouldn't be a case of winning the battle to only lose the war. Utilizing the existing brand equity for a new launch is straightforward and efficient. But the new product could be weighed down by the existing brand's baggage. A new brand may offer a fresh slate to start with, yet it would need resources to bring it on par with other brands in the portfolio. Think of it, the time and efforts needed to create a strong impression on the customer for a new brand is tough. If it is supposed to be done in unfamiliar geography or terrain, the complexity is incomprehensible. Even if the decision is taken to go with a new brand, the inevitable is just postponed. This new brand during the course of time will face a similar dilemma of being replaced by another new brand or live long enough to be irrelevant in the grand scheme of things. There are many scenarios that could come to categorize the Decline Stage. This conundrum does put a spin on the old age adage that even destruction is onerous as creation. Creation and destruction are two sides of the coin that are in a continuous cycle.

The Circle of Kalki

Death is never the end, just the beginning of another journey. The concepts related to time, life, and death are cyclic by nature as per the Hindu philosophy. Folks who stumble upon this truth lead fruitful lives, taking control of their actions. Stories across diverse mythologies deal with the concept of death in a mature fashion. While they deal with individual anecdotes, the destruction of the universe is baked into the creation story.

The creation of the universe is the responsibility of Lord Brahma. And the lifetime of the universe is tied to the lifeforce of Lord Brahma, with the smallest unit of measure being a *Mahayuga* consisting of four yugas – Satya, Treta, Dwapara, and Kali. As per the scripture, currently we are in Kali Yuga, the last and shortest period in the Mahayuga cycle. The end of Kali Yuga leads for the decks to be cleared for a new Satya Yuga to spring up and the cycle goes on, unperturbed till the death of Lord Brahma. Even the creator of the known universe is destined to meet his demise. In that instant, the whole universe goes into destruction mode. Only from its ashes, the embers of creation are stoked anew.

Humanity has witnessed all the prime nine avatars of Lord Vishnu, but the tenth avatar is yet to happen. Scriptures state that Lord Vishnu would take on the avatar of Kalki - the fearsome warrior whose very presence would send trembles to his enemies. This avatar would eventually appear as proclaimed by Vyasa Maharshi, the author of *Mahabharata.* As one begins to move to the end of Kali Yuga, one cannot hear *Swahakaram, Vshatkaram* (the sounds of *Swaha* and *Vshat* uttered during yagnas). Nor could one witness any sort of yagnas or poojas to be performed. If anything, king Mahabali demonstrated the power of yagnas in the story of Vamana avatar. Humanity would denounce things and living beings that were once considered holy and divine by the ancients. Cows would be treated as a pariah and they are massacred for food. The institution of marriage would not survive the ebb of Kali. Neither the husband nor the wife would respect each other to continue in the lifelong partnership. Children would no longer care for their parents. The concept of family turns into a joke for all to witness. The lifespan of men reduces to just eighteen years, while the longevity of women reduces further down. With no religious or social support, the society crumbles down on its own weight of expectations. Anarchy would be the rule of the day and might survive to fight another day. There is no place for truth or compassion or respect.

It's unthinkable to imagine a society with no redeeming qualities at all. In such a bleak scenario, the Kalki avatar is prophesied to arrive. In a village named Shambala, Kalki would be born as a son to a brahmin named Vishnuyasudu. This would be the intermediate time between the end of Kali Yuga and the start of Satya Yuga. His birth is heralded by signs if one is careful to observe. Sinners would be affected by a disease that makes them shed out blood from the body and they would fall down like insects. All kinds of diseases would be on a rampage in the form of a pandemic. Only the citizens who have managed to stay true to their hearts without being corrupted would survive to see the dawn of Satya Yuga.

Atop a pristine white horse, with the saffron flag in one hand and wielding a fiery sword, Kalki would go on a campaign of the entire world. All the kingdoms that have managed to survive the rampage of pandemics and have been living in an *adharmic* way would have to answer his sword. In Kali Yuga, man would lose all the principles he once stood for in the golden ages of Satya Yuga, the ideals he valued in the silver ages of Treta Yuga, and the learnings he gained in the bronze ages of Dwapara Yuga. The survivors of the carnage would lead into the new Satya Yuga and would be provided with necessary guidance to start a new way of life, after obliterating every essence of the chaotic Kali yuga.

The spirit of Kalki's account is not about absolute annihilation or salvation. It's not even about Dharma and Adharma. The lord will always find a way to protect Dharma and preserve the order. The essence of this avatar is about the fact that creation and destruction go hand in hand. A variation of this is also found in the *Gita* – The one who is born cannot escape death and the one who has died cannot be stopped from being born again. It is a cycle that must continue without any breaks.

Vysa Maharshi and *Puranas* (ancient Hindu texts) offer information on the details of the Kalki avatar and what he is destined to do. Yet it doesn't offer too much information on how Kalki avatar would lead the remaining virtuous humanity into the new age. What would the new Satya Yuga look like? How would life be shaped in that age? What would be the structure of the society fabric? The questions are aplenty. Signs that need to be monitored for the arrival of Lord Kalki on the face of the earth have been chronicled, yet comprehending them completely would lead to a fantasy adventure born of pure thought.

The mere mention of Kalki's avatar is a gentle reminder that every journey has an end and every end is an opportunity for a new beginning. No brand or business can operate in perpetuity in the same form without any form of change happening. If at all a brand/ business has to deal with the eventuality, then what is the best way to react to such a situation? How would the new Satya Yuga look for the brand/ business? While Kalki avatar highlights the happenings of Kali Yuga, it doesn't offer too much details on how he plans to herald the new Satya Yuga. Hence, we turn towards other stories of Lord Vishnu drawn from the rich mythology that offer insights on how best to tackle situations in the face of inevitability. After all, not everyone can choose the timing of one's death like Bhishma Pitamah.

Till the End

The timeline for any brand in its PLC journey may vary from case to case, but if it manages to reach the 'Maturity Stage' then its ultimate destination would be the 'Decline Stage'. In a few instances, the brand could find itself in the Decline Stage without even crossing all the stages. One can wonder how a brand/company that has been exceeding its expectations could find itself in the embargo of the Decline Stage? Not all can read the tea leaves at hand and the signs emerging out from various quarters to provide a complete picture for the management to take a call on the state of affairs. The scenarios of how the Decline would happen are countless – a popular brand is not able to rake sales anymore, a company having a different core competency is not able to manage the needs of a particular brand, a brand is not able to fight in a competitive market, the product portfolio is heavy enough for a company to weigh down, the brand's offering turns out outdated in an ever-changing environment, etc. Depending upon the circumstances, the brands can take a call whether to go out in all glory or end up with a sad state of affairs with only being dedicated to case studies as a footnote. Below are a few illustrations that point out the scenarios of how the PLC journey would end for a brand.

Un-glorious Purpose...

Mergers and acquisitions happen to be one of the major reasons for a brand to write its obituary. Any acquiring company performs due diligence before making an offer. A company could be acquired for its core competencies or to ensure that there is consolidation amongst the competition or to stave off a future threat. This could happen in normal circumstances in the search for synergy or when a firm is on the verge of bankruptcy and is looking for resources to stay alive in the competition.

It's a given fact that the acquiring company gets a final say on how the firm would be managed unless any specific clauses are baked into the contract. Rather than the intangible assets like brand equity, intellectual properties and goodwill, a firm might be more interested in the tangible assets that add value to its existing portfolio. In a way it's a subtle discarding of the existing brand presence and looking only at how best the company/ brand would serve the acquirer. For example, when the Indian business of Hutch was acquired by Vodafone, it wasted no time in rebranding everything as Vodafone, leading to the death of brand Hutch. Probably the brand Hutch remained only in the collective consciousness of the customers due to its memorable advertisements with a pug dog and a catchy tagline, 'Wherever you go, we will follow you'. Its physical assets might have added value to Vodafone, but Hutch was dead as a brand. In a way, Hutch found a new purpose even after its demise, but it didn't exist anymore in its original form.

This instance bears a close resemblance to the creation of *vajra*, the weapon of Lord Indra which is formidable to strike fear amongst his enemies. Long ago, when Indra had just ascended the heavens as its ruler, his capital city Amaravati was attacked by Vritra, the serpent demon. Vritra defeated the armies of Devas and imprisoned all the cloud cattle.

Droughts, famines were a common sight for people who had no water to grow food. With life withering away, Devas set out to find a solution. Upon guidance from Lord Brahma, the gods assembled in the holy forests of Naimisharanya on earth. A group of sages welcomed them to their abode and enquired about the purpose of the visit. Devas wanted to meet a sage named Dadichi Mahamuni. The sages led them to the old monk who was meditating in the deeper parts of the ashram. The mood turned somber when the Devas narrated to Dadichi about their ordeal and sought his reply. He didn't even flinch for a second and agreed. Devas intended to fashion a weapon out of Dadichi's backbone and it would be powered by the ultimate sacrifice. Lord Indra used this weapon vajra, to defeat Vritra and bring back rain to nourish life on earth. Dadichi may have had intellectual capabilities or wisdom beyond the ages, but he was a frail, old man whose body was powered by this meditation prowess. He transformed into the weapon that serves as a guardian for the heavens against its enemies.

The above story has certain similarities with one of the recent acquisitions of Uber Eats by Zomato in India. Zomato got access to Uber Eats fleet and operational expertise in an all-stock buyout, while the brand Uber Eats ceased to exist anymore. Uber Eats may not exist in its current form, but it indirectly aids in the growth of Zomato.

For the Greater Good

Earlier we have witnessed where a company is forced to seek external help because its financials are not robust and not in a position to keep up with the ever-changing market. No matter how glorious the brand is, if it doesn't solve the customer's problem and doesn't contribute to the top line of the balance sheet, then it is for nothing. There are other ways in how a brand could witness its end. One such particular scenario is where the brand doesn't die, but the association with the parent company does. It comes to reality when a company would have bitten off more than it could chew.

To capitalize on the momentum in the market or have the uttermost belief in its capabilities, companies indulge in entering new categories with diversified product offerings and splutter the market with brand extensions. These moves may seem prudent in the short term, but the firm would be spreading itself thin in terms of resources and focus to shore up its complete product portfolio. Earlier, it could be spending INR 200 crores on two brands, but that spend per brand decreases if the brands increase from two to five. A firm could land up with a potential multi-billion-dollar brand, but it doesn't have the capacity or the needed muscle to make the potential come true. Or worse, it is never a focus of the top-level management bull's eye which delegates the respective brand to a low status within the firm. The brand never gets the attention it deserves with a lot going on in the company. With fewer resources and not much focus, the brand may not be in a position to rake in revenues, thus going into a vicious cycle. The brand doesn't have enough budget to put itself in front of the customers. This reduces the sales numbers, which in turn justifies the budget cuts in the first place.

Intra departmental turf wars could also take away the sheen from the battle chest. Imagine fighting for brand ambassadors, media spaces, product offering similarities, budgets amongst the company brands, real estate within the company's digital assets. For example, Lux having to fight with Dove to get a fair share of representation within HUL's planning, just because both belong to the soaps category. Managing multiple brands with competing agendas that contribute to disproportionate revenues is a task in itself.

This is one of the moves a company can do when it is faced with a multi-brand dilemma. The firm puts its brands out on the block so that they deserve a place where the brands can utilize their potential. And the company doesn't exactly do this from a position of weakness, unlike in the earlier scenario. The premise is pretty simple - this brand could have a better life in your house, than mine given the circumstances. Of course, the parent company wouldn't be doing this out of their goodwill. They would be left with a reduced portfolio which helps them in focusing on larger objectives, plus gains a hefty sum on the side. Not always a successful brand is on the block for sale, but the acquiring company witnesses possibilities in retaining the brand as it is without stripping it away to its bones. Hypothetically, if a company X acquires Coca-Cola, it wants to retain Coca-Cola as is, for its brand has some value in the consumer's mind space. Yet, no brand has the same essence once a change of management is on the cards. Change of some form is eventual and it cannot be avoided. In such a scenario, this would be the death of a brand as it was known, before being launched into the market again.

The story of Karna, the demigod son of Surya in *Mahabharata* also emphasizes this point. When sage Durvasa, the most feared amongst the rishis visited Kuntibhoja, an ancient kingdom of Bharatavarsha, his hospitality knew no limits, thanks to princess Kunti. Pleased with her service and devotion, sage Durvasa granted her a mantra that can be used to invoke any of the Devas to grant her a child with powers that are unparalleled in the mortal realm. Unconvinced, she tried out the mantra on Lord Surya. She was shocked when Lord Surya turned up due to the effect of the mantra. She pleaded with the Lord to go away as it was a mistake. But, Lord Surya couldn't do anything as he was bound by the powers of the mantra to provide the invoker with a child. He provided her with a child born with golden *kavachakundalas* (armour and earrings) that grant invincibility. Unfortunately, Kunti was not in a position to be happy about the turn of events for she was an unmarried woman who was not supposed to have a child. Everyone would be asking thousands of questions and the unbearable humiliation that would follow was the only thought in her mind. With a heavy heart, she kissed the baby boy one last time and left him in a basket along the waters of river Ganga. The water currents carried the baby to Athiratha, who happened to be a chariot driver in the army of Hastinapura, working directly for King Dhritarashtra. Athiratha and his wife Radha were childless. When he found the baby, his joy knew no bounds, for his prayers were finally answered. The little boy grew up to be warrior Karna who went to make a name for himself beyond the annals of time. The grounded upbringing of Athiratha was very much visible in Karna. Had Karna grown up as Kunti's son, he may have been a different character altogether, for he could have led a different life. But he found his home in a place where he was loved and cherished by his foster parents. Kunti abandoning Karna was almost inhumane, for she could have done many other things, but that is not the point of discussion. If she hadn't done what she had done, the story of *Mahabharata* would be unrecognizable.

Handing over brands that have been crafted from scratch in the light of low performance or due to lack of alignment with the management vision is unseasonable. However, tough calls need to be made for the greater good. One such example is that of P&G (Procter and Gamble). The company was established in 1837 by Willian Procter and James Proctor in Cincinnati who were heading their small candle making and soap making business, respectively. It started off with making soaps first and grew to span across continents into an untamable beast that had to resort to drastic measures. As the company began to grow, it added brands that would help it win in each geography. On a smaller scale, the company was doing well for itself and its business decisions of launching brands made sense. But when one looks at the big picture, it was not exactly rosy. With a diverse portfolio, P&G was not able to manage its internal complexities or the grappling issues with the supply chain or the challenges in marketing. It resembled a giant beast whose momentum was paused due to its own internal weight. That was when P&G intended to simplify its product portfolio to realize benefits from its efficiencies. It took a step back and looked at all its brands from all possible perspectives. Based on the results of the exercise, the management took the hard call of pulling the plug on some of their brands that didn't bring in the desired level of revenues, or the ones that didn't fit with the focus categories. P&G decided that it wanted to focus on the categories of beauty & grooming, household care, and health & well-being. It took the hard call of divesting wherever there's an interested buyer and discontinuing where P&G itself doesn't see a potential, as the count of brands was over a hundred.

Pringles, the famous geometric-shaped potato wafer snack found its new home in Kelloggs, which led to it being the second-largest brand in terms of volume in the chips segment. Pringles was in the snacks category, which was not in the new focus area of P&G. Duracell (a battery brand known for its rabbit mascot in the commercials) was sold off to Berkshire, Rembrandt (a stain-removal toothpaste to make the teeth whiter and make enamel stronger) to Johnson & Johnson, IAMS – the complete pet division to Mars, etc., and P&G retained only the brands that were in a position to manage lucidly. Most of these hundred brands were crafted by P&G themselves over the years or got acquired and developed by P&G. But when the time came for the greater good of the company, they chopped off the hand so that the body may live.

Even though the company is acquiring these brands because they see an inherent value in adding the brand to its portfolio, the essence of how it is envisaged is slightly different. One instance in recent memory is the acquisition of brand Horlicks by HUL from GSK. From the era of GSK, Horlicks was always known as a children's malt-based nutrition brand with the catchy tagline – "Taller, stronger, and sharper". The recent advertisements from HUL portray a slightly different approach moving away from the iconic tagline, and positioning it a bit more closely as a nutritional addition to a kid's diet. Instead of being abstract about how Horlicks helps in the child's growth, the HUL is envisaging the brand as a nutritional supplement to the kid. While the intent of using the brand might be the same, the narrow differences are hard to ignore. Comparing the benefits of Horlicks to a permutation of nutrients derived from spinach, milk, and orange in one of the advertisements is a testament to this.

A brand may earn a new lease of life when it finds a new house where it receives the attention it deserves. But it may not be the same brand as it was before as the acquiring company decides on how best to portray it to its customers in line with its company's objectives and processes. That is a subtle sign of a brand's death in the eyes of customers who remember it differently. And the brand gets an opportunity to shine again in front of an entirely new audience, in addition to the old ones.

Phoenix is in the Making

"What is dead may never die. But will rise again stronger", is a quote from a popular television series. Death happens to be just a starting point in a divergent journey as per the Hindu line of thought. This principle holds for brands in certain scenarios also. Earlier it was illustrated how external agents precipitate the decline of a brand. On the other hand, in the absence of white knights or saviors, a brand may be put to rest by its internal stakeholders. Pulling out the plug would be a conscious call that would be noticed gradually. The death of a brand is never easy. It wouldn't happen in a neat fashion where the brand disappears from the face of the earth one fine day. Its supply would be slowly curbed to a point where the shopkeepers have no interest in stocking them or customers would get frustrated in waiting for supply. The marketing spends are sloshed off to ensure that it would never get the focus. The supply and manufacturing lines are reduced to curb the production. All the moves are in tandem to slow down the demand. Very few companies admit that they are killing off a brand. Some companies go for the quiet kill where the product would never be found again. The human capital associated with the brand would be reduced slowly. Any media associations, website links, or other information would be purged from official company pages. It would be as if the brand never existed in their collective consciousness. Internally the brand would be called a 'sunset' brand, lying around till a new brand takes its place.

This may be the usual end of the story, however, in certain instances, firms decide to bring back 'dead' brands in a different time and place. Bajaj bought back its classic Chetak scooter brand to launch its electric vehicle portfolio. Chetak was popular with its iconic tagline Humara Bajaj, but it was discontinued in the early '90s after motorcycles started coming into fashion. Did Bajaj always intend to re-launch Chetak to a new generation, or did it merely take an opportunity with the rising EV trends? Probably the answer to this question would never be known. Either way, Bajaj had a choice to make – to spend a hefty amount in making a new brand from scratch or bring back a classic with a twist at a much lesser cost. Leaving aside the financial aspect of the decision, the discussion would have credibility only if the yesteryear brand was popular in its heyday. Usually, that is the benchmark for any brand to warrant a rebirth, but that is not the only parameter. A firm may decide to give an old brand a new lease of life to make it relevant to the current times. Otherwise, every company would be stuck in a loop of reviving its portfolio in newer forms for a fresh audience, without even breaking the proverbial ceiling.

In the tales of mythology, there have been incidents where devout disciples have defied death, powerful sages cracked the code to immortality. But one character that stood relevant to Treta Yuga and Dwapara Yuga was Jambavant. The old bear king who was born from the yawn of Lord Brahma went on to play pivotal roles in the lives of Lord Rama and Lord Krishna, who lived in two different times. In Treta Yuga, he was critical in making Hanuman realize his potential by awakening his hidden powers, which helped the vanara army know the whereabouts of Sita. Once the army knew about Lanka, the major action was about how Ravana's forces were vanquished. However, without this piece of information, they would have been roaming around in circles. In Dwapara Yuga, Jambavant was instrumental in clearing Lord Krishna's name when he was accused of stealing Samantaka Mani, a legendary gem powered by the energy of the sun. The gem was rumoured to bestow its owner with unimaginable wealth and resources. The gem ended up in Jambavant's cave when a lion ventured into the surroundings. The lion killed off the person holding the jewel who was hunting alone in the forest. Jambavant and Krishna fought furiously due to a misunderstanding when Krishna turned up at the cave in search of the trail. After a while, Jambavant understood that Krishna was none other than the incarnation of Lord Rama in this age, as the essence of the Lord Protector - Vishnu. As a token, he handed over the jewel and even gave his daughter, Jambavati's hand in marriage.

Jambavant wasn't exactly dead and brought back to life in a different era. However, he was instrumental in two different eras, displaying the same core strength but tweaking it according to the circumstance. In the end, any resurrected brand has to mean something to the customers of that time. Otherwise, the whole exercise would be moot. In hindsight,

Chetak was not the only brand that was bought back in the automobile industry. Mahindra went on a bid to reintroduce Jawa motorcycles in the country, as a clear competition for Royal Enfield, capitalizing on its nostalgia factor for the older and new generations alike.

In certain instances, not only the brand is resurrected in a new avatar, but product offerings are bought back for the cherishing of a whole new audience. The reason movies or TV shows turn popular and attain cult status is because they are introduced to a fresh set of consumers who would fall in love with them once again. Similar incidents are witnessed in the usual line of business too. Once a fan of Parle Rol-a-Cola petitioned on Twitter for Parle to bring back the favorite product. Rol-a-Cola was a coke-flavoured candy that mimicked the taste of carbonated drinks. Parle responded to the customer saying that it would consider the request only if the tweet got more than 10,000 retweets. The fan went on a publicity spree, completely organic and based on word of mouth, tagging celebrities, asking them to share the tweet, and helping in spreading the word about his crusade to bring back a favoured product. In the end, the tweet went viral and got the required target in no time. Parle brought back the product on popular demand and is continuing to capitalize on this. If only various fans start petitioning the same for various other products that were considered classic, maybe then the companies would rethink their strategy for once.

The decision to bring back a dead brand or a product is never a piece of cake. The main challenge would be to go against the rationale which killed the brand in the first place. Nonetheless, it would be a phoenix that was given a new lease of life, for not all brands receive a second chance in this line of business.

Signing Note

One profound question that may arise is – what is the point of everything if it ends in the decline stage. Some philosophers tried to provide a solution claiming that it is the journey that matters and not the destination. Kalki avatar represents the herald of destruction, the precursor for a new dawn. The death of a brand or a business is part of the cycle. Not understanding the simple fact or disrespecting it would only delay the inevitable, but never stop it. Turns out, creation and destruction are the very primal forces of the universe.

Below are a few key takeaways from the avatar of Kalki from the perspective of PLC.

- Any brand or a business needs to have a competitive advantage that makes it lucrative for potential suitors.
- Marketers should take pragmatic calls to trim down the product portfolio to ensure a sharper focus on objectives.
- Any second chance for a brand should be consciously taken only if it stands to have relevance for a new set of customers.
- All in all, the ebb of business never ceases for a second. The tales from the annals of history serve as a pathfinder for those who wish to see them.

Mythology Glossary

Abhimanyu	Warrior son of Arjuna, the third Pandava prince
Aditi	Wife of Sage Kashyapa
Agni Pariksha	Trial by fire
Airavat	Celestial mount of Indra
Ajax	Greek warrior who fought in the trojan war
Amaravati	A heavenly abode, capital city of Devas
Amazon	A race of female Greek warriors known for their prowess
Amba	Princess of Kashi, reborn as Shikhandi during Mahabharata
Amritha	Nectar of immortality
Arjuna	Demi-god son of Indra – the king of Gods, the third Pandava prince, renowned for his archery skills
Ashwamedha Yagna	A yagna performed by emperors as a tool of conquest. During this yagna a ceremonial horse is unleashed upon the lands. The land that the horse sets foot on would become a part of the empire. If opposed, the king of that land would have to face the army and defeat them. The yagna is completed only after the horse returns in twelve months
Ashwatthama	Son of Guru Dronacharya
Asuras	A race of divine beings, in constant war with Devas
Balarama	Elder brother of Lord Krishna
Bali Chakravarti	Grandson of Prahalad, an asura

Bharata	Son of Queen Kaikeyi and King Dasharatha
Bhargava Rama	Another name for Lord Parashuram
Bheema	Demi-god son of Vayu – the God of air, the second Pandava prince, renowned for his strength
Bhishma	Demi-god son of Ganga – the river Goddess, grand old man of Kuru clan
Brahma	God of Creation
Bhu Devi	Goddess Earth
Bodhi Vriksha	The tree under which Lord Buddha attained enlightenment
Buddha	The ninth avatar of Lord Vishnu
Chakravyuh	A deadly military strategy adopted by Guru Drona in the Mahabharata war
Charanas	A unit of time measurement
Chitrakoot Hill	A hill in the north west part of the country
Dadichi Mahamuni	A great sage who sacrificed his life to make the powerful weapon Vajra
Daksha Prajapati	A lieutenant of Lord Brahma, who helped him with creation duties. Father of Goddess Sati - first wife of Lord Siva
Dandakaranya	A fearsome forest which is full of wild animals, demons and rakshasas
Dantavakra	An ally of King Shishupala in Dwapara Yuga, an incarnation of Jaya-Vijaya due to their curse, killed by Krishna avatar
Dasharatha	Father of Rama, king of Ayodhya and a descendant of Ikshavaku clan
Dashavatar	Ten avatars taken by Lord Vishnu to save the world
David	A youngling and a famous underdog who defeated Goliath the giant

Devaki	Mother of Lord Krishna
Dhristadyunma	Son of Drupada and heir to the Panchala kingdom
Dhritarashtra	Bling king of the Kuru clan, father of Duryodhana
Draupadi	Daughter of Drupada, Queen of the Pandavas
Dronacharya	Teacher for the Kuru princes – Kauravas and Pandavas
Drupada	King of Panchala
Durvasa Maharshi	A sage known for his prowess
Duryodhana	Eldest of the Kauravas
Dwapara Yuga	The third of the yugas in a 'Mahayuga', characterized as the Bronze age of mankind
Dwaraka	Capital of the Yadava kingdom
Gandaberunda	Fearsome two headed bird avatar taken by Lord Shiva
Gandharva	A race of celestial beings
Ganga	Holy River that passes through the heart of the subcontinent. Legend says that she descended from heavens due to the efforts of Bhagiratha
Garuda	King of birds, Vehicle of Lord Vishnu and the mortal enemy of all snakes
Ghatotkach	Rakshasa son of Bheema
Goliath	A giant warrior who was defeated by a puny David
Govardhanagiri	A hill near the Vrindavan village in Dwapara Yuga
Halahal	A powerful, potent poison that turned up during the ocean churning exercise

Hanuman	A Vanara blessed with divine powers and the son of Vayu, the god of air
Hari	Another name for Lord Vishnu
Hastinapur	Capital city of the Kuru kingdom
Hayagreeva	A horse headed demon who stole the Vedas from Lord Brahma
Hiranyakashyapa	An incarnation of Jaya-Vijaya due to their curse, killed by Narasimha avatar
Hiranyakshya	An incarnation of Jaya-Vijaya due to their curse, killed by Narasimha avatar
Ikshavaku clan	The lineage of King Ikshavaku
Indra	King of the Devas and the heaven
Indraprastha	Capital city of Pandavas short lived kingdom
Jamadagni Maharshi	Father of Parashurama
Jambavant	Old bear king, born out of Brahma's yawn
Jambavati	Daughter of Jambhavanth
Janaka	King of Mithila, adoptive father of Lady Sita
Jarasandha	King of Mathura and the brother-in-law of Kansa
Jatayu	A loyal vulture bird whose sacrifice was indistinguishable
Jaya	Door-keeper of the Vaikuntha doors
Jayadrath	Brother-in-law of the Kauravas
Kaikeyi	Youngest queen of King Dasharatha
Kali Yuga	The third of the yugas in a 'Mahayuga', characterized as the Bronze age of mankind
Kalki	The tenth avatar of Vishnu
Kamadhenu	The bountiful divine cow which blesses the hosts by providing them with food and healing

Kansa	Uncle of Lord Krishna, brother of Devaki
Karna	Demi-god son of Lord Surya, a warrior skilled in archery
Kartaveeryajuna	The 100 handed warriors ruled the kingdom of Haihayas kingdom
Kashyapa Rishi	A renowned sage, one of the Sapta rishis and the father of Devas, Rakshasas and Manavas
Kauravas	Hundred sons of King Dhritarashtra and Queen Gandhari
Kaushalya	Eldest queen of King Dasharatha and mother of Lord Rama
Kayadhu	Mother of Prince Prahalad and Queen of King Hiranyakashyapa
Kuntibhoja	Father of Kunti
Kishkindha	Kingdom of Vanaras
Krishna	Eight avatar of Lord Vishnu
Ksheer Sagar Manthan	Divine acting of churning the milk ocean in the search of nectar of immortality
Kumaras	Powerful sons of Lord Brahma created by the power of thought
Kumbhakarna	Brother of the asura king Ravana
Kunti	Mother of Pandavas and Queen of Pandu
Kurma	Second avatar of Lord Vishnu
Kuru	The collective name given to the lineage of Hastinapur
Kurukshetra	Place where the final battle was fought between Kauravas and Pandavas
Kusha	Son of Lord Rama and Lady Sita
Lakshmana	Brother of Rama, eldest son of Queen Sumitra and King Dasharatha
Lanka	Kingdom of Asuras ruled by Ravana

Luva	Son of Lord Rama and Lady Sita
Maha Yuga	A combination of Krita, Tretha, Dwapara and Kali yugas
Mahabharata	The epic which chronicles the war and the events leading to it written by Sage Vyasa
Mahendragiri Parvat	A set of hills where Lord Parashuram did his penance
Manthara	Handmaiden to Queen Kaikeyi
Maryada Purshottam	Another name for Lord Rama
Matsya	First avatar of Lord Vishnu
Mritsanjeevani Mantra	The chant that grants immortality
Narada Muni	Son of Lord Brahma, a staunch devotee of Lord Vishnu
Narasimha	Fourth avatar of Lord Vishnu
Narayani Sena	A fabled army of Dwaraka led by Lord Balarama and Lord Krishna, known for its battle prowess
Neelkanth	Another name for Lord Shiva for his blue throat which houses the poison – 'Halahal'
Nike	Greek goddess of Victory
Nirvana	Eternal bliss
Panchala	Kingdom of Drupada which housed the children of Draupadi and Pandavas during the latter's exile
Panchavati	Forests near the river Godavari
Pandavas	Five sons of King Pandu and Queen Kunti
Parashuram	Sixth avatar of Lord Vishnu
Pashupatastra	Divine weapon of Lord Shiva
Prahalad	Grandfather of King Bali and an ardent devotee of Lord Vishnu

Prajapatis	Celestial rulers tasked by Lord Brahma for creation
Pratyingira Devi	An avatar of Shakti, powerful enough to stop the quarrel between Lord Shiva and Lord Vishnu
Puranas	Ancient texts chronicling the stories related to Hindu mythology
Radha	Childhood friend of Lord Krishna
Rama Rajya	A term used to compare to the glorious rule of Lord Rama
Ramayana	Story of Lord Rama written by Sage Valmiki
Ravana	King of Lanka
Renuka	Mother of Lord Parashurama
Rishyamukha Parvat	Hill near Kishkinda where Sugreeva took refuge
Samantaka Mani	A divine gem made from the power of Sun
Sampati	Brother of Jatayu who lived near the southernmost tip of the sub-continent
Sandeepan Rishi	Guru to lord Krishna
Sapta Rishis	A group of seven sages
Satya Yuga	The first of the yugas in a 'Mahayuga', characterized as the Golden age of mankind
Satyavrat Manu	First manu in the history of mankind, who rescued and established life after the great deluge
Sharabha	Fierce bird avatar taken by Lord Vishnu to fight Lord Shiva
Shikhandi	An incarnation of Lady Amba
Shiva	God of Destruction
Shukracharya	Guru of Rakshasas

Sibi Chakravarthi	An ancient king known for his ability to carry out promises no matter what
Siddhartha	Original name of Lord Buddha, before he went on searching for enlightenment
Sisupala	An ally of King Dantavakra in Dwapara Yuga, an incarnation of Jaya-Vijaya due to their curse, killed by Krishna avatar
Srushti Dharma	Natural order of creation
Subhadra	Sister of Lord Krishna, wife of Arjuna
Sudama	Childhood friend of Lord Krishna
Sugreeva	Brother of Vaali – the vanara king
Sundara Kanda	Chapter of Ramayana which deals with the adventures of Hanuman after crossing the mighty ocean in the search of Sita
Surpanakha	Sister of King Ravana
Surya Deva	The sun god
Suryavanshi	Descendants from the Sun god
Treta Yuga	The second of the yugas in a 'Mahayuga', characterized as the Silver age of mankind
Trojan War	Bloody war fought between Greeks and the city of Troy
Ucchaishravas	The seven headed horse which emerged from the churning of the milk ocean
Uttara Kanda	An extension of Ramayana which deals with King Rama after his coronation
Vaikuntha	The heavenly abode of Lord Vishnu
Vajra	Divine weapon of Lord Indra capable of destroying his enemies
Vali	King of Vanaras and the Kishkinda kingdom
Valmiki Maharishi	Sage who has written Ramayana
Vamana Avatar	Fifth avatar of Lord Vishnu

Varaha Avatar	Third avatar of Lord Vishnu
Varuna Dev	God of rains and water
Vasudeva	Father of Lord Krishna
Vasuki	King of serpents used for churning of the milk ocean
Vayu Dev	God of Air
Vedas	Holy texts of Sanatana Dharma/Hindu religion which contain the complete knowledge about everything
Vijaya	Door-keeper of the Vaikuntha doors
Virata	King of Matsya kingdom where Pandavas spent a year of their exile in incognito mode
Vishnu	God of preservation who is known to take avatars to establish Dharma
Vishwamitra Maharishi	Raj guru of Ayodhya
Vritha	Demon who imprisoned all the clouds in a conquest of the heavens
Yagnas	A holy ceremony using fire as the carrier to give our offerings to Gods
Yudhishtir	Demi-god son of Yama – the god of Death, the eldest Pandava prince, renowned for his practice of Dharma
Yugas	A unit of time measurement

Brands and Companies

Chapter 1

Chik	DMart	Dunzo	Epigamia
Future Group	Google	GPay	iD
ITC	More	OnePlus	OYO
Premji Trust	Reliance Retail	Spencers	Tiny Owl

Chapter 2

Amazon	Britannia	DS Group	Fitso
Flipkart	Foodiebay.com	HyperPure	ITC
Kacha Aam	Mango Bite	Mondelez	Mont Blanc
Nestle	Nirma	Parle	Pass Pass
Perfetti Van Melle	Pulse	Rajanigandha	Sunfeast: Dark Fantasy
Swiggy	Swiggy Genie	Zomato	Zomato Pro

Chapter 3

Dubsmash	Fevicol	Micromax	Pidilite
Reynolds	Samsung	Tik Tok	

Chapter 4

Fizz	Frooti	Galaxy Note 10 &10+	Hippo
HPCL	Instagram	Jet Airways	Jio
Kingfisher	Lays	Maggi	Maggi Hot Heads
Monaco	Netflix	Parle G	Subway
Twitter	Uber Eats		

Chapter 5

Ajio	Amazon Pay	Android	Bharat Pe
Big Basket	Coke	Diet Coke	Kodak
Nokia	Oxigen	Paytm	PhonePe
Samsung	Snapdeal	Zerodha	

Chapter 6

Ariel	Eicher Motors	Ghadi	Hindustan Lever
Hootsuite	ITC	Maggi Fusion	Maggi Special Masala
Maggi Tomatina	Marcio	Parachute	Royal Enfield
Sprinklr	Surf Excel	TATA Nihar	TOMCO
Wheel	Yippee		

Chapter 7

Airbnb	Airtel	Amazon Prime	AMD
Apollo Hospitals	Classic Coke	Coke	Colgate
Facebook	Fair & Lovely	Flipkart	Glow & Lovely
Google	Idea	Indian Express	Instagram
Intel	Jio	Juggernaut	Kwality Walls
Lionsgate	LIV.AI	Local Mind	Lovefilm.com
McDonald's	Mondelez	Myntra	Nokia
Oreo	Patanjali	PepsiCo	Reliance
The Hindu	Vodafone	WhatsApp	Zee 5

Chapter 8

AMUL	Avenger	Bajaj Chetak	BM 100
Boxer	CavinKare	Dairy Milk Silk	Discover 125

Dominos	Gillette	Godrej	Harley Davidson
Honda	Husqvarna	Kelloggs'	KTM
Maggi	Maggi Fusion	Maggi Hot Heads	Maxima
McD	Netflix	OLA	P&G
Pulsar	Qute	Royal Enfield	Unilever
Vespa	Vicks	Virgin Airlines	Wheel
Yamaha			

Chapter 9

Airtel	AMUL	Apple	Azure
Bing	Coca Cola	Facebook	Google
Microsoft	Nike	Thums Up	

Chapter 10

Bajaj Chetak	Berkshire	Dove	Duracell
GSK	Horlicks	Hutch	Jawa
Johnson & Johnson	Kelloggs'	Lux	Mahindra
P&G	Parle	Pringles	Rol-a-Cola
Vodafone			

References

Chapter 1

- Vernon, R. (1966). Product Life-Cycle Theory. The Quarterly Journal of Economics
- https://timesofindia.indiatimes.com/business/india-business/d-mart-ipo-subscribed-105-times/articleshow/57581783.cms
- https://scholar.google.com/scholar?hl=en&as_sdt=0%2C5&q=porter+forces&oq=porter+1979 (Porter 5 Forces, 1979 Actual Year)
- Kim, W. C. (2005). Blue ocean strategy: from theory to practice. California management review, 47(3), 105-121.
- Porter's, V. C. M. (1985). What Is Value Chain. E-Commer., 1-13.
- https://www.businessinsider.in/retail/news/dmarts-growth-momentum-could-be-impacted-by-high-inflation/articleshow/92747965.cms
- https://yourstory.com/2018/09/id-fresh-grew-50-sq-ft-store-rs-182-crore-brand
- https://www.indianretailer.com/article/whats-hot/marvels/how-technology-helped-id-fresh-food-become-a-direct-to-retailer-brand.a8146
- https://yourstory.com/2015/11/id-fresh
- https://www.livemint.com/Companies/I85uaLoEVT5moWc2NdEG6L/iD-Fresh-Foods-to-expand-product-portfolio.html
- https://www.forbesindia.com/article/startups/dunzo-googles-chosen-one/49499/1
- https://www.financialexpress.com/business/blockchain-google-invests-in-indian-startup-dunzo-heres-how-the-app-can-help-you-get-things-done-962139/
- https://edition.cnn.com/2019/11/28/tech/dunzo-india-app-google/index.html

Chapter 2

- https://www.forbesindia.com/article/special/meet-the-batman-of-biscuits/62461/1

- ITC Annual Reports - 2010 to 2015
- Britannia Annual Reports - 2010 to 2015
- https://stories.flipkart.com/first-flipkart-customer/
- https://www.afaqs.com/news/advertising/29162_sunfeast-dark-fantasy-a-feast-for-the-senses
- https://economictimes.indiatimes.com/news/company/corporate-trends/10-year-milestone-reached-but-zomato-gets-hungry-for-more/the-origin-story/slideshow/64942723.cms?from=mdr
- https://www.thehindu.com/business/food-delivery-platform-zomato-to-acquire-blinkit-in-4447-cr-deal/article65562376.ece
- https://www.afaqs.com/news/marketing/47821_how-pulse-candy-captured-the-market-the-full-story
- https://m.economictimes.com/consumer-legal/success-story-of-the-favourite-candy-in-town-pulse/everybodys-eye-candy/slideshow/57533879.cms
- https://economictimes.indiatimes.com/industry/cons-products/fmcg/cavinkare-rolls-out-hand-sanitizers-at-re-1-hopes-to-repeat-shampoo-sachet-story/articleshow/74906295.cms
- https://economictimes.indiatimes.com/magazines/panache/the-rise-and-fall-of-tinyowl-lessons-that-start-up-founder-saurabh-goyal-learnt/articleshow/60069036.cms

Chapter 3

- Core Competence, Prahalad, C. K., & Hamel, G. (1997). The core competence of the corporation (pp. 969-987). Physica-Verlag HD.
- Competitive Advantage Theory, Porter, M. E. (1985). Technology and competitive advantage. Journal of business strategy, 5(3), 60-78.
- https://brandequity.economictimes.indiatimes.com/news/advertising/fevicol-turns-60-how-the-adhesive-brand-stole-the-heart-of-indian-consumer-with-its-quirky-ads/70755164
- https://www.forbesindia.com/article/super-50-companies-2016/by-sticking-to-basics-pidilite-continues-to-dominate-the-adhesives-market/43949/1
- https://economictimes.indiatimes.com/magazines/panache/micromax-ropes-in-hugh-jackman-as-the-brand-ambassador/articleshow/40307496.cms

- https://www.livemint.com/Technology/KsUB8dksllxzBqcUCFfySJ/How-Chinese-mobile-phones-took-over-the-Indian-market.html
- https://www.business-standard.com/article/companies/failed-to-match-pricing-offered-by-chinese-firms-micromax-s-rahul-sharma-120110301975_1.html

Chapter 4

- https://www.coursera.org/articles/4-ps-of-marketing (McCarthy 4Ps, 1960)
- https://economictimes.indiatimes.com/tech/software/know-how-fast-is-tez-googles-new-mobile-payments-app/articleshow/60728161.cms
- https://www.livemint.com/Consumer/RFboOY15QvQNWP9ZsS3w1J/You-can-buy-OnePlus-One-through-invites-only-in-India.html
- https://timesofindia.indiatimes.com/city/lucknow/hpcl-introduces-rasoi-ghar-concept/articleshow/31903779.cms
- HPCL's Rasoi Ghar Project; Mart Global Management Solutions LLP
- https://www.business-standard.com/article/press-releases/parle-agro-launches-first-ad-campaign-for-its-snack-brand-hippo-110021100099_1.html
- https://www.campaignasia.com/article/case-study-parle-agros-hippo-turns-to-twitter-to-track-inventory-and-replenish/214608
- https://www.afaqs.com/news/social-media/samsung-pulls-a-netflix-with-a-bandersnatch-like-instagram-story-ad

Chapter 5

- VUCA, Barber, H. F. (1992). Developing strategic leadership: The US army war college experience. Journal of Management Development, 11(6), 4-12.
- Levitt, T. (2004). Marketing myopia. Harvard business review., 82(7/8), 138-149, Actual 1960, Republished in 2004
- https://www.livemint.com/news/india/india-saw-record-of-rs-149-5-trillion-upi-card-transactions-in-2022-this-city-tops-the-list-11681789465771.html
- https://indianexpress.com/article/technology/gadgets/the-evolution-of-digital-cameras-from-kodaks-1975-digital-camera-prototype-to-iphone-5727036/

- https://www.businessoutreach.in/we-do-miss-kodak-but-let-us-understand/
- https://www.moneycontrol.com/news/business/personal-finance/paying-with-your-mobile-wallet-to-get-simpler-with-interoperable-qr-codes-6026991.html
- https://www.ft.com/content/17433c60-2d31-11e0-9b0f-00144feab49a
- https://www.fortuneindia.com/long-reads/how-zerodha-went-from-zero-tohero/111627
- https://www.forbesindia.com/article/bharatiya-vidya-bhavan039s-spjimr/the-curious-case-study-of-zerodhas-blue-ocean-strategy/77457/1

Chapter 6

- BCG, http://boston-consulting-group-brightspot.s3.amazonaws.com/img-src/BCG_Classics_Revisited_The_Growth_Share_Matrix_Jun_2014_tcm9-84453.pdf
- https://www.livemint.com/Companies/1JKHsutTXLWtTcVwdIDg0H/The-Maggi-ban-How-Indias-favourite-twominute-noodles-lost.html
- https://www.thehindubusinessline.com/companies/with-or-without-maggi-yippee-noodles-is-doing-well-says-itc/article7919867.ece
- Harsh Realities, Harsh Mariwala & Ram Charan, Penguin Publications (2021)

Chapter 7

- Sarkar, C., & Kotler, P. (2020). Brand activism: From purpose to action. Idea Bite Press.
- https://www.livemint.com/companies/news/mondelez-hul-partner-to-launch-crackle-ice-cream-under-kwality-walls-11624269790093.html
- https://indianexpress.com/article/business/supreme-court-agr-vodafone-airtel-telecom-6267665/
- https://www.livemint.com/companies/news/pepsico-and-airtel-announce-offers-ahead-of-festive-season-11662547723802.html
- https://indianexpress.com/article/technology/myntra-logo-change-new-logo-myntra-7167927/

- https://www.moneycontrol.com/news/business/whats-in-a-name-if-its-all-glow-and-lovely-hul-wouldnt-mind-6027671.html
- https://www.forbes.com/sites/parmyolson/2014/10/06/facebook-closes-19-billion-whatsapp-deal/
- https://www.wsj.com/articles/SB10001424052702303815404577333840377381670
- https://www.ft.com/content/9aa7315e-2482-11e0-8c0e-00144feab49a
- https://www.livemint.com/Companies/G3xizf7B81qqaU3INYC49L/Flipkart-buys-AI-startup-Livai.html
- https://www.businessinsider.com/airbnb-local-business-localmind-nabewise-acquisition-2012-12

Chapter 8

- 4As, Prahalad, C. K. (2012). Bottom of the pyramid as a source of breakthrough innovations. Journal of product innovation management, 29(1), 6-12.
- https://www.thehindubusinessline.com/companies/hindustan-unilevers-women-empowerment-project-shakti-rises-by-50-over-the-last-3-years/article66357525.ece
- https://www.businessinsider.com/unilevers-shakti-women-fight-pg-in-india-2012-7
- https://www.dailymail.co.uk/news/article-2443191/Gillette-spent-fortune-Indian-razor-forgetting-countrys-running-water.html
- https://www.thehindubusinessline.com/companies/humara-bajaj-becomes-the-worlds-favourite-indian/article26052825.ece
- https://www.moneycontrol.com/news/trends/features/storyboard18-from-being-hamara-bajaj-to-the-worlds-favourite-indian-the-true-legacy-of-rahul-bajaj-8085971.html
- https://www.livemint.com/Industry/TahDU0s1uWwBCPEYLSfmmI/Bajaj-KTM-expand-partnership-to-make-Husqvarna-Motorcycles.html
- https://www.hul.co.in/planet-and-society/case-studies/enhancing-livelihoods-through-project-shakti/

Chapter 9

- https://www.financialexpress.com/business/brandwagon/airtel-targets-zero-questions-with-new-campaign/1996084/
- https://www.forbesindia.com/article/forbes-global-2000/satya-nadella-no-more-mr-mean-guy/37956/1
- https://www.bbc.com/news/technology-47078013
- https://www.forbes.com/sites/laurarittenhouse/2019/03/21/how-the-most-underrated-ceo-became-a-winner/
- https://www.latimes.com/business/technology/story/2019-12-21/satya-nadella-reinvigorated-microsoft
- https://fortune.com/longform/amazon-web-services-ceo-adam-selipsky-cloud-computing/

Chapter 10

- https://www.ft.com/content/0c6cb68a-fdb1-11db-8d62-000b5df10621
- https://www.forbes.com/sites/abrambrown/2012/02/15/kellogg-to-buy-pringles-for-2-7-billion/
- https://www.livemint.com/Companies/z4Q2wkDfcUNq4uPsdyxAPP/PG-plans-to-eliminate-100-brands-to-focus-on-top-performers.html
- https://www.livemint.com/auto-news/bajaj-chetak-electric-scooter-launched-check-price-booking-date-features-mileage-11578989366235.html
- https://www.livemint.com/companies/news/parle-s-rola-cola-candy-makes-a-comeback-after-13-years-prompted-by-a-tweet-11570019204373.html

Acknowledgement

The seeds for the book were laid way before the pandemic, but it finally bore fruit as you are holding this book. As cliche as it sounds, it's not a singular effort that went into the creation of this book. Just saying thank you to all of them wouldn't be enough, but we can start somewhere.

Dr. Prateek and I went on tinkering with varied disparate ideas before settling on a structured narrative that drew inspiration from annals of Vaikuntha to simplify marketing. Not sure what was more difficult - Knowing what to write condensing the whole marketing journey or penning it down in the first place!

For starters, we would like to thank our families for being our constant support amidst multiple brainstorming sessions, writing and editing marathons and rewrites (The first draft never makes the cut. Hazards of being an author, you can't share your work unless you are personally happy with it).

Thank you Srishti Publishers, for taking a bet on us.

Arup Bose and Stuti, thank you for investing so much of your time and interest in this manuscript.

A person of varied interests, Prof. Himanshu Rai (Director - IIM Indore) is an inspiration for many. Thank you for making time to go through the early versions and graciously penning down the Foreword.

We would also like to thank Dr. Naveen Maheshwari (Director, ALLEN Career Institute Pvt. Ltd) for sharing his views on the manuscript and providing constant support.

Special mention to CA. Siva Prasad V.R.K.S for ensuring that all the mythological stories referred to in the book are extracted from appropriate ancient texts.

We are fortunate to have remarkable individuals from the corporate world - Mohit Malhotra (CEO, Dabur); K.V. Rao (Resident Director ASEAN, TATA Sons); Sudeep Singh (MD, Accenture Consulting); Keshav Maheswari (MD, Allen Overseas); Nishant Sekhar (MD and Partner, BCG India), among others, sharing their valuable views.

From the earliest rough drafts to the final manuscript, there are folks who do not need any introduction, who have been our sounding boards, which helped in crafting the narrative.

Any book you see in the market is an effort by some hundreds of invisible hands who ensure that it reaches your hands. This book is no different. Just saying thank you to all of them wouldn't be enough, but we can start somewhere.

Dr. Prateek Maheshwari

A passionate teacher and mentor, he has more than ten years of academic and a couple of years of corporate experience. He is currently working as an assistant professor (Marketing) at the Indian Institute of Foreign Trade (IIFT), New Delhi. An advocate of collaborative and experiential learning, he strongly believes that 'The True Purpose of Education is to Make Minds, Not Careers'. He has published several research papers in prestigious refereed journals and has presented/attended many conferences and seminars at the national and international levels in the field of marketing and general management. He has also delivered/ attended various workshops, seminars, conclaves, short-term courses and management development programs (MDPs), and faculty development programs (FDPs) at the institutes of national and international repute. His areas of interest include Educational/ Pedagogical Innovation, Advertising, Rural Marketing, Marketing of Financial Services, General Management and International Marketing.

Sagar Venkateshwar Nemani

Marketer by day, writer by night and doodler always, Sagar Venkateshwar grew up amidst stories from childhood in the 'City of Destiny' – Visakhapatnam. Fantasy and myths have always held a special place for him, which resulted in his first book - *Untold Myths of India*. His second book *Vampire's Vanity* bagged #1 bestseller rank on Amazon (2019). He also runs a blog 'Marketing Raven', a one-stop place for all curated stories and business insights related to the world of marketing. An MBA graduate from Indian Institute of Foreign Trade (IIFT), New Delhi and an electrical engineer from NIT Patna, he loves to doodle in his free time whenever he isn't reading or writing.